The Women

of the

French Salons

Also from Westphalia Press

westphaliapress.org

The Women
of the
French Salons

Amelia Gere Mason

WESTPHALIA PRESS
An imprint of Policy Studies Organization

Westphalia Press
An imprint of Policy Studies Organization
1527 New Hampshire Ave., NW
Washington, D.C. 20036
info@ipsonet.org

ISBN-13: 978-1-63391-370-7
ISBN-10: 1-63391-370-8

Cover design by Taillefer Long at Illuminated Stories:
www.illuminatedstories.com

Daniel Gutierrez-Sandoval, Executive Director
PSO and Westphalia Press

Updated material and comments on this edition
can be found at the Westphalia Press website:
www.westphaliapress.org

The Women
of the
French Salons

BY

AMELIA GERE MASON

T. FISHER UNWIN, LONDON
THE CENTURY CO. NEW YORK
1891

Louise Henriette de Bourbon-Conti
Duchesse d'Orléans

PREFACE.

*I*T has been a labor of love with many distinguished Frenchmen to recall the memories of the women who have made their society so illustrious, and to retouch with sympathetic insight the features which time was beginning to dim. One naturally hesitates to enter a field that has been gleaned so carefully, and with such brilliant results, by men like Cousin, Sainte-Beuve, Goncourt, and others of lesser note. But the social life of the two centuries in which women played so important a rôle in France is always full of human interest, from whatever point of view one may regard it. If there is not a great deal to be said that is new, old facts may be grouped afresh, and old modes of life and thought measured by modern standards.

In searching through the numerous memoirs, chronicles, letters, and original manuscripts in which the records of these centuries are hidden away, nothing has struck me so forcibly as the remarkable mental vigor and the far-reaching influence of women whose theater was mainly a social one. Though society has its frivolities, it has also its serious side, and it is through the phase of social evolution that was begun in the salons that women have attained the position they hold to-day. However beautiful, or valuable, or poetic may have been the feminine types of other nationalities, it is in France that we find the forerunners of the intelligent, self-poised, clear-sighted, independent modern woman. It is possible that in the search for larger fields the smaller but not less important ones have been in a measure forgotten. The great stream of civilization flows from a thousand unnoted rills that make sweet music in their course, and swell the current as surely as the more noisy torrent. The conditions of the past cannot be revived, nor are they desirable. The present has its own theories and its own methods. But at a time when the reign of luxury is rapidly establishing false standards, and the best intellectual life makes hopeless struggles against an ever aggressive

*materialism, it may be profitable as well as interesting to consider the pos-
sibilities that lie in a society equally removed from frivolity and pretension,
inspired by the talent, the sincerity, and the moral force of American women,
and borrowing a new element of fascination from the simple and charming
but polite informality of the old salons.*

*It has been the aim in these studies to gather within a limited compass the
women who represented the social life of their time, on its most intellectual
side, and to trace lightly their influence upon civilization through the avenues of literature and manners. Though the work may lose something in fullness from the effort to put so much into so small a space, perhaps there is some
compensation in the opportunity of comparing, in one gallery, the women
who exercised the greatest power in France for a period of more than two
hundred years. The impossibility of entering into the details of so many
lives in a single volume is clearly apparent. Only the most salient points
can be considered. Many who would amply repay a careful study have simply been glanced at, and others have been omitted altogether. As it would
be out of the question in a few pages to make an adequate portrait of women
who occupy so conspicuous a place in history as Mme. de Maintenon and
Mme. de Staël, the former has been reluctantly passed with a simple allusion,
and the latter outlined in a brief résumé not at all proportioned to the rela-
tive interest or importance of the subject.*

*I do not claim to present a complete picture of French society, and without
wishing to give too rose-colored a view, it has not seemed to me necessary to
dwell upon its corrupt phases. If truth compels one sometimes to state unpleasant facts in portraying historic characters, it is as needless and unjust
as in private life to repeat idle and unproved tales, or to draw imaginary
conclusions from questionable data. The conflict of contemporary opinion on
the simplest matters leads one often to the suspicion that all personal history is more or less disguised fiction. The best one can do in default of direct records is to accept authorities that are generally regarded as the most
trustworthy.*

*This volume is affectionately dedicated to the memory of my mother, who
followed the work with appreciative interest in its early stages, but did not
live to see its conclusion.*

AMELIA GERE MASON.

Paris, July 6, 1891.

TABLE OF CONTENTS

CHAPTER V

A Literary Salon at Port Royal

CHAPTER VI

Madame de Sévigné

CHAPTER VII

Madame de La Fayette

CHAPTER VIII

Salons of the Eighteenth Century

CHAPTER IX

An Antechamber of the Académie Française

LIST OF ILLUSTRATIONS

List of Illustrations.

The Women
of the
French Salons

CHAPTER I

SALONS OF THE SEVENTEENTH CENTURY

Characteristics of French Women — Gallic Genius for Conversation — Social Conditions — Origin of the Salons — Their Power — Their Composition — Their Records.

"INSPIRE, but do not write," said Le Brun to women. Whatever we may think to-day of this rather superfluous advice, we can readily pardon a man living in the atmosphere of the old French salons, for falling somewhat under the special charm of their leaders. It was a charm full of subtle flattery. These women were usually clever and brilliant, but their cleverness and brilliancy were exercised to bring into stronger relief the talents of their friends. It is true that many of them wrote, as they talked, out of the fullness of their own hearts or their own intelligence, and with no thought of a public; but it was only an incident in their lives, another form of diversion, which left them quite free from the dreaded taint of feminine authorship. Their peculiar gift was to inspire others, and much of the fascination that gave them such power in their day still clings to their memories. Even at this distance, they have a perpetual interest for us. It may be that the long perspective lends them a certain illusion which a closer view might partly dispel. Something also may be due to the dark background against which they were out-lined. But, in spite of time and change, they stand out upon the pages of history, glowing with an ever-fresh vitality, and personifying the genius of a civilization of which they were the fairest flower.

The Gallic genius is eminently a social one, but it is, of all others, the most difficult to reproduce. The subtle grace of manner, the magic of spoken words, are gone with the moment. The conversations of two centuries ago are to-day like champagne which has lost its sparkle. We may recall their tangible forms—the facts, the accessories, the thoughts, even the words, but the flavor is not there. It is the volatile essence of gaiety and wit, that especially characterizes French society. It glitters from a thousand facets, it surprises us in a thousand delicate turns of thought, it appears in countless movements and shades of expression. But it refuses to be imprisoned. Hence the impossibility of catching the essential spirit of the salons. We know something of the men and women who frequented them, as they have left many récords of themselves. We have numerous pictures of their social life from which we may partially reconstruct it and trace its influence. But the nameless attraction that held for so long a period the most serious men of letters as well as the gay world still eludes us.

We find the same elusive quality in the women who presided over these reunions. They were true daughters of a race of which Mme. de Graffigny wittily said that it "escaped from the hands of Nature when there had entered into its composition only air and fire." They certainly were not faultless;

indeed, some of them were very faulty. Nor were they, as a rule, remarkable for learning. Even the leaders of noted literary salons often lacked the common essentials of a modern education. But if they wrote badly and spelled badly, they had an abundance of that delicate combination of intellect and wit which the French call *esprit.* They had also, in superlative measure, the social gifts which women of genius reared in the library or apart from the world, are apt to lack. The close study of books leads to a knowledge of man rather than of men. It tends towards habits of introspection which are fatal to the clear and swift vision required for successful leadership of any sort. Social talent is distinct, and implies a happy poise of character and intellect; the delicate blending of many gifts, not the supremacy of one. It implies taste and versatility, with fine discrimination, and the tact to sink one's personality as well as to call out the best in others. It was this flexibility of mind, this active intelligence tempered with sensibility and the native instinct of pleasing, that distinguished the French women who have left such enduring traces upon their time. "It is not sufficient to be wise, it is necessary also to please," said the witty and penetrating Ninon, who thus very aptly condensed the feminine philosophy of her race. Perhaps she has revealed the secret of their fascination, the indefinable something which is as difficult to analyze as the perfume of a rose.

A history of the French salons would include the history of the entire period of which they were so prominent a factor. It would make known to us its statesmen and its warriors; it would trace the great currents of thought; it would give us glimpses of every phase of society, from the diversions of the old *noblesse,* with their sprinkling of literature and philosophy, to the familiar life of the men of letters, who cast about their intimate coteries the halo of their own genius. These salons were closely interwoven with the best intellectual life of more than two hundred years. Differing in tone according to the rank, taste, or character of their leaders, they were rallying points for the most famous men and women of their time. In these brilliant centers, a new literature had its birth. Here was found the fine critical sense that put its stamp on a new poem

or a new play.   Here ministers were created and deposed,
authors and artists were brought into vogue, and vacant chairs
in the Académie Française were filled.   Here the great philosophy of the eighteenth century was cradled.   Here sat the
arbiters of manners, the makers of social success.   To these
high tribunals came, at last, every aspirant for fame.

It was to the refinement, critical taste, and moral force of a
rare woman, half French and half Italian, that the first literary
salons owed their origin and their distinctive character.   In
judging of the work of Mme. de Rambouillet, we have to consider that in the early days of the seventeenth century knowledge was not diffused as it is to-day.   A new light was just
dawning upon the world, but learning was still locked in the
brains of *savants,* or in the dusty tomes of languages that were
practically obsolete.   Men of letters were dependent upon the
favors of noble but often ignorant patrons, whom they never
met on a footing of equality.   The position of women was as
inferior as their education, and the incredible depravity of
morals was a sufficient answer to the oft-repeated fallacy that
the purity of the family is best maintained by feminine seclusion.   It is true there were exceptions to this reign of illiteracy.
With the natural disposition to glorify the past, the writers of
the next generation liked to refer to the golden era of the Valois
and the brilliancy of its voluptuous court.   Very likely they exaggerated a little the learning of Marguerite de Navarre, who
was said to understand Latin, Italian, Spanish, even Greek and
Hebrew.   But she had rare gifts, wrote religious poems, besides the very secular *Heptaméron* which was not eminently
creditable to her refinement, held independent opinions, and
surrounded herself with men of letters.   This little oasis of
intellectual light, shadowed as it was with vices, had its influence, and there were many women in the solitude of remote
châteaux who began to cultivate a love for literature.   " The
very women and maidens aspired to this praise and celestial
manna of good learning," said Rabelais.   But their reading
was mainly limited to his own unsavory satires, to Spanish
pastorals, licentious poems, and their books of devotion.   It
was on such a foundation that Mme. de Rambouillet began to

rear the social structure upon which her reputation rests. She
was eminently fitted for this rôle by her pure character and
fine intelligence ; but she added to these the advantages of
rank and fortune, which gave her ample facilities for creating

MARGUERITE DE VALOIS, QUEEN OF NAVARRE, AND OF FRANCE.
FROM AN OIL PORTRAIT.

a social center of sufficient attraction to focus the best intellectual life of the age, and sufficient power to radiate its light.
Still it was the tact and discrimination to select from the wealth
of material about her, and quietly to reconcile old traditions
with the freshness of new ideas, that especially characterized
Mme. de Rambouillet.

It was this richness of material, the remarkable variety and originality of the women who clustered round and succeeded their graceful leader, that gave so commanding an influence to the salons of the seventeenth century. No social life has been so carefully studied, no women have been so minutely portrayed. The annals of the time are full of them. They painted one another, and they painted themselves, with realistic fidelity. The lights and shadows are alike defined. We know their joys and their sorrows, their passions and their follies, their tastes and their antipathies. Their inmost life has been revealed. They animate, as living figures, a whole class of literature which they were largely instrumental in creating, and upon which they have left the stamp of their own vivid personality. They appear later in the pages of Cousin and Sainte-Beuve, with their radiant features softened and spiritualized by the touch of time. We rise from a perusal of these chronicles of a society long passed away, with the feeling that we have left a company of old friends. We like to recall their pleasant talk of themselves, of their companions, of the lighter happenings, as well as the more serious side of the age which they have illuminated. We seem to see their faces, note their manner, watch the play of intellect and feeling, while they speak. The variety is infinite and full of charm.

Mme. de Sévigné talks upon paper, of the trifling affairs of every-day life, adding here and there a sparkling anecdote, a bit of gossip, a delicate characterization, a trenchant criticism, a dash of wit, a touch of feeling, or a profound thought. All this is lighted up by her passionate love of her daughter, and in this light we read the many-sided life of her time for twenty-five years. Mme. de La Fayette takes the world more seriously, and replaces the playful fancy of her friend by a richer vein of imagination and sentiment. She sketches for us the court of which Madame* is the central figure — the unfortunate Princess Henrietta whom she loved so tenderly, and who died so tragically in her arms. She writes novels too ; not profound studies of life, but fine and exquisite pictures of that side of the century which appealed most to her poetic sensi-

---

* Title given to the wife of the king's brother.

bility. We follow the leading characters of the age through the ten-volume romances of Mlle. de Scudéry, which have mostly long since fallen into oblivion. Doubtless the portraits are a trifle rose-colored, but they accord, in the main, with more veracious history. The Grande Mademoiselle describes herself and her friends, with the curious naïveté of a spoiled child who thinks its smallest experiences of interest to all the world. Mme. de Maintenon gives us another picture, more serious, more thoughtful, but illuminated with flashes of wonderful insight.

Most of these women wrote simply to amuse themselves and their friends. It was only another mode of their versatile expression. With rare exceptions, they were not authors consciously or by intention. They wrote spontaneously, and often with reckless disregard of grammar and orthography. But the people who move across their gossiping pages are alive. The century passes in review before us as we read. The men and women who made its literature so brilliant and its salons so famous, become vivid realities. Prominent among the fair faces that look out upon us at every turn, from court and salon, is that of the Duchesse de Longueville, sister of the Grand Condé, and heroine of the Fronde. Her lovely blue eyes, with their dreamy languor and "luminous awakenings," turn the heads alike of men and women, of poet and critic, of statesman and priest. We trace her brief career through her pure and ardent youth, her loveless marriage, her fatal passion for La Rochefoucauld, the final shattering of all her illusions; and when at last, tired of the world, she bows her beautiful head in penitent prayer, we too love and forgive her, as others have done. Were not twenty-five years of suffering and penance an ample expiation? She was one of the three women of whom Cardinal Mazarin said that they were "capable of governing and overturning three kingdoms." The others were the intriguing Duchesse de Chevreuse, who dazzled the age by her beauty and her daring escapades, and the fascinating Anne de Gonzague, better known as the Princesse Palatine, of whose winning manners, conversational charm, penetrating intellect, and loyal character Bossuet spoke so eloquently at her death. We

catch pleasant glimpses of Mme. Deshoulières, beautiful and a
poet; of Mme. Cornuel, of whom it was said that "every sin
she confessed was an epigram"; of Mme. de Choisy, witty and
piquante; of Mme. de Coulanges, also a wit and *femme d'esprit*.

DRAWN BY KENYON COX.　　　　　　　　JANUARY - 1890

JACQUELINE ARNAULD — MÈRE ANGÉLIQUE.

FROM AN OIL PORTRAIT.

Linked with these by a thousand ties of sympathy and affection were the worthy counterparts of Pascal and Arnauld, of
Bossuet and Fénelon, the devoted women who poured out their
passionate souls at the foot of the cross, and laid their earthly
hopes upon the altar of divine love. We follow the devout
Jacqueline Pascal to the cloister in which she buries her bril-

liant youth to die at thirty-five of a wounded conscience and a broken heart.   Many a bruised spirit, as it turns from the gay world to the mystic devotion which touches' a new chord in its jaded sensibilities, finds support and inspiration in the strong and fervid sympathy of Jacqueline Arnauld, better known as Mère Angélique of Port Royal.   This profound spiritual passion was a part of the intense life of the century, which gravitated from love and ambition to the extremes of penitence and asceticism.

A multitude of minor figures, graceful and poetic, brilliant and *spirituelles*, flit across the canvas, leaving the fragrance of an exquisite individuality, and tempting one to extend the list of the versatile women who toned and colored the society of the period.   But we have to do, at present, especially with those who gathered and blended this fresh intelligence, delicate fancy, emotional wealth, and religious fervor, into a society including such men as Corneille, Balzac, Bossuet, Richelieu, Condé, Pascal, Arnauld, and La Rochefoucauld — those who are known as leaders of more or less celebrated salons.   Of these, Mme. de Rambouillet and Mme. de Sablé were among the best representative types of their time, and the first of the long line of social queens who, through their special gift of leadership, held so potent a sway for two centuries.

The Women
of the
French Salons

CHAPTER II

THE HÔTEL DE RAMBOUILLET

*Mme. de Rambouillet — The Salon Bleu — Its Habitués — Its
Diversions — Corneille — Balzac — Richelieu — Romance of
the Grand Condé — The Young Bossuet — Voiture — The
Duchesse de Longueville — Angélique Paulet — Julie d'An-
gennes — Les Précieuses Ridicules — Decline of the Salon —
Influence upon Literature and Manners.*

THE Hôtel de Rambouillet has been called the
"cradle of polished society," but the personality
of its hostess is less familiar than that of many
who followed in her train. This may be partly
due to the fact that she left no record of herself
on paper. She aptly embodied the kind advice
of Le Brun. It was her special talent to inspire others and
to combine the various elements of a brilliant and complex
social life. The rare tact which enabled her to do this lay
largely in a certain self-effacement and the peculiar harmony
of a nature which presented few salient points. She is best

represented by the salon of which she was the architect and the animating spirit; but even this is better known to-day through its faults than its virtues. It is a pleasant task to clear off a little dust from its memorials, and to paint in fresh colors one who played so important a rôle in the history of literature and manners.

Catherine de Vivonne was born at Rome, in 1588. Her father, the Marquis de Pisani, was French ambassador, and she

COURTYARD OF THE HÔTEL RAMBOUILLET.

belonged through her mother to the old Roman families of Strozzi and Savelli. Married at sixteen to the Count d'Angennes, afterwards Marquis de Rambouillet, she was introduced to the world at the gay court of Henry IV. But the coarse and depraved manners which ruled there were altogether distasteful to her delicate and fastidious nature. At twenty she retired from these brilliant scenes of gilded vice, and began to gather round her the coterie of choice spirits which later became so famous.

Filled with the poetic ideals and artistic tastes which had been nourished in a thoughtful and elegant seclusion, it seems to have been the aim of her life to give them outward expres-

sion. Her mind, which inherited the subtle refinement of the
land of her birth, had taken its color from the best Italian and
Spanish literature, but she was in no sense a learned woman.
She was once going to study Latin, in order to read Virgil,
but was prevented by ill-health. It is clear, however, that she
had a great diversity of gifts, with a basis of rare good sense
and moral elevation. "She was revered, adored," writes Mme.
de Motteville; "a model of courtesy, wisdom, knowledge, and
sweetness." She is always spoken of in the chronicles of her
time as a loyal wife, a devoted mother, the benefactor of the
suffering, and the sympathetic adviser of authors and artists.
The poet Segrais says: "She was amiable and gracious, of a
sound and just mind; it is she who has corrected the bad customs
which prevailed before her. She taught politeness to all those
of her time who frequented her house. She was also a good
friend, and kind to every one." We are told that she was beautiful, but we know only that her face was fair and delicate, her
figure tall and graceful, and her manner stately and dignified.
Her Greek love of beauty expressed itself in all her appointments. The unique and original architecture of her *hôtel,*—
which was modeled after her own designs,— the arrangement
of her salon, the pursuits she chose, and the amusements she
planned, were all a part of her own artistic nature. This was
shown also in her code of etiquette, which imposed a fine courtesy upon the members of her coterie, and infused into life the
spirit of politeness, which one of her countrymen has called the
"flower of humanity." But this esthetic quality was tempered
with a clear judgment, and a keen appreciation of merit and
talent, which led her to gather into her society many not "to
the manner born." Sometimes she delicately aided a needy
man of letters to present a respectable appearance—a kindness
much less humiliating in those days of patronage than it would be
to-day. As may readily be imagined, these new elements often
jarred upon the tastes and prejudices of her noble guests, but in
spite of this it was considered an honor to be received by her,
and, though not even a duchess, she was visited by princesses.

Adding to this spirit of noble independence the prestige
of rank, beauty, and fortune; a temper of mingled sweetness

and strength; versatile gifts controlled by an admirable reason; a serene and tranquil character; a playful humor, free from the caprices of a too exacting sensibility; a perfect *savoir-faire*, and we have the unusual combination which enabled her to hold her sway for so many years, without a word of censure from even the most scandal-loving of chroniclers.

"We have sought in vain," writes Cousin, "for that which is rarely lacking in any life of equal or even less brilliancy, some calumny or scandal, an equivocal word, or the lightest epigram. We have found only a concert of warm eulogies which have run through many generations. . . . She has disarmed Tallemant himself. This caricaturist of the seventeenth century has been pitiless towards the *habitués* of her illustrious house, but he praises her with a warmth which is very impressive from such a source."

The modern spirit of change has long since swept away all vestiges of the old Rue Saint-Thomas-du-Louvre and the time-honored dwellings that ornamented it. Conspicuous among these, and not far from the Palais Royal, was the famous Hôtel de Rambouillet. The *salon bleu* has become historic. This "sanctuary of the Temple of *Athène*," as it was called in the stilted language of the day, has been illuminated for us by the rank, beauty, and talent of the Augustan age of France. We are more or less familiar with even the minute details of the spacious room, whose long windows, looking across the little garden towards the Tuileries, let in a flood of golden sunlight. We picture to ourselves its draperies of blue and gold, its curious cabinets, its choice works of art, its Venetian lamps, and its crystal vases always filled with flowers that scatter the perfume of spring.

It was here that Mme. de Rambouillet held her court for nearly thirty years, her salon reaching the height of its power under Richelieu, and practically closing with the Fronde. She sought to gather all that was most distinguished, whether for wit, beauty, talent, or birth, into an atmosphere of refinement and simple elegance, which should tone down all discordant elements and raise life to the level of a fine art. There was a strongly intellectual flavor in the amusements, as well as in the discussions of this salon, and the place of honor was given to genius, learning, and good manners, rather than to rank. But it was by no means purely literary. The exclusive spirit of the old aristocracy, with its *hauteur* and its lofty patronage, found itself face to face with fresh ideals. The position of the hostess enabled her to break the traditional barriers, and form a society upon a new basis, but in spite of the mingling of classes hitherto separated, the dominant life was that of the *noblesse.* Women of rank gave the tone and made the laws. Their code of etiquette was severe. They aimed to combine the graces of Italy with the chivalry of Spain. The model man must have a keen sense of honor, and wit without pedantry; he must be brave, heroic, generous, gallant, but he must also possess good breeding and gentle courtesy. The coarse passions which had disgraced the court were refined into subtle sentiments, and women were raised upon a pedestal, to be respectfully and platonically adored. In this reaction from extreme license, familiarity was forbidden, and language was subjected to a critical censorship. It was here that the word *précieuse* was first used to signify a woman of personal distinction, accomplished in the highest sense, with a perfect accord of intelligence, good taste, and good manners. Later, when pretension crept into the inferior circles which took this one for a model, the term came to mean a sort of intellectual *parvenue,* half prude and half pedant, who affected learning, and paraded it like fine clothes, for effect.

"Do you remember," said Fléchier, many years later, in his funeral oration on the death of the Duchesse de Montausier, " the salons which are still regarded with so much veneration, where the spirit was purified, where virtue was revered under the name of the incomparable Arthénice; where people of merit and quality assembled, who composed a select court, numerous without confusion, modest without constraint, learned without pride, polished without affectation?"

Whatever allowance we may be disposed to make for the friendship of the eminent abbé, he spoke with the authority of personal knowledge, and at a time when the memories of the Hôtel de Rambouillet were still fresh. It is true that those

who belonged to this professed school of morals were not all
patterns of decorum. But we cannot judge by the Anglo-
Saxon standards of the nineteenth century the faults of an age
in which a Ninon de L'Enclos lives on terms of veiled intimacy with a strait-laced Mme. de Maintenon, and, when age
has given her a certain title to respectability, receives in her
salon women of as spotless reputation as Mme. de La Fayette.
Measured from the level of their time, the lives of the Rambouillet coterie stand out white and shining. The pure character of the Marquise and her daughters was above reproach,
and they were quoted as "models whom all the world cited, all
the world admired, and every one tried to imitate." To be a
précieuse was in itself an evidence of good conduct.

"This salon was a resort not only for all the fine wits, but
for every one who frequented the court," writes Mme. de Motteville. "It was a sort of academy of *beaux esprits*, of gallantry,
of virtue, and of science," says St. Simon ; "for these things
accorded marvelously. It was a rendezvous of all that was
most distinguished in condition and in merit ; a tribunal with
which it was necessary to count, and whose decisions upon the
conduct and reputation of people of the court and the world,
had great weight."

Corneille read most of his dramas here, and, if report be
true, read them very badly. He says of himself:

> Et l'on peut rarement m'écouter sans ennui,
> Que quand je me produis par la bouche d'autrui.

He was shy, awkward, ill at ease, not clear in speech, and
rather heavy in conversation ; but the chivalric and heroic character of his genius was quite in accord with the lofty and rather
romantic standards affected by this circle, and made him one
of its central literary figures. Another was Balzac, whose fine
critical taste did so much for the elegance and purity of the
French language, and who was as noted in his day as was
his namesake, the brilliant author of the *Comédie Humaine*,
two centuries later. His long letters to the Marquise, on the
Romans, were read and discussed in his absence, and it was
through his influence, added to her own classic ideals, that

CORNEILLE READING "POLYEUCTE" AT THE HÔTEL RAMBOUILLET.

Roman dignity and urbanity were accepted as models in the new code of manners; indeed, it was he who introduced the word *urbanité* into the language. Armand du Plessis, who aimed to be poet as well as statesman, read here in his youth a thesis on love. When did a Frenchman ever fail to write with facility upon this fertile theme? After he became Cardinal de Richelieu he feared the influence of the Hôtel de Rambouillet, and sent a request to its hostess to report what was said of him there. She replied with consummate tact, that her guests were so strongly persuaded of her friendship for his Eminence, that no one would have the temerity to speak ill of him in her presence.

Even the Grand Condé courted the muses, and wrote verses which were bad for a poet, though fairly good for a warrior. If it be true that every man is a poet once in his life, we may infer that this was about the time of his sad little romance with the pretty and charming Mlle. du Vigean, who was one of the youthful attractions of this coterie. Family ambition stood in the way of their marriage, and the prince yielded to the wishes of his friends. The Grande Mademoiselle tells us that this was the only veritable passion of the brave young hero of many battles, and that he fainted at the final separation. United to a wife he did not love, and whom he did not scruple to treat very ill, he gave himself to glory and, it must be added, to unworthy intrigues. The pure-hearted young girl buried her beauty and her sorrows in the convent of the Carmelites, and was no more heard of in the gay world.

It is evident that the great soldier sometimes forgot the urbanity which was so strongly insisted upon in this society. He is said to have carried the impetuosity of his character into his conversation. When he had a good cause, he sustained it with grace and amiability. If it was a bad one, however, his eyes flashed, and he became so violent that it was thought prudent not to contradict him. It is related that Boileau, after yielding one day in a dispute, remarked in a low voice to a friend : " Hereafter I shall always be of the opinion of the Prince when he is wrong."

Bossuet, when a boy of seventeen, improvised here one evening a sermon on a given theme, which was so eloquent

3

that it held the company until near midnight. "I have never heard any one preach so early and so late," remarked the witty Voiture, as he congratulated the youthful orator at the close.

This famous *bel esprit* played a very prominent part here. His rôle was to amuse, and his talents gave him great vogue, but at this distance his small vanities strike one much more vividly than the wit which flashed out with the moment, or the *vers de société* on which his fame rests. He owed his social success to a rather high-flown love-letter which he evidently thought too good to be lost to the world. He sent it to a friend, who had it printed and circulated. What the lady thought does not appear, but it made the fortune of the poet. Though the son of a wine-merchant, and without rank, he had little more of the spirit of a courtier than Voltaire, and his biting epigrams were no less feared. "If he were one of us, he would be insupportable," said Condé. But his caprices were tolerated for the sake of his inexhaustible wit, and he was petted and spoiled to the end.

A list of the men of letters who appeared from time to time at the Hôtel de Rambouillet would include the most noted names of the century, besides many which were famous in their day, but at present are little more than historical shadows. The conversations were often learned, doubtless sometimes pretentious. One is inclined to wonder if these noble cavaliers and high-born women did not yawn occasionally over the scholarly discourse of Corneille and Balzac upon the Romans, the endless disputes about rival sonnets, and the long discussions on the value of a word. "Doubtless it is a very beautiful poem, but also very tiresome," said Mme. de Longueville, after Chapelain had finished reading his *Pucelle* — a work which aimed to be the Iliad of France, but succeeded only in being very long and rather heavy.

This lovely young Princess, who at sixteen had the exaltation of a *religieuse*, and was with difficulty won from her dreams of renunciation and a cloister, had become the wife of a man many years her senior, whom she did not love, and the idol of the brilliant world in which she lived. La Rochefoucauld had not yet disturbed the serenity of her heart, nor political intrigues her peace of mind. It was before the Fronde, in which she was destined to play so conspicuous a part, and she was still content with the rôle of a reigning beauty; but she

ANNE-GENEVIÈVE DE BOURBON, DUCHESSE DE LONGUEVILLE.
FROM AN ENGRAVING AFTER THE PORTRAIT BY MIGNARD.

was not at all averse to the literary entertainments of this salon, in which her own fascinations were so delightfully sung. She found the flattering verses of Voiture more to her taste than the stately epic of Chapelain, took his side warmly against Benserade in the famous dispute as to the merits of their two sonnets, *Job* and *Urania*, and won him a doubtful victory. The poems of Voiture lose much of their flavor in translation, but I venture to give a verse in the original, which was addressed to

the charming *Princesse*, and which could hardly fail to win the
favor of a young and beautiful woman.

De perles, d'astres, et de fleurs,
Bourbon, le ciel fit tes couleurs,
Et mit dedans tout ce mélange
L'esprit d'une ange.

ANGÉLIQUE PAULET.
FROM AN ENGRAVING ON STEEL.

But the diversions were by no means always grave or literary.   Life was represented on many sides, one secret, doubtless, of the wide influence of this society.   The daughters of
Mme. de Rambouillet, and her son, the popular young Marquis
de Pisani, formed a nucleus of youth and gaiety.   To these we
may add the beautiful Angélique Paulet, who at seventeen had
turned the head of Henri IV., and escaped the fatal influence
of that imperious sovereign's infatuation by his timely, or untimely, death.   Fair and brilliant, the best singer of her time,
skilled also in playing the lute, and gifted with a special dramatic talent, she was always a favorite, much loved by her

friends and much sung by the poets. Her proud and impetuous character, her frank and original manners, together with her luxuriance of blonde hair, gained her the *sobriquet* of *la belle lionne*. Nor must we forget Mlle. de Scudéry, one of the most constant literary lights of this salon, and in some sense its chronicler; nor the fastidious Mme. de Sablé.

The brightest ornament of the Hôtel de Rambouillet, however, was Julie d'Angennes, the petted daughter of the house, the devoted companion and clever assistant of her mother. Her gaiety of heart, amiable temper, ready wit, and gracious manners surrounded her with an atmosphere of perpetual sunshine. Fertile in resources, of fine intelligence, winning the love alike of men and women, she was the soul of the serious conversations, as well as of the amusements which relieved them. These amusements were varied and often original. They played little comedies. They had mythological *fêtes*, draping themselves as antique gods and goddesses. Sometimes they indulged in practical jokes and surprises, which were more laughable than dignified. Malherbe and Racan, the latter sighing hopelessly over the attractions of the dignified Marquise, gave her the romantic name of Arthénice, and forthwith the other members of the coterie took some *nom de Parnasse*, by which they were familiarly known. They read the *Astrée* of d'Urfé, that platonic dream of a disillusioned lover; discussed the romances of Calprenède and the sentimental *Bergeries* of Racan. Such Arcadian pictures seemed to have a singular fascination for these courtly dames and plumed cavaliers. They tried to reproduce them. Assuming the characters of the rather insipid Strephons and Florimels, they made love in pastoral fashion, with pipe and lute—these rustic diversions serving especially to while away the long summer days in the country at Rambouillet, at Chantilly, or at Ruel. They improvised sonnets and madrigals; they praised each other in verse; they wrote long letters on the slightest pretext. As a specimen of the badinage so much in vogue, I quote from a letter written by Voiture to one of the daughters of Mme. de Rambouillet, who was an abbess, and had sent him a present of a cat.

"Madame, I was already so devoted to you that I supposed you knew there was no need of winning me by presents, or trying to take me like a rat, with a cat. Nevertheless, if there was anything in my thought that was not wholly yours, the cat which you have sent me has captured it." After a eulogy upon the cat, he adds: "I can only say that it is very difficult to keep, and for a cat religiously brought up it is very little inclined to seclusion. It never sees a window without wishing to jump out, it would have leaped over the wall twenty times if it had not been prevented, and no secular cat could be more lawless or more self-willed."

The wit here is certainly rather attenuated; but the subject is an ungrateful one. Mme. de Sévigné finds Voiture "*libre, badin, charmant,*" and disposes of his critics by saying, "So much the worse for those who do not understand him." One is often puzzled to detect this rare *spirituelle* quality; but it is fair to presume that it was of the volatile sort that evaporates with time.

All this sentimental masquerading and exaggerated gallantry suggests the vulnerable side of the Hôtel de Rambouillet, and the side which its enemies have been disposed to make very prominent. Among those who tried to imitate this salon, Spanish chivalry doubtless degenerated into a thousand absurdities, and it must be admitted that the salon itself was not free from reproach on this point. It became the fashion to write and talk in the language of hyperbole. Sighing lovers were consumed with artificial fires, and ready to die with affected languors. Like the old poets of Provence, whose spirit they caught and whose phrases they repeated, they were dying of love they did not feel. The eyes of Phyllis extinguished the sun. The very nightingales expired of jealousy, after hearing the voice of Angélique.

It would be difficult, perhaps, to find anywhere a company of clever people bent upon amusing themselves and passing every day more or less together, whose sayings and doings would bear to be exactly chronicled. The literary diversions and poetic ideals of this circle, too, gave a certain color to the charge of affectation, among people of less refined instincts,

JULIE D'ANGENNES, DUCHESSE DE MONTAUSIER.

FROM AN ETCHING IN THE "GUIRLANDE DE JULIE" OF OCTAVE UZANNE.

who found its *esprit* incomprehensible, its manners prudish, and its virtue a tacit reproach ; but the dignified and serious character of many of its constant *habitués* should be a sufficient guarantee that it did not greatly pass the limits of good taste and good sense.   The only point upon which Mme. de Rambouillet seems to have been open to criticism was a certain formal reserve and an over-fastidious delicacy ; but, in an age when the standards of both refinement and morals were so low, this implies a virtue rather than a defect.   Nor does her character appear to have been at all tinged with pretension.   " I should fear from your example to write in a style too elevated," says Voiture, in a letter to her.   But traditions are strong, and people do not readily adapt themselves to new models.   Charracter and manners are a growth.   That which is put on, and not ingrained, is apt to lack true balance and proportion. Hence it is not strange that this new order of things resulted in many crudities and exaggerations.

It is not worth while to criticize too severely the plumed knights who took the heroes of Corneille as models, played the harmless lover, and paid the tribute of chivalric deference to women.   The strained politeness may have been artificial, and the forms of chivalry very likely outran the feeling, but they served at least to keep it alive, while the false platonism and ultra-refined sentiment were simply moral protests against the coarse vices of the time.   The prudery which reached a satirical climax in *Les Précieuses Ridicules* was a natural reaction from the sensuality of a Marguerite and a Gabrielle.   Mme. de Rambouillet saw and enjoyed the first performance of this celebrated play, nor does it appear that she was at all disturbed by the keen satire which was generally supposed to have been directed toward her salon.   Molière himself disclaims all intention of attacking the true *précieuse ;* but the world is not given to fine discrimination, and the true suffers from the blow aimed at the false.   This brilliant comedian, whose manners were not of the choicest, was more at home in the lax and epicurean world of Ninon and Mme. de la Sablière—a world which naturally did not find the decorum of the *précieuses* at all to its taste ; the witticism of Ninon, who defined them as the " Jansenists of love," is well known. It is not unlikely that Molière shared her dislike of the powerful and fastidious coterie whose very virtues might easily have furnished salient points for his scathing wit.

But whatever affectations may have grown out of the new code of manners, it had a more lasting result in the fine and stately courtesy which pervaded the later social life of the century. We owe, too, a profound gratitude to these women who exacted and were able to command a consideration which with many shades of variation has been left as a permanent heritage to their sex. We may smile at some of their follies: have we not our own which some nineteenth century Molière may serve up for the delight and possible misleading of future generations?

There is a warm human side to this daily intercourse, with its sweet and gracious courtesies. The women who discuss grave questions and make or unmake literary reputations in the salon, are capable of rare sacrifices and friendships that seem quixotic in their devotion. Cousin, who has studied them so carefully and so sympathetically, has saved from oblivion many private letters which give us pleasant glimpses of their everyday life. As we listen to their quiet exchange of confidences, we catch the smile that plays over the light badinage, or the tear that lurks in the tender words.

A little son of Mme. de Rambouillet has the small-pox, and his sister Julie shares the care of him with her mother, when every one else has fled. At his death, she devotes herself to her friend Mme. de Longueville, who soon after her marriage is attacked with the same dreaded malady. Mme. de Sablé is afraid of contagion, and refuses to see Mlle. de Rambouillet, who writes her a characteristic letter. As it gives us a vivid idea of her *esprit* as well as of her literary style, I copy it in full, though it has been made already familiar to the English reader by George Eliot, in her admirable review of Cousin's *Life of Mme. de Sablé.*

Mlle. de Chalais * will please read this letter to Mme. la Marquise, out of the wind.

Madame, I cannot begin my treaty with you too early, for I am sure that between the first proposition made for me to see you, and the conclusion, you will

* *Dame de compagnie* to the Marquise.

have so many reflections to make, so many physicians to consult, and so many fears to overcome, that I shall have full leisure to air myself. The conditions which I offer are, not to visit you until I have been three days absent from the Hôtel de Condé, to change all my clothing, to choose a day when it has frozen, not to approach you within four paces, not to sit down upon more than one seat. You might also have a great fire in your room, burn juniper in the four corners, surround yourself with imperial vinegar, rue, and wormwood. If you can feel safe under these conditions, without my cutting off my hair, I swear to you to execute them religiously ; and if you need examples to fortify you, I will tell you that the Queen saw M. de Chaudebonne when he came from Mlle. de Bourbon's room, and that Mme. d'Aiguillon, who has good taste and is beyond criticism on such points, has just sent me word that if I did not go to see her, she should come after me.

Mme. de Sablé retorts in a satirical vein, that her friend is too well instructed in the needed precautions, to be quite free from the charge of timidity, adding the hope that since she understands the danger, she will take better care of herself in the future.

This calls forth another letter, in which Mlle. de Rambouillet says, "One never fears to see those whom one loves. I would have given much, for your sake, if this had not occurred." She closes this spicy correspondence, however, with a very affectionate letter which calms the ruffled temper of her sensitive companion.

Mme. de Sablé has another friend, Mlle. d'Attichy, who figures quite prominently in the social life of a later period, as the Comtesse de Maure. This lady was just leaving Paris to visit her in the country, when she learned that Mme. de Sablé had written to Mme. de Rambouillet that she could conceive of no greater happiness than to pass her life alone with Julie d'Angennes. This touches her sensibilities so keenly that she changes her plans, and refuses to visit one who could find her pleasure away from her. Mme. de Sablé tries in vain to appease her exacting friend, who replies to her explanations by a long letter in which she recalls their tender and inviolable friendship, and closes with these words:

> Malheureuse est l'ignorance,
> Et plus malheureux le savoir.

Having thus lost a confidence which alone rendered life supportable to me, I cannot dream of taking the journey so much talked of ; for there would be no propriety in traveling sixty leagues at this season, in order to burden you with a person so uninteresting to you, that after years of a passion without parallel you cannot help thinking that the greatest pleasure would consist in passing life without her. I return then into my solitude, to examine the faults which cause me so much unhappiness, and unless I can correct them I should have less joy than confusion in seeing you. I kiss your hands very humbly.

How this affair was adjusted does not appear, but as they remained devoted friends through life, unable to live apart, or pass a day happily without seeing each other, it evidently did not end in a serious alienation. It suggests, however, a delicacy and an exaltation of feeling which we are apt to accord only to love, and which go far toward disproving the verdict of Montaigne, that "the soul of a woman is not firm enough for so durable a tie as friendship."

We like to dwell upon these inner phases of a famous and powerful coterie, not only because they bring before us so vividly the living, moving, thinking, loving women who composed it, letting us into their intimate life with its quiet shadings, its fantastic humors, and its wayward caprices, but because they lead us to the fountain-head of a new form of literary expression. We have seen that the formal letters of Balzac were among the early entertainments of the Hôtel de Rambouillet, and that Voiture had a witty or sentimental note for every occasion. Mlle. de Scudéry held a ready pen, and was in the habit of noting down in her letters to absent friends the conversation, which ran over a great variety of topics, from the gossip of the moment to the gravest questions. There was no morning journal with its columns of daily news, no magazine with its sketches of contemporary life, and these private letters were passed from one to another to be read and discussed. The craze for clever letters spread. Conversations literally overflowed upon paper. A romantic adventure, a bit of scandal, a drawing-room incident, or a personal pique, was a fruitful theme. Everybody aimed to excel in an art which brought a certain prestige. These letters, most of which had their brief day, were often gathered into little volumes. Many have long since disappeared, or found burial in the dust of old libraries from which they are occasionally exhumed to throw fresh light upon some forgotten nook and by-way of an age whose habits and manners, virtues and follies, they so faithfully record. A few, charged with the vitality of genius, retain their freshness, and live among the enduring monuments of the society that gave them birth. The finest outcome of this prevailing taste was Mme. de Sévigné, who still reigns as the queen of graceful letter-writers. Although her maturity belongs to a later period, she was familiar with the Rambouillet circle in her youth, and inherited its best spirit.

The charm of this literature is its spontaneity. It has no ulterior aim, but delights in simple expression. These people write because they like to write. They are original because they sketch from life. There is something naïve and fresh in their vivid pictures. They give us all the accessories. They tell us how they lived, how they dressed, how they thought, how they acted. They talk of their plans, their loves, and their private piques, with the same ingenuous frankness. They condense for us their worldly philosophy, their sentiments, and their experience. The style of these letters is sometimes heavy and stilted, the wit is often strained and far-fetched, but many of them are written with an easy grace and a lightness of touch as fascinating as inimitable.

The marriage of Julie d'Angennes, in 1645, deprived the Hôtel de Rambouillet of one of its chief attractions. It was only through the earnest wish of her family that, after a delay of thirteen years, she yielded at last to the persevering suit of the Marquis, afterwards the Duc de Montausier, and became his wife. She was then thirty-eight, and he three years younger. The famous *Guirlande de Julie*, which he dedicated and presented to her, still exists, as the unique memorial of his patient and enduring love. This beautiful volume, richly bound, decorated with a flower exquisitely painted on each of the twenty-nine leaves and accompanied by a madrigal written by the Marquis himself or by some of the poets who frequented her house, was a remarkable tribute to the graces of the woman whose praises were so delicately sung. The faithful lover, who was a Protestant, gave a crowning proof of his devotion, in changing his religion. So much adoration could hardly fail to touch the most capricious and obdurate of hearts.

We cannot dismiss this woman, whom Cousin regards as the most accomplished type of the society she adorned; without a word more. Though her ambition was gratified by the honors that fell upon her husband, who after holding many high positions was finally entrusted with the education of the Dauphin; and though her own appointment of *dame d'honneur* to the Queen gave her an envied place at court, we trace with regret the close of her brilliant career. As has been already indicated, she added to much *esprit* a character of great sweetness, and manners facile, gracious, even caressing. With less elevation, less independence, and less firmness than her mother, she had more of the sympathetic quality, the frank unreserve, that wins the heart. No one had so many adorers; no one scattered so many hopeless passions; no one so gently tempered these into friendships. She knew always how to say the fitting word, to charm away the clouds of ill-humor, to conciliate opposing interests. But this spirit of complaisance which, however charming it may be, is never many degrees removed from the spirit of the courtier, proved to be the misfortune of her later life. Too amiable, perhaps too diplomatic, to frown openly upon the King's irregularities, she was accused, whether justly or otherwise, of tacitly favoring his relations with Mme. de Montespan. The husband of this lady took his wife's infidelity very much to heart, and, failing to find any redress, forced himself one day into the presence of Madame de Montausier, and made a violent scene which so affected her that she fell into a profound melancholy and an illness from which she never rallied. There is always an air of mystery thrown about this affair, and it is difficult to fathom the exact truth; but the results were sufficiently tragical to the woman who was quoted by her age as a model of virtue and decorum.

In 1648, the troubles of the Fronde, which divided friends and added fuel to petty social rivalries, scattered the most noted guests of the Hôtel de Rambouillet. Voiture was dead; Angélique Paulet died two years later. The young Marquis de Pisani, the only son and the hope of his family, had fallen with many brave comrades on the field of Nordlingen. Of the five daughters, three were abbesses of convents. The health of the Marquise, which had always been delicate, was still further enfeebled by the successive griefs which darkened her closing years.   Her husband, of whom we know little save that he was sent on various foreign missions, and "loved his wife always as a lover," died in 1652.   She survived him thirteen years, living to see the death of her youngest daughter, Angélique, wife of the Comte de Grignan who was afterwards the son-in-law of Mme. de Sévigné.   She witnessed the elevation of her favorite Julie, but was spared the grief of her death which occurred five or six years after her own.   The aged Marquise, true to her early tastes, continued to receive her friends in her *ruelle,* and her salon had a brief revival when the Duchesse de Montausier returned from the provinces, after the second Fronde; but its freshness had faded with its draperies of blue and gold.   The brilliant company that made it so famous was dispersed, and the glory of the *salon bleu* was gone.

There is something infinitely pathetic in the epitaph this much-loved and successful woman wrote for herself when she felt that the end was near:

> Ici gît Arthénice, exempte des rigueurs
> Dont la rigueur du sort l'a toujours poursuivie.
> Et si tu veux, passant, compter tous ses malheurs,
> Tu n'aura qu'à compter les moments de sa vie.

The spirit of unrest is there beneath the calm exterior. It may be some hidden wound; it may be only the old, old weariness, the inevitable burden of the race.   "Mon Dieu!" wrote Mme. de Maintenon, in the height of her worldly success, "how sad life is!   I pass my days without other consolation than the thought that death will end it all."

Mme. de Rambouillet had worked unconsciously toward a very important end.   She found a language crude and inelegant, manners coarse and licentious, morals dissolute and vicious.   Her influence was at its height in the age of Corneille and Descartes, and she lived almost to the culmination of the era of Racine and Molière, of Boileau and La Bruyère, of Bossuet and Fénelon, the era of simple and purified language, of refined and stately manners, and of at least outward respect for morality. To these results she largely contributed. Her salon was the social and literary power of the first half of the century. In an age of political espionage, it maintained its position and its dignity. It sustained Corneille against the persecutions of Richelieu, and numbered among its *habitués* the founders of the Académie Française, who continued the critical reforms begun there.

As a school of politeness, it has left permanent traces. This woman of fine ideals and exalted standards exacted of others the purity of character, delicacy of thought, and urbanity of manner, which she possessed in so eminent a degree herself. Her code was founded upon the best instincts of humanity, and whatever modifications of form time has wrought its essential spirit remains unchanged. "Politeness does not always inspire goodness, equity, complaisance, gratitude," says La Bruyère, "but it gives at least the appearance of these qualities, and makes man seem externally what he ought to be internally."

It was in this salon, too, that the modern art of conversation, which has played so conspicuous a part in French life, may be said to have had its birth. Men and women met on a footing of equality, with similar tastes and similar interests. Different ranks and conditions were represented, giving a certain cosmopolitan character to a society which had hitherto been narrow in its scope and limited in its aims. Naturally conversation assumed a new importance, and was subject to new laws. To quote again from La Bruyère, who has so profoundly penetrated the secrets of human nature: "The *esprit* of conversation consists much less in displaying itself than in drawing out the wit of others. . . . Men do not like to admire you, they wish to please; they seek less to be instructed or even to be entertained, than to be appreciated and applauded, and the most delicate pleasure is to make that of others." "To please others," says La Rochefoucauld, "one must speak of the things they love and which concern them, avoid disputes upon indifferent matters, ask questions rarely, and never let them think that one is more in the right than themselves."

Many among the great writers of the age touch in the same tone upon the philosophy underlying the various rules of man-

ners and conversation which were first discussed at the Hôtel
de Rambouillet, and which have passed into permanent though
unwritten laws — unfortunately a little out of fashion in the
present generation.

It is difficult to estimate the impulse given to intelligence
and literary taste by this breaking up of old social crystalliza-
tions. What the *savant* had learned in his closet passed more
or less into current coin. Conversation gave point to thought,
clearness to expression, simplicity to language. Women of
rank and recognized ability imposed the laws of good taste,
and their vivid imaginations changed lifeless abstractions into
something concrete and artistic. Men of letters, who had held
an inferior and dependent position, were penetrated with the
spirit of a refined society, while men of the world, in a circle
where wit and literary skill were distinctions, began to aspire
to the rôle of a *bel esprit*, to pride themselves upon some intellectual gift and the power to write without labor and without
pedantry, as became their rank. Many of them lacked seriousness, dealing mainly with delicate fancies and trivial incidents,
but pleasures of the intellect and taste became the fashion.
Burlesques and *chansons* disputed the palm with madrigals and
sonnets. A neatly turned epigram or a clever letter made a
social success.

Perhaps it was not a school for genius of the first order. Society favors graces of form and expression rather than profound
and serious thought. No Homer, nor Æschylus, nor Milton,
nor Dante is the outgrowth of such a soil. The prophet
or seer shines by the light of his own soul. He deals with
problems and emotions that lie deep in the pulsing heart of
humanity, but he does not best interpret his generation. It
is the man living upon the level of his time, and finding his
inspiration in the world of events, who reflects its life, marks
its currents, and registers its changes. Matthew Arnold has
aptly said that "the qualities of genius are less transfer-
able than the qualities of intelligence, less can be immediately
learned and appropriated from their product; they are less
direct and stringent intellectual agencies, though they may be
more beautiful and divine." It was this quality of intelligence

that eminently characterized the literature of the seventeenth century. It was a mirror of social conditions, or their natural outcome. The spirit of its social life penetrated its thought, colored its language, and molded its forms. We trace it in the letters and *vers de société* which were the pastime of the Hôtel de Rambouillet and the *Samedis* of Mlle. de Scudéry, as well as in the romances which reflected their sentiments and pictured their manners. We trace it in the literary portraits which were the diversion of the coterie of Mademoiselle, at the Luxembourg, and in the voluminous memoirs and chronicles which grew out of it. We trace it also in the *Maxims* and *Thoughts* which were polished and perfected in the convent salon of Mme. de Sablé, and were the direct fruits of a wide experience and observation of the great world. It would be unfair to say that anything so complex as the growth of a new literature was wholly due to any single influence, but the intellectual drift of the time seems to have found its impulse in the salons. They were the alembics in which thought was fused and crystallized. They were the schools in which the French mind cultivated its extraordinary clearness and flexibility.

As the century advanced, the higher literature was tinged and modified by the same spirit. Society, with its follies and affectations, inspired the mocking laughter of Molière, but its unwritten laws tempered his language and refined his wit. Its fine urbanity was reflected in the harmony and delicacy of Racine, as well as in the critical decorum of Boileau. The artistic sentiment ruled in letters, as in social life. It was not only the thought that counted, but the setting of the thought. The majestic periods of Bossuet, the tender persuasiveness of Fénelon, gave even truth a double force. The moment came when this critical refinement, this devotion to form, passed its limits, and the inevitable reaction followed. The great literary wave of the seventeenth century reached its brilliant climax and broke upon the shores of a new era. But the seeds of thought had been scattered, to spring up in the great literature of humanity that marked the eighteenth century.

The Women
of the
French Salons

CHAPTER III

MADEMOISELLE DE SCUDÉRY AND THE *Samedis*

Salons of the Noblesse — "The Illustrious Sappho" — Her Romances — The Samedis — Bons Mots of Mme. Cornuel — Estimate of Mlle. de Scudéry.

HERE were a few contemporary salons among the *noblesse*, modeled more or less after the Hôtel de Rambouillet, but none of their leaders had the happy art of conciliating so many elements. They had a literary flavor, and patronized men of letters, often, doubtless, because it was the fashion and the name of a well-known *littérateur* gave them a certain éclat; but they were not cosmopolitan, and have left no marked traces. One of the most important of these was the Hôtel de Condé, over which the beautiful Charlotte de Montmorency presided with such dignity and grace, during the youth of her daughter, the Duchesse de Longueville. Another was the Hôtel de Nevers, where the gifted Marie de Gonzague, afterward Queen of Poland, and her charming sister, the Princesse Palatine, were the central attractions of a brilliant and intellectual society. Richelieu, recognizing the power of the Rambouillet circle, wished to transfer it to the salon of his niece at the Petit Luxembourg. We have a glimpse of the young and still worldly Pascal, explaining here his discoveries in mathematics and his experiments in physics. The tastes of this courtly company were evidently rather serious, as we find another celebrity, of less enduring fame, discoursing upon the immortality of the soul. But the rank, talent, and masterful

MLLE. DE SCUDÉRY.

FROM AN ENGRAVING.

character of the Duchesse d'Aiguillon did not suffice to give her salon the wide influence of its model; it was tainted by her own questionable character, and always hampered by the suspicion of political intrigues.

There were smaller coteries, however, which inherited the spirit and continued the traditions of the Hôtel de Rambouillet. Prominent among these was that of Madeleine de Scudéry, who held her *Samedis* in modest fashion in the Marais. These famous reunions lacked the prestige and the fine tone of their model, but they had a definite position, and a wide though not altogether favorable influence.　As the forerunner of Mme. de La Fayette and Mme. de Sévigné, and one of the most eminent literary women of the century with which her life ran parallel, Mlle. de Scudéry has a distinct interest for us and it is to her keen observation and facile pen that we are indebted for the most complete and vivid picture of the social life of the period.

The "illustrious Sappho," as she was pleased to be called, certainly did not possess the beauty popularly accorded to her namesake and prototype.　She was tall and thin, with a long, dark, and not at all regular face; Mme. Cornuel said that one could see clearly "she was destined by Providence to blacken paper, as she sweat ink from every pore."　But, if we may credit her admirers, who were numerous, she had fine eyes, a pleasing expression, and an agreeable address.　She evidently did not overestimate her personal attractions, as will be seen from the following quatrain, which she wrote upon a portrait made by one of her friends.

> Nanteuil, en faisant mon image,
> A de son art divin signalé le pouvoir;
> Je hais mes yeux dans mon miroir,
> Je les aime dans son ouvrage.

She had her share, however, of small but harmless vanities, and spoke of her impoverished family, says Tallemant, "as one might speak of the overthrow of the Greek empire."　Her father belonged to an old and noble house of Provence, but removed to Normandy, where he married and died, leaving two children with a heritage of talent and poverty.　A trace of the Provençal spirit always clung to Madeleine, who was born in 1607, and lived until the first year of the following century. After losing her mother, who is said to have been a woman of some distinction, she was carefully educated by an uncle in all the accomplishments of the age, as well as in the serious studies which were then unusual.　According to her friend Conrart she was a veritable encyclopedia of knowledge both useful and ornamental.　"She had a prodigious imagination," he writes, "an excellent memory, an exquisite judgment, a lively temper, and a natural disposition to understand everything curious which she saw done, and everything laudable which she heard talked of. She learned the things that concern agriculture, gardening, housekeeping, cooking, and a life in the country: also the causes and effects of maladies, the composition of an infinite number of remedies, perfumes, scented waters and distillations useful or agreeable. She wished to play the lute, and took some lessons with success." In addition to all this, she mastered Spanish and Italian, read extensively and conversed brilliantly. At the death of her uncle and in the freshness of her youth, she went to Paris with her brother who had some pretension as a poet and dramatic writer. He even posed as a rival of Corneille, and was sustained by Richelieu, but time has long since relegated him to comparative oblivion. His sister, who was a victim of his selfish tyranny, is credited with much of the prose which appeared under his name; indeed, her first romances were thus disguised. Her love for conversation was so absorbing, that he is said to have locked her in her room, and refused her to her friends until a certain amount of writing was done. But, in spite of this surveillance, her life was so largely in the world that it was a mystery when she did her voluminous work.

Of winning temper and pleasing address, with this full equipment of knowledge and imagination, versatility and ambition, she was at an early period domesticated in the family of Mme. de Rambouillet as the friend and companion of Julie d'Angennes. Her graces of mind and her amiability made her a favorite with those who frequented the house, and she was thus brought into close contact with the best society of her time. She has painted it carefully and minutely in the *Grand Cyrus*, a romantic allegory in which she transfers the French aristocracy and French manners of the seventeenth century to an oriental court. The Hôtel de Rambouillet plays an important part as the Hôtel Cléomire. When we consider that the central figures were the Prince de Condé and his lovely sister the Duchesse de Longueville, also that the most distinguished men and women of the age saw their own portraits, somewhat idealized but quite recognizable, through the thin disguise of Persians, Greeks, Armenians, or Egyptians, it

is easy to imagine that the ten volumes of rather exalted sentiment were eagerly sought and read. She lacked incident
and constructive power, but excelled in vivid portraits, subtle
analysis, and fine conversations. She made no attempt at
local color; her plots were strained and unnatural, her style
heavy and involved. But her penetrating intellect was thoroughly tinged with the romantic spirit, and she had the art
of throwing a certain glamour over everything she touched.
Cousin, who has rescued the memory of Mlle. de Scudéry from
many unjust aspersions, says that she was the "creator of the
psychological romance." Unquestionably her skill in character-
painting set the fashion for the pen-portraits which became a
mania a few years later.

She depicts herself as Sappho, whose opinions may be supposed to reflect her own. In these days, when the position of
women is discussed from every possible point of view, it may
be interesting to know how it was regarded by one who
represented the thoughtful side of the age in which their social
power was first distinctly asserted. She classes her critics and
enemies under several heads. Among them are the "light and
coquettish women whose only occupation is to adorn their persons and pass their lives in fêtes and amusements — women
who think that scrupulous virtue requires them to know nothing but to be the wife of a husband, the mother of children,
and the mistress of a family; and men who regard women as
upper servants, and forbid their daughters to read anything but
their prayer-books."

"One does not wish women to be coquettes," she writes
again, "but permits them to learn carefully all that fits them
for gallantry, without teaching them anything which can fortify
their virtue or occupy their minds. They devote ten or a dozen
years to learning to appear well, to dress in good style, to
dance and sing, for five or six; but this same person, who
requires judgment all her life and must talk until her last
sigh, learns nothing which can make her converse more agreeably, or act with more wisdom."

But she does not like a *femme savante*, and ridicules, under
the name of *Damophile*, a character which might have been

the model for Molière's *Philaminte*. This woman has five or six masters, of whom the least learned teaches astrology. She poses as a Muse, and is always surrounded with books, pencils, and mathematical instruments, while she uses large words in a grave and imperious tone, although she speaks only of little things. After many long conversations about her, Sappho concludes thus: "I wish it to be said of a woman that she knows a hundred things of which she does not boast, that she has a well-informed mind, is familiar with fine works, speaks well, writes correctly, and knows the world; but I do not wish it to be said of her that she is a *femme savante*. The two characters have no resemblance." She evidently recognized the fact that when knowledge has penetrated the soul, it does not need to be worn on the outside, as it shines through the entire personality.

After some further discussion, to the effect that the wise woman will conceal superfluous learning and especially avoid pedantry, she defines the limit to which a woman may safely go in knowledge without losing her right to be regarded as the "ornament of the world, made to be served and adored."

One may know some foreign languages and confess to reading Homer, Hesiod, and the works of the illustrious Aristée (Chapelain), without being too learned. One may express an opinion so modestly that, without offending the propriety of her sex, she may permit it to be seen that she has wit, knowledge, and judgment. That which I wish principally to teach women is not to speak too much of that which they know well, never to speak of that which they do not know at all, and to speak reasonably.

We note always a half-apologetic tone, a spirit of compromise between her conscious intelligence and the traditional prejudice which had in no wise diminished since Martial included, in his picture of a domestic *ménage*, a wife "not too learned." She is not willing to lose a woman's birthright of love and devotion, but is not quite sure how far it might be affected by her ability to detect a solecism. Hence, she offers a great deal of subtle flattery to masculine self-love. With curious *naïveté* she says:

Whoever should write all that was said by fifteen or twenty women together would make the worst book in the world, even if some of them were women of

ÉLISABETH SOPHIE CHÉRON — MME. LE HAY.
FROM AN ENGRAVING.

intelligence. But if a man should enter, a single one, and not even a man of distinction, the same conversation would suddenly become more *spirituelle* and more agreeable.   The conversation of men is doubtless less sprightly when there are no women present ; but ordinarily, although it may be more serious, it is still rational, and they can do without us more easily than we can do without them.

She attaches great importance to conversation, as " the bond of society, the greatest pleasure of well-bred people, and the best means of introducing, not only politeness into the world, but a purer morality." She dwells always upon the necessity of " a spirit of urbanity, which banishes all bitter railleries, as well as everything that can offend the taste," also of a certain " *esprit de joie.*"

We find here the code which ruled the Hôtel de Rambouillet, and the very well-defined character of the *précieuse.* But it may be noted that Mlle. de Scudéry, who was among the *avant-coureurs* of the modern movement for the advancement of women, always preserved the forms of the old traditions, while violating their spirit. True to her Gallic instincts, she presented her innovations sugar-coated. She had the fine sense of fitness which is the conscience of her race, and which gave so much power to the women who really revolutionized society without antagonizing it.

Her conversations, which were full of wise suggestions and showed a remarkable insight into human character, were afterwards published in detached form and had a great success. Mme. de Sévigné writes to her daughter: "Mlle. de Scudéry has just sent me two little volumes of conversations; it is impossible that they should not be good, when they are not drowned in a great romance."

When the Hôtel de Rambouillet was closed, Mlle. de Scudéry tried to replace its pleasant reunions by receiving her friends on Saturdays. These informal receptions were frequented by a few men and women of rank, but the prevailing tone was literary and slightly *bourgeois.* We find there, from time to time, Mme. de Sablé, the Duc and Duchesse de Montausier, and others of the old circle who were her lifelong friends. La Rochefoucauld is there occasionally, also Mme. de La Fayette, Mme. de Sévigné, and the young Mme. Scarron whose brilliant future is hardly yet in her dreams. Among those less known to-day, but of note in their age, were the Comtesse de la Suze, a favorite writer of elegies, who changed her faith and became a Catholic, as she said, that she "might not meet her husband in this world or the next"; the versatile Mlle. Chéron who had some celebrity as poet, musician, and painter; Mlle. de la Vigne and Mme. Deshoulières, also poets; Mlle. Descartes, niece of the great philosopher; and, at rare intervals, the clever Abbess de Rohan who tempered her piety with a little sage worldliness. One of the most brilliant lights in this galaxy of talent was Mme. Cornuel, whose *bons mots* sparkle from so many pages in the chronicles of the period.

A woman of high *bourgeois* birth and of the best associations, she had a swift vision, a penetrating sense, and a clear intellect prompt to seize the heart of a situation. Mlle. de Scudéry said that she could paint a grand satire in four words. Mme. de Sévigné found her admirable, and even the grave Pomponne begged his friend not to forget to send him all her witticisms. Of the agreeable but rather light Comtesse de Fiesque, she said : " What preserves her beauty is that it is salted in folly." Of James II. of England, she remarked, " The Holy Spirit has eaten up his understanding." The saying that the eight generals appointed at the death of Turenne were "the small change for Turenne " has been attributed to her. It is certainly not to a woman of such keen insight and ready wit that one can attach any of the affectations which later crept into the *Samedis*.

The poet Sarasin is the Voiture of this salon. Conrart, to whose house may be traced the first meetings of the little circle of lettered men which formed the nucleus of the Académie Française, is its secretary; Pellisson, another of the founders and the historian of the same learned body, is its chronicler. Chapelain is quite at home here, and we find also numerous minor authors and artists whose names have small significance to-day. The *Samedis* follow closely in the footsteps of the Hôtel de Rambouillet. It is the aim there to speak simply and naturally upon all subjects grave or gay, to preserve always the spirit of delicacy and urbanity, and to avoid vulgar intrigues. There is a superabundance of sentiment, some affectation, and plenty of *esprit*.

They converse upon all the topics of the day, from fashion to politics, from literature and the arts to the last item of gossip. They read their works, talk about them, criticize them, and vie with one another in improvising verses. Pellisson takes notes and leaves us a multitude of madrigals, sonnets, *chansons* and letters, of varied merit. He says there reigned a sort of epidemic of little poems. " The secret influence began to fall with the dew. Here, one recites four verses ; there, one writes a dozen. All this is done gaily and without effort. No one bites his nails, or stops laughing and talking. There are challenges, responses, repetitions, attacks, repartees. The pen passes from

ANTOINETTE DE LIGIER DE LA GARDE—MME. DESHOULIÈRES.

FROM THE OIL PORTRAIT BY PIERRE MIGNARD.

hand to hand, and the hand does not keep pace with the mind. One makes verses for every lady present." Many of these verses were certainly not of the best quality, but it would be difficult, in any age, to find a company of people clever enough to divert themselves by throwing off such poetic trifles on the spur of the moment.

In the end, the *Samedis* came to have something of the character of a modern literary club, and were held at different houses. The company was less choice, and the *bourgeois* coloring more pronounced. These reunions very clearly illustrated the fact that no society can sustain itself above the average of its members. They increased in size, but decreased in quality, with the inevitable result of affectation and pretension. Intelligence, taste, and politeness were in fashion. Those who did not possess them put on their semblance, and, affecting an intellectual tone, fell into the pedantry which is sure to grow out of the effort to speak above one's altitude. The fine-spun theories of Mlle. de Scudéry also reached a sentimental climax in *Clélie*, which did not fail of its effect. Platonic love and the *ton galant* were the texts for innumerable follies which finally reacted upon the *Samedis*. After a few years, they lost their influence and were discontinued. But Mlle. de Scudéry retained the position which her brilliant gifts and literary fame had given her, and was the center of a choice circle of friends until a short time before her death at the ripe age of ninety-four. Even Tallemant, writing of the decline of these reunions, says, "Mlle. de Scudéry is more considered than ever." At sixty-four she received the first *Prix d'Eloquence* from the Académie Française, for an essay on Glory. This prize was founded by Balzac, and the subject was specified. Thus the long procession of laureates was led by a woman.

In spite of her subtle analysis of love, and her exact map of the Empire of Tenderness, the sentiment of the "Illustrious Sappho" seems to have been rather ideal. She had numerous adorers, of whom Conrart and Pellisson were among the most devoted. During the long imprisonment of the latter for supposed complicity with Fouquet, she was of great service to him, and the tender friendship ended only with his life, upon which she wrote a touching eulogy at its close. But she never married. She feared to lose her liberty. " I know," she writes, " that there are many estimable men who merit all my esteem and who can retain a part of my friendship; but as soon as I regard them as husbands I regard them as masters, and so apt to become tyrants that I must hate them from that moment; and I thank the gods for giving me an inclination very much averse to marriage."

It was the misfortune of Mlle. de Scudéry to outlive her literary reputation. The interminable romances which had charmed the eloquent Fléchier, the Grand Condé in his cell at Vincennes, the ascetic d'Andilly at Port Royal, as well as the dreaming maidens who sighed over their fanciful descriptions and impossible adventures, passed their day. The touch of a merciless criticism stripped them of their already fading glory. Their subtle analysis and etherealized sentiment were declared antiquated, and fashion ran after new literary idols. It was Boileau who gave the severest blow. " This Despréaux," said Segrais, " knows how to do nothing else but talk of himself and criticise others; why speak ill of Mlle. de Scudéry as he has done ? "

There has been a disposition to credit the founder of the *Samedis* with many of the affectations which brought such deserved ridicule upon their *bourgeois* imitators, and to trace in her the original of Molière's *Madelon*. But Cousin has relieved her of such reproach, and does ample justice to the truth and sincerity of her character, the purity of her manners, and the fine quality of her intellect. He calls her "a sort of French sister of Addison." Perhaps her resemblance to one of the clearest, purest, and simplest of English essayists is not quite apparent on the surface; but as a moralist and a delineator of manners she may have done a similar work in her own way.

Sainte-Beuve, who has left so many vivid and exquisite portraits of his countrywomen, does not paint Mlle. de Scudéry with his usual kindly touch. He admits her merit, her accomplishments, her versatility, and the perfect innocence of her life; but he finds her didactic, pedantic, and tiresome as a writer, and without charm or grace as a woman. Doubtless one would

find it difficult to read her romances to-day. She lacks the
genius which has no age and belongs to all ages. Her literary
life pertains to the first half of the seventeenth century, when
style had not reached the Attic purity and elegance of a later
period. She was teacher rather than artist; but no one could
be farther from a *bas bleu*, or more severe upon pedantry or
pretension of any sort. She takes the point of view of her time,
and dwells always upon the wisdom of veiling the knowledge
she claims for her sex behind the purely feminine graces. How
far she practised her own theories, we can know only from the
testimony of her contemporaries. It is not possible to perpetuate so indefinable a thing as personal charm, but we are
told repeatedly that she had it in an eminent degree. It is
certain that no woman without beauty, fortune, or visible rank,
living simply and depending mainly upon her own talents, could
have retained such powerful and fastidious friends, during a long
life, unless she had had some rare attractions. That she was
much loved, much praised, and much sought, we have sufficient
evidence among the writers of her own time. She was familiarly
spoken of as the tenth Muse, and she counted among her personal friends the greatest men and women of the century.
Leibnitz sought her correspondence. The Abbé de Pure, who
was not friendly to the *précieuses* and made the first severe
attack upon them, thus writes of her: "One may call Mlle.
de Scudéry the muse of our age and the prodigy of her sex. It
is not only her goodness and her sweetness, but her intellect
shines with so much modesty, her sentiments are expressed with
so much reserve, she speaks with so much discretion, and all
that she says is so fit and reasonable, that one cannot help both
admiring and loving her. Comparing what one sees of her,
and what one owes to her personally, with what she writes, one
prefers, without hesitation, her conversation to her works.
Although she has a wonderful mind, her heart outweighs it.
It is in the heart of this illustrious woman that one finds true
and pure generosity, an immovable constancy, a sincere and
solid friendship."

The loyalty of her character was conspicuously shown in
her brave devotion to the interests of the Condé family, through

all the reverses of the Fronde. In one of her darkest moments
Mme. de Longueville received the last volume of the "Grand
Cyrus," which was dedicated to her, and immediately sent her
own portrait encircled with diamonds, as the only thing she
had left worthy of this friend who, without sharing ardently her
political prejudices, had never deserted her waning fortunes.
The same rare quality was seen in her unwavering friendship for
Fouquet, during his long disgrace and imprisonment. Mme.
de Sévigné, whose satire was so pitiless toward affectation of
any sort, writes to her in terms of exaggerated tenderness.

"In a hundred thousand words, I could tell you but one
truth, which reduces itself to assuring you, Mademoiselle, that
I shall love you and adore you all my life ; it is only this word
that can express the idea I have of your extraordinary merit.
I am happy to have some part in the friendship and esteem of
such a person. As constancy is a perfection, I say to myself
that you will not change for me ; and I dare to pride myself
that I shall never be sufficiently abandoned of God not to be
always yours. . . . I take to my son your conversations. I wish
him to be charmed with them, after being charmed myself."

Mlle. de Scudéry is especially interesting to us as marking
a transition point in the history of women ; as the author of the
first romances of any note written by her sex ; as a moral teacher
in an age of laxity; and as a woman who combined high aspirations, fine ideals, and versatile talents with a pure and unselfish character. She aimed at universal accomplishments —
from the distillation of a perfume to the writing of a novel,
from the preparation of a rare dish to fine conversation, from
playing the lute to the dissection of the human heart. In this
versatility she has been likened to Mme. de Genlis, whom she
resembled also in her moral teaching and her factitious sensibility. She was, however, more genuine, more amiable, and
far superior in true elevation of character. She was full of
theories and loved to air them, hence the people who move
across the pages of her novels are often lost in a cloud of speculation. But she gave a fresh impulse to literature, adding a
fine quality of grace, tenderness, and pure though often exaggerated sentiment. Mme. de La Fayette, who had more clear-

ness of mind as well as a finer artistic sense, gave a better form
to the novel and pruned it of superfluous matter.   The sentiment which casts so soft and delicate a coloring over her romances was more subtle and refined.   It may be questioned,
however, if she wrote so much that has been incorporated in
the thought of her time.

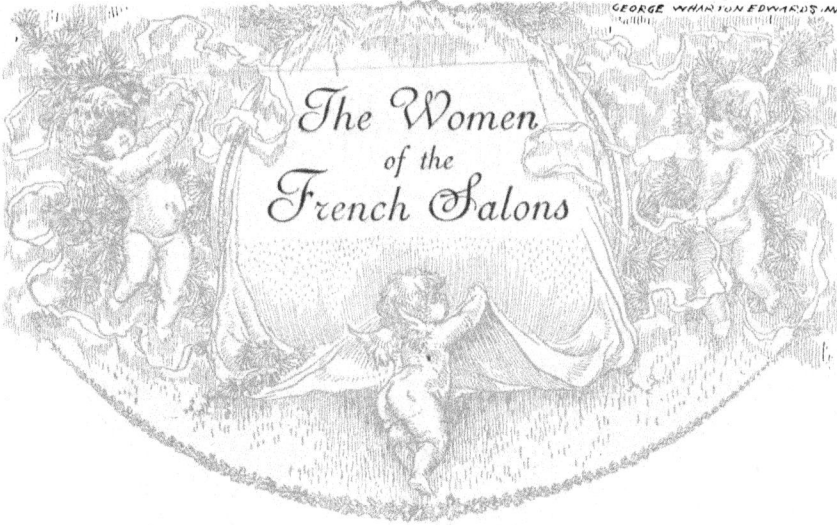

The Women
of the
French Salons

CHAPTER IV

LA GRANDE MADEMOISELLE

*Her Character—Her Heroic Part in the Fronde—Her Exile
— Literary Diversions of her Salon — A Romantic Episode.*

HERE are certain women preëminently distinguished by diversity of gifts, who fail to leave behind them a fame at all commensurate with their promise. It may be from a lack of unity, resulting from a series of fragmentary efforts, no one of which is of surpassing excellence; it may be that the impression of power they give is quite beyond any practical manifestation of it; or it may be that talents in themselves remarkable are cast into the shade by some exceptional brilliancy of position. The success of life is measured by the harmony between its ideals and its attainments. It is the symmetry of the temple that gives the final word, not the breadth of its foundations nor the wealth of its material.

It was this lack of harmony and fine proportion which marred the career of a woman who played a very conspicuous

7

ANNE MARIE LOUISE D'ORLÉANS. DUCHESSE DE MONTPENSIER.

CALLED LA GRANDE MADEMOISELLE. FROM AN OIL PAINTING.

part in the social and political life of her time, and who belongs to my subject only through a single phase of a stormy and eventful history. No study of the salons would be complete without that of the Grande Mademoiselle, but it was not as the leader of a coterie that she held her special claim to recognition. By the accident of birth she stood apart, subject to many limitations that modified the character of her salon and narrowed its scope, though they emphasized its influence. It was only an incident of her life, but through the quality of its *habitués* and their unique diversions it became the source of an important literature.

Anne Marie Louise d'Orléans, Duchesse de Montpensier, has left a very distinct record of herself in letters, romances, memoirs, and portraits, written out of an abounding fullness of nature, but with infinite detail and royal contempt for precision and orthography. She talks naïvely of her happy childhood, of her small caprices, of the love of her grandmother, Marie de Medicis, of her innocent impressions of the people about her. She dwells with special pleasure upon a grand fête at the Palais Royal, in which she posed as an incipient queen. She was then nineteen. "They were three entire days in arranging my costume," she writes. "My robe was covered with diamonds, and trimmed with rose, black and white tufts. I wore all the jewels of the crown and of the Queen of England, who still had some left. No one could be better or more magnificently attired than I was that day, and many people said that my beautiful figure, my imposing mien, my fair complexion, and the splendor of my blonde hair did not adorn me less than all the riches which were upon my person." She sat resplendent upon a raised dais, with the proud consciousness of her right and power to grace a throne. Louis XIV., then a child, and the Prince of Wales, afterwards Charles II., were at her feet. The latter was a devoted suitor. "My heart as well as my eyes regarded the prince *de haut en bas*," she says. "I had the spirit to wed an emperor."

There were negotiations for her marriage with the Emperor of Austria, and she thought it wise to adapt herself in advance to his tastes. She had heard that he was religious, and immediately began to play the part of a *devoté* so seriously, that she was seized with a violent desire to become a veritable *religieuse* and enter the convent of the Carmelites. She could neither eat nor sleep, and it was feared that she would fall dangerously ill. " I can only say that, during those eight days, the empire was nothing to me," she writes. But she confesses to a certain feeling of vanity at her own spirit of self-sacrifice, and the sensibility which made her weep at the thought of leaving those she loved. This access of piety was of short duration, however, as her father quickly put to flight all her exalted visions of a cloister. Her dreams of an emperor for whom she lost a prospective king were alike futile.

" She had beauty, talent, wealth, virtue, and a royal birth," says Mme. de Motteville. " Her face was not without defects, and her intellect was not one which always pleases. Her vivacity deprived all her actions of the gravity necessary to people of her rank, and her mind was too much carried away by her feelings. As she was fair, had fine eyes, a pleasing mouth, was of good height, and blonde, she had quite the air of a great beauty." But it was beauty of a commanding sort, without delicacy, and dependent largely upon the freshness of youth. The same veracious writer says that " she spoiled all she went about by the eagerness and impatience of her temper. She was always too hasty and pushed things too far." What she may have lacked in grace and charm, she made up by the splendors of rank and position.

A princess by birth, closely related to three kings, and glowing with all the fiery instincts of her race, the Grande Mademoiselle curiously blended the courage of an Amazon with the weakness of a passionate and capricious woman. As she was born in 1627, the most brilliant days of her youth were passed amid the excitements of the Fronde. She casts a romantic light upon these trivial wars, which were ended at last by her prompt decision and masculine force. We see her at twenty-five, riding victoriously into the city of Orléans at the head of her troops and, later, ordering the cannon at the Bastile turned against the royal forces, and opening the gates of Paris to the exhausted army of Condé. This adventure gives us the key-note to her haughty and imperious character. She would have posed well for the heroine of a great drama; indeed, she posed all her life in real dramas.

At this time she had hopes of marrying the Prince de Condé, whom she regarded as a hero worthy of her. His wife, an amiable woman who was sent to a convent after her marriage to learn to read and write, was dangerously ill, and her illustrious husband did not scruple to make tacit arrangements to supply her place. Unfortunately for these plans, and fortunately perhaps for a certain interesting phase of literature, she recovered. Soon afterwards, Mademoiselle found the reward of her heroic adventures in a sudden exile to her estates at Saint Fargeau. The country life, so foreign to her tastes, pressed upon her very heavily at first, the more so as she was deserted by most of her friends. " I received more compliments than visits," she writes. " I had made everybody ill. All those who did not dare send me word that they feared to embroil themselves with the court pretended that some malady or accident had befallen them." By degrees, however, she adapted herself to her situation, and in her loneliness and disappointment betook herself to pursuits which offered a strong contrast to the dazzling succession of magnificent fêtes and military episodes which had given variety and excitement to her life at the Tuileries. When she grew tired of her parrots, her dogs, her horses, her comedians and her violins, she found solace in literature, beginning the *Memoirs*, which were finished thirty years later, and writing romances, after the manner of Mlle. de Scudéry. The drift of the first one, *Les Nouvelles françaises et les Divertissements de la princesse Aurélie*, is suggested by its title. It was woven from the little stories or adventures which were told to amuse their solitude by the small coterie of women who had followed the clouded fortunes of Mademoiselle. A romance of more pretension was the *Princesse de Paphlagonie*, in which the writer pictures her own little court, and introduces many of its members under fictitious names. These romances have small interest for the world to-day, but the exalted position of their author and their personal character made them much talked of in their time.

It was in quite another fashion, however, that the Grande Mademoiselle made her most important contribution to literature. One day in 1657, while still in the country, she proposed to her friends to make pen-portraits of themselves, and set the fashion by writing her own, with a detailed description of her physical, mental, and moral qualities. This was followed by carefully drawn pictures of others, among whom were Louis XIV., Monsieur, and the Grand Condé. All were bound in honor to give the lights and shadows with the same fidelity, though it would be hardly wise to call them to too strict an account on this point. As may be readily imagined, the result was something piquant and original. That the amusement was a popular one goes without saying. People like to talk of themselves, not only because the subject is interesting, but because it gives them an opportunity of setting in relief their virtues and tempering their foibles. They like also to know what others think of them — at least, what others say of them. It is too much to expect of human nature, least of all, of French human nature, that an agreeable modicum of subtle flattery should not be added under such conditions.

When Mademoiselle opened her salon in the Luxembourg, on her return from exile, these portraits formed one of its most marked features. The salon was limited mainly to the nobility, with the addition of a few men of letters. Among those who frequented it on intimate terms were the Marquise de Sablé, the Comtesse de Maure, the beautiful and pure-hearted Mme. de Hautefort, the *dame d'honneur* of Anne of Austria, so hopelessly adored by Louis XIII., and Mme. de Choisy, the witty wife of the chancellor of the Duc d'Orléans. Its most brilliant lights were Mme. de Sévigné, Mme de La Fayette, and La Rochefoucauld. It was here that Mme. de La Fayette made the vivid portrait of her friend Mme. de Sévigné. "It flatters me," said the latter long afterwards, "but those who loved me sixteen years ago may have thought it true." The beautiful Comtesse de Brégy, who was called one of the muses of the time, portrayed the Princess Henrietta and the irrepressible Queen Christine of Sweden. Mme. de Châtillon, known later as the Duchesse de Mecklenbourg, who was mingled with all the intrigues of this period, traces a very agreeable sketch of herself, which may serve as a specimen of this interesting diversion. After minutely describing her person, which she evidently regards with much complacence, she continues:

"I have a temper naturally cheerful and a little given to raillery; but I correct this inclination, for fear of displeasing. I have much *esprit*, and enter agreeably into conversation. I have a pleasant voice and a modest air. I am very sincere and do not fail my friends. I have not a trifling mind, nor do I cherish a thousand small malices against my neighbor. I love glory and fine actions. I have heart and ambition. I am very sensitive to good and ill, but I never avenge myself for the ill that has been done me, although I might have the inclination; I am restrained by self-love. I have a sweet disposition, take pleasure in serving my friends, and fear nothing so much as the petty drawing-room quarrels which usually grow out of little nothings. I find my person and my temper constructed something after this fashion; and I am so satisfied with both, that I envy no one. I leave to my friends or to my enemies the care of seeking my faults."

It was under this stimulating influence that La Rochefoucauld made the well-known pen-portrait of himself. "I will lack neither boldness to speak as freely as I can of my good qualities," he writes, "nor sincerity to avow frankly that I have faults." After describing his person, temper, abilities, passions, and tastes, he adds with curious candor: "I am but little given to pity, and do not wish to be so at all. Nevertheless there is nothing I would not do for an afflicted person; and I sincerely believe one should do all one can to show sympathy for misfortune, as miserable people are so foolish that this does them the greatest good in the world; but I also hold that we should be content with expressing sympathy, and carefully avoid having any. It is a passion that is wholly worthless in a well-regulated mind, that only serves to weaken the heart, and should be left to people, who, never doing anything from reason, have need of passion to stimulate their actions. I love my friends; and I love them to such an extent that I would not for a moment weigh my interest against theirs. I condescend to them, I patiently endure their bad temper. But I do not make much of their caresses, and I do not feel great uneasiness at their absence."

It would be interesting to quote in full this sample of the close and not always flattering self-analysis so much in fashion, but its length forbids. Its revelation of the hidden springs of character is at least unique.

The poet Segrais, who was attached to Mademoiselle's household, collected these graphic pictures for private circulation, but they were so much in demand that they were soon printed for the public under the title of *Divers Portraits*. They served the double purpose of furnishing to the world faithful delineations of many more or less distinguished people and of setting a literary fashion. The taste for pen-portraits, which originated in the romances of Mlle. de Scudéry, and received a fresh impulse from this novel and personal application, spread rapidly among all classes. It was taken up by men of letters and men of the world, the nobility, and the *bourgeoisie*. There were portraits of every grade of excellence and every variety of people, until they culminated, some years later, in *Les Caractères* of La Bruyère, who dropped personalities and gave them the form of permanent types. It is a literature peculiarly adapted to the flexibility and fine perception of the French mind, and one in which it has been preëminent, from the analytic but diffuse Mlle. de Scudéry, and the clear, terse, spirited Cardinal de Retz, to the fine, penetrating, and exquisitely finished Sainte-Beuve, the prince of modern critics and literary artists. It was this skill in vivid delineation that gave such point and piquancy to the memoirs of the period, which are little more than a series of brilliant and vigorous sketches of people outlined upon a shifting background of events. In this rapid characterization the French have no rivals. It is the charm of their fiction as well as of their memoirs. Balzac, Victor Hugo, and Daudet, are the natural successors of La Bruyère and Saint-Simon.

The marriage of Louis XIV. shattered one of the most brilliant illusions of the Grande Mademoiselle, and it was about this time that she wrote a characteristic letter to Mme. de

FRANÇOISE BERTAUT, MME. DE MOTTEVILLE.

FROM AN OIL PAINTING.

8

Motteville, picturing an Arcadia in some beautiful forest,
where people are free to do as they like. The most ardent
apostle of socialism could hardly dream of an existence more
democratic or more Utopian. These favored men and women
lead a simple, pastoral life. They take care of the house and
the garden, milk the cows, make cheese and cakes, and tend
sheep on pleasant days. But this rustic community must have
its civilized amusements. They visit, drive, ride on horseback,
paint, design, play on the lute or clavecin, and have all the new
books sent to them. After reading the lives of heroes and
philosophers, the princess is convinced that no one is perfectly
happy, and that Christianity is desirable, as it gives hope for
the future. Her platonic and Christian republic is composed
of "amiable and perfect people," but it is quite free from the
entanglements of love and the "vulgar institution of marriage."
Mme. de Motteville replies very gracefully, accepting many of
these ideas, but as it is difficult to repress love altogether, she
thinks "one will be obliged to permit that error which an
old custom has rendered legitimate, and which is called marriage." This curious correspondence takes its color from the
Spanish pastorals which tinged the romantic literature of the
time as well as its social life. The long letters, carefully written on large and heavy sheets yellow with age, have a peculiarly old-time flavor, and throw a vivid light upon the woman
who could play the rôle of a heroine of Corneille or of a sentimental shepherdess, as the caprice seized her.

A tragical bit of romance colored the mature life of the
Grande Mademoiselle. She had always professed a great aversion to love, regarding it as "unworthy of a well-ordered soul."
She even went so far as to say that it was better to marry from
reason or any other thing imaginable, dislike included, than
from passion that was, in any case, short-lived. But this princess of intrepid spirit, versatile gifts, ideal fancies, and platonic theories, who had aimed at an emperor and missed a
throne; this amazon, with her *penchant* for glory and contempt
for love, forgot all her sage precepts, and at forty two fell a
victim to a violent passion for the Comte de Lauzun. She has
traced its course to the finest shades of sentiment. Her pride,

her infatuation, her scruples, her new-born humility — we are made familiar with them all, even to the *finesse* of her respectful adorer, and the reluctant confession of love which his discreet silence wrings from her at last. Her royal cousin, after much persuasion, consented to the unequal union. The impression this affair made upon the world is vividly shown in a letter written by Mme. de Sévigné to her daughter:

> I am going to tell you a thing the most astonishing, the most surprising, the most marvelous, the most miraculous, the most triumphant, the most astounding, the most unheard of, the most singular, the most extraordinary, the most incredible, the most unexpected, the grandest, the smallest, the rarest, the most common, the most dazzling, the most secret even until to-day, the most brilliant, the most worthy of envy . . . . a thing in fine which is to be done Sunday, when those who see it will believe themselves dazed; a thing which is to be done Sunday and which will not perhaps have been done Monday. . . . M. de Lauzun marries Sunday, at the Louvre — guess whom? . . . . He marries Sunday at the Louvre, with the permission of the King, Mademoiselle, Mademoiselle de, Mademoiselle: guess the name; he marries Mademoiselle, *ma foi, par ma foi, ma foi jurée*, Mademoiselle, la grande Mademoiselle, Mademoiselle, daughter of the late Monsieur, Mademoiselle, grand-daughter of Henry IV., Mademoiselle d'Eu, Mademoiselle de Dombes, Mademoiselle de Montpensier, Mademoiselle d'Orléans, Mademoiselle, cousin of the king, Mademoiselle, destined to the throne, Mademoiselle, the only *parti* in France worthy of Monsieur. *Voilà* a fine subject for conversation. If you cry out, if you are beside yourself, if you say that we have deceived you, that it is false, that one trifles with you, that it is a fine bit of raillery, that it is very stupid to imagine, if, in fine, you abuse us, we shall find that you are right; we have done as much ourselves.

In spite of the prudent warnings of her friends, the happy princess could not forego the éclat of a grand wedding, and before the hasty arrangements were concluded, the permission was withdrawn. Her tears, her entreaties, her cries, her rage, and her despair, were of no avail. Louis XIV. took her in his arms, and mingled his tears with hers, even reproaching her for the two or three days of delay; but he was inexorable. Ten years of loyal devotion to her lover, shortly afterward imprisoned at Pignerol, and of untiring efforts for his release which was at last secured at the cost of half her vast estates, ended in a brief reunion. A secret marriage, a swift discovery that her idol was of very common clay, abuse so violent that she was obliged to forbid him forever her presence, and the disenchantment was complete. The sad remnant of her existence was devoted to literature and to conversation; the latter she regarded as "the greatest pleasure in life, and almost the only one." When she died, the Count de Lauzun wore the deepest mourning, had portraits of her everywhere, and adopted permanently the subdued colors that would fitly express the inconsolable nature of his grief.

Without tact or fine discrimination, the Grande Mademoiselle was a woman of generous though undisciplined impulses, loyal disposition, and pure character; but her egotism was colossal. Under different conditions, one might readily imagine her a second Joan of Arc, or a heroine of the Revolution. She says of herself: "I know not what it is to be a heroine; I am of a birth to do nothing that is not grand or elevated. One may call that what one likes. As for myself, I call it to follow my own inclination and to go my own way. I am not born to take that of others." She lacked the measure, the form, the delicacy of the typical *précieuse;* but her quick, restless intellect and ardent imagination were swift to catch the spirit of the Hôtel de Rambouillet, and to apply it in an original fashion. Though many subjects were interdicted in her salon, and many people were excluded, it gives us interesting glimpses into the life of the literary *noblesse,* and furnishes a complete gallery of pen-portraits of more or less noted men and women. With all the brilliant possibilities of her life, it was through the diversion of her idle hours that this princess, author, amazon, prospective queen, and disappointed woman has left the most permanent trace upon the world.

The Women
of the
French Salons

CHAPTER V

A LITERARY SALON AT PORT ROYAL

Mme. de Sablé — Her Worldly Life — Her Retreat — Her Friends — Pascal — The Maxims of La Rochefoucauld — Last Days of the Marquise.

HE transition from the restless character and stormy experiences of the Grande Mademoiselle, to the gentler nature and the convent salon of her friend and literary *confidante*, Mme. de Sablé, is a pleasant one. Perhaps no one better represents the true *précieuse* of the seventeenth century, the happy blending of social *savoir-faire* with an amiable temper and a cultivated intellect. Without the genius of Mme. de Sévigné or Mme. de La Fayette, without the force or the rare attractions of Mme. de Longueville, without the well-poised character and catholic sympathies of Mme. de Rambouillet, she played an important part in the life of her time, through her fine insight and her consummate tact in bringing together the choicest spirits, and turning their thoughts into channels that were fresh and unworn. Born in 1599, Madeleine de Souvré passed her childhood in Touraine, of which province her father was governor. In the brilliancy of her youth, we find her in Paris, among the early favorites of the Hôtel de Rambouillet, and on terms of lifelong intimacy with its hostess and her daughter Julie. Beautiful, versatile, generous, but fastidious and exacting in her friendships, with a dash of coquetry — inevitable when a woman is fascinating and French — she repeated the oft-played rôle of a *mariage de convenance* at sixteen, a few brilliant years of social triumphs marred by domestic neglect and suffering, a period of enforced seclusion after the death of her unworthy husband, a brief return to the world, and an old age of mild and comfortable devotion.

"The Marquise de Sablé," writes Mme. de Motteville, "was one of those whose beauty made the most sensation when the Queen (Anne of Austria) came into France. But if she was amiable, she desired still more to appear so. Her self-love rendered her a little too sensible to that which men professed for her. There was still in France some remnant of the politeness which Catherine de Médicis had brought from Italy, and Mme. de Sablé found so much delicacy in the new dramas, as well as in other works, in prose and verse, which came from Madrid, that she conceived a high idea of the gallantry which the Spaniards had learned from the Moors. She was persuaded that men may without wrong have tender sentiments for women ; that the desire of pleasing them leads men to the greatest and finest actions, arouses their spirit, and inspires them with liberality and all sorts of virtues ; but that, on the other side, women, who are the ornaments of the world, and made to be served and adored, ought to permit only respectful attentions. This lady, having sustained her views with much talent and great beauty, gave them authority in her time."

The same writer says that she has "much light and sincerity," with "penetration enough to unfold all the secrets of one's heart."

Mlle. de Scudéry introduces her in the *Grand Cyrus*, as *Parthénie*, "a tall and graceful woman, with fine eyes, the most beautiful throat in the world, a lovely complexion, blonde hair, and a pleasant mouth, with a charming air, and a fine and eloquent smile, which expresses the sweetness or the bitterness

MADELEINE DE SOUVRÉ, MARQUISE DE SABLÉ.

FROM AN OIL PAINTING.

of her soul." She dwells upon her surprising and changeful beauty, upon the charm of her conversation, the variety of her knowledge, the delicacy of her tact, and the generosity of her tender and passionate heart. One may suspect this portrait of being idealized, but it seems to have been in the main correct.

Of her husband we know very little, excepting that he belonged to the family of Montmorency, passed from violent

CATHERINE DE MÉDICIS, REINE DE FRANCE.
FROM AN OIL PAINTING.

love to heart-breaking indifference, and died about 1640, leaving her with four children and shattered fortunes. To recruit her failing health, and to hide her chagrin and sorrow at seeing herself supplanted by unworthy rivals, she had lived for some time in the country, where she had leisure for the reading and reflection which fitted her for her later life. But after the death of her husband she was obliged to sell her estates, and we find her established in the Place Royale with her devoted friend, the Comtesse de Maure, and continuing the traditions of the Hôtel de Rambouillet. Her tastes had been formed in this circle, and she had also been under the instruction of the Chevalier de Méré, a *littérateur* and courtier who had great vogue, was something of an oracle, and molded the character and manners of divers women of this period, among others the future Mme. de Maintenon. His confidence in his own power of bringing talent out of mediocrity was certainly refreshing. Among his pupils was the Duchesse de Lesdiguières, who said to him one day, "I wish to have *esprit.*"—"Eh bien, Madame," replied the complaisant chevalier, "you shall have it."

How much Mme. de Sablé may have been indebted to this modest *bel esprit* we do not know, but her finished manner, fine taste, exquisite tact, cultivated intellect, and great experience of the world made her an authority in social matters. To be received in her salon was to be received everywhere. Cardinal Mazarin watched her influence with a jealous eye. "Mme. de Longueville is very intimate with the Marquise de Sablé," he writes in his private note-book. "She is visited constantly by d'Andilly, the Princesse de Guéméné, d'Enghien and his sister, Nemours, and many others. They speak freely of all the world. It is necessary to have some one who will advise us of all that passes there."

But the death of her favorite son—a young man distinguished for graces of person, mind, heart, and character, who lost his life in one of the battles of his friend and comrade, the Prince de Condé—together with the loss of her fortune and the fading of her beauty, turned the thoughts of the Marquise to spiritual things. We find many traces of the state of mind which led her first into a mild form of devotion, serious but not too ascetic, and later into pronounced Jansenism. In a note to a friend who had neglected her, she dwells upon "the misery and nothingness of the world," recalls the strength of their long friendship, the depth of her own affection, and tries to account for the disloyalty to herself, by the inherent weakness and emptiness of human nature, which renders it impossible for even the most perfect to do anything that is not defective. All this is very charitable, to say the least, as well as a little abstract. Time has given a strange humility and forgivingness

9

to the woman who broke with her dearest friend, the unfortunate Duc de Montmorency, because he presumed to lift his eyes to the Queen, saying that she "could not receive pleasantly the regards which she had to share with the greatest princess in the world."

The fashion of the period furnished a peaceful and dignified refuge for women, when their beauty waned and the "terrible forties" ended their illusions. To go into brief retreat for penitence and prayer was at all times a graceful thing to do, besides making for safety. It was only a step further to retire altogether from the scenes of pleasure which had begun to pall. The convent offered a haven of repose to the bruised heart, a fresh aim for drooping energies, a needed outlet for devouring emotions, and a comfortable sense of security, not only for this world, but for the next. It was the next world which was beginning to trouble Mme. de Sablé. She had great fear of death, and, after many penitential retreats to Port Royal, she finally obtained permission to build a suite of apartments within its precincts, and retired there about 1655, to prepare for that unpleasant event which she put off as long as possible by the most assiduous care of her health. "If she was not devoted, she had the idea of becoming so," said Mademoiselle. But her devotion was in quite a mundane fashion. Her pleasant rooms were separate and independent, thus enabling her to give herself not only to the care of her health and her soul, but to a select society, to literature, and to conversation. She never practised the severe asceticism of her friend, Mme. de Longueville. With a great deal of abstract piety, the iron girdle and the hair shirt were not included. She did not even forego her delicate and fastidious tastes. Her elegant dinners and her dainty *confitures* were as famous as ever. "Will the anger of the Marquise go so far, in your opinion, as to refuse me her recipe for salad?" writes Mme. de Choisy at the close of a letter to the Comtesse de Maure, in which she has ridiculed her friend's Jansenist tendencies; "If so, it will be a great inhumanity, for which she will be punished in this world and the other." She had great skill in delicate cooking, and was in the habit of sending cakes, jellies, and other dainties, prepared by herself, to her intimate friends. La Rochefoucauld says, "If I could hope for two dishes of those preserves, which I did not deserve to eat before, I should be indebted to you all my life." Mme. de Longueville, who is about to visit her, begs her not to give a feast, as she has "scruples about such indulgence."

This spice of worldliness very much tempered the austerity of her retreat, and lent an added luster to its intellectual attractions. But the Marquise had many conflicts between her luxurious tastes and her desire to be devout. Her dainty and epicurean habits, her extraordinary anxiety about her health, and her capricious humors were the subject of much light badinage among her friends. The Grande Mademoiselle sketches these traits with a satiric touch, in the *Princesse de Paphlagonie*, where she introduces her with the Comtesse de Maure. "There are no hours when they do not confer together upon the means of preventing themselves from dying, and upon the art of rendering themselves immortal," she writes. "Their conferences are not like those of other people; the fear of breathing an air too cold or too hot, the apprehension that the wind may be too dry or too damp, a fancy that the weather is not as moderate as they judge necessary for the preservation of their health—these are sufficient reasons for writing from one room to another. . . . If one could find this correspondence, one might derive great advantages in every way; for they were princesses who had nothing mortal, except the knowledge of being so. . . . Of Mme. de Sablé she adds: "The Princesse *Parthénie* had a taste as dainty as her mind; nothing equaled the magnificence of her entertainments; all the viands were exquisite, and her elegance was beyond anything that one could imagine." The fastidious Marquise suffered, with all the world, from the defects of her qualities. Her extreme delicacy and sensibility appear under many forms and verge often upon weakness; but it is an amiable weakness that does not detract greatly from her fascination. She was not cast in a heroic mold, and her faults are those which the world is pleased to call essentially feminine.

The records of her life were preserved by Conrart, also by her friend and physician, Valant. They give us a clear picture of her character, with its graces and its foibles, as well as of her pleasant intercourse and correspondence with many noted men and women.   They give us, too, interesting glimpses of her salon.   We find there the celebrated Jansenists Nicole and Arnauld, the eminent lawyer Domat, Esprit, sometimes Pascal, with his sister, Mme. Périer; the Prince and Princesse de Conti, the Grand Condé, La Rochefoucauld, the penitent Mme. de Longueville, Mme. de La Fayette, and many others among the cultivated *noblesse*, who are attracted by its tone of *bel esprit* and graceful, but by no means severe, devotion.   The Duc d'Orléans and the lovely but unfortunate Madame were intimate and frequent visitors.

In this little world, in which religion, literature, and fashion are curiously blended, they talk of theology, morals, physics, Cartesianism, friendship, and love.   The youth and gaiety of the Hôtel de Rambouillet have given place to more serious thoughts and graver topics.   The current which had its source there is divided.   At the *Samedis*, in the Marais, they are amusing themselves about the same time with letters and *vers de société*.   At the Luxembourg, a more exclusive coterie is exercising its mature talent in sketching portraits.   These salons touch at many points, but each has a channel of its own.   The reflective nature of Mme. de Sablé turns to more serious and elevated subjects, and her friends take the same tone.   They make scientific experiments, discuss Calvinism, read the ancient moralists, and indulge in dissertations upon a great variety of topics.   Mme. de Brégy, poet, *dame d'honneur* and *femme d'esprit*, who amused the little court of Mademoiselle with so many discreetly flattering pen-portraits, has left two badly written and curiously spelled notes upon the merits of Socrates and Epictetus, which throw a ray of light upon the tastes of this aristocratic and rather speculative circle.   Mme. de Sablé writes an essay upon the education of children, which is very much talked about, also a characteristic paper upon friendship.   The latter is little more than a series of detached sentences, but it indicates the drift of her thought, and might have served as an antidote to the selfish philosophy of La Rochefoucauld.   It calls out an appreciative letter from

ANNÉ D'AUTRICHE, REINE DE FRANCE.
FROM AN OIL PAINTING.

d'Andilly, who, in his anchorite's cell, continues to follow the sayings and doings of his friends in the little salon at Port Royal.

"Friendship," she writes, "is a kind of virtue which can only be founded upon the esteem of people whom one loves— that is to say, upon qualities of the soul, such as fidelity, generosity, discretion, and upon fine qualities of mind."

After insisting that it must be reciprocal, disinterested, and based upon virtue, she continues: "One ought not to give the name of friendship to natural inclinations, because they do not depend upon our will or our choice; and, though they render our friendships more agreeable, they should not be the foundation of them. The union which is founded upon the same pleasures and the same occupations does not deserve the name of friendship, because it usually comes from a certain egotism which causes us to love that which is similar to ourselves, however imperfect we may be." She dwells also upon the mutual offices and permanent nature of true friendship, adding, "He who loves his friend more than reason and justice, will on some other occasion love his own pleasure and profit more than his friend."

The Abbé Esprit, Jansenist and academician, wrote an essay upon *Des Amitiés en apparence les plus saintes des Hommes avec les Femmes*, which was doubtless suggested by the conversations in this salon, where the subject was freely discussed. The days of chivalry were not so far distant, and the subtle blending of exalted sentiment with thoughtful companionship, which revived their spirit in a new form, was too marked a feature of the time to be overlooked. These friendships, half intellectual, half poetic, and quite platonic, were mostly formed in mature life, on a basis of mental sympathy. "There is a taste in pure friendship which those who are born mediocre do not reach," said La Bruyère. Mme. de Lambert speaks of it as "the product of a perfect social culture, and, of all affections, that which has most charm."

The well-known friendship of Mme. de La Fayette and La Rochefoucauld, which illustrates the mutual influence of a critical man of intellect and a deep-hearted, thoughtful woman who has passed the age of romance, began in this salon. Its nature was foreshadowed in the tribute La Rochefoucauld paid to women, in his portrait of himself. "Where their intellect is cultivated," he writes, "I prefer their society to that of men. One finds there a gentleness one does not meet with among ourselves; and it seems to me, beyond this, that they express themselves with more neatness, and give a more agreeable turn to the things they talk about."

Mme. de Sablé was herself, in less exclusive fashion, the intimate friend and adviser of Esprit, d'Andilly, and La Rochefoucauld. The letters of these men show clearly their warm regard, as well as the value they attached to her opinions. "Indeed," wrote Voiture to her, many years before, "those who decry you on the side of tenderness must confess that if you are not the most loving person in the world, you are at least the most obliging. True friendship knows no more sweetness than there is in your words." Her character, so delicately shaded and so averse to all violent passions, seems to have been peculiarly fitted for this calm and enduring sentiment which cast a soft radiance, as of Indian summer, over her closing years.

At a later period, the sacred name of friendship was unfortunately used to veil relations that had lost all the purity and delicacy of their primitive character. This fact has sometimes been rather illogically cited, as an argument not only against the moral influence of the salons but against the intellectual development of women. There is neither excuse nor palliation to be offered for the Italian manners and the recognized system of *amis intimes*, which disgraced the French society of the next century. But, while it is greatly to be deplored that the moral sense has not always kept pace with the cultivation of the intellect, there is no reason for believing that license of manners is in any degree the result of it. There is striking evidence to the contrary, in the incredible ignorance and laxity that found its reaction in the early salons; also in the dissolute lives of many distinguished women of rank who had no pretension to wit or education. The fluctuation of morals, which has always existed, must be traced to quite other causes. Virtue

has not invariably accompanied intelligence, but it has been
still less the companion of ignorance.

It was Mme. de Sablé who set the fashion of condensing
the thoughts and experiences of life into maxims and epigrams.
This was her specific gift to literature; but her influence was
felt through what she inspired others to do, rather than through
what she did herself. It was her good fortune to be brought
into contact with the genius of a Pascal and a La Rochefoucauld,—men who reared immortal works upon the pastime
of an idle hour. One or two of her own maxims will suffice to
indicate her style, as well as to show the estimate she placed
upon form and measure in the conduct of life.

A bad manner spoils everything, even justice and reason. The *how* constitutes the best part of things, and the air which one gives them gilds, modifies,
and softens the most disagreeable.

There is a certain command in the manner of speaking and acting, which
makes itself felt everywhere, and which gains, in advance, consideration and
respect.

We find here the spirit that underlies French manners, in
which form counts for so much.

There is another, which suggests the delicate flavor of sentiment then in vogue.

Wherever it is, love is always the master. It seems truly that it is to the soul
of the one who loves, what the soul is to the body it animates.

Among the eminent men who lent so much brilliancy to
this salon was the great jurist Domat. He adds his contribution and falls into the moralizing vein.

A little fine weather, a good word, a praise, a caress, draws me from a profound sadness from which I could not draw myself by any effort of meditation.
What a machine is my soul, what an abyss of misery and weakness!

Here is one by the Abbé d'Ailly, which foreshadows the
thought of the next century.

Too great submission to books, and to the opinions of the ancients, as to
the eternal truths revealed of God, spoils the head and makes pedants.

The finest and most vigorous of these choice spirits was
Pascal, who frequented more or less the salon of Mme. de
Sablé, previous to his final retirement to the gloom and aus-

terity of the cloister. His delicate platonism and refined spirituality go far towards offsetting the cold cynicism of La Rochefoucauld. Each gives us a different phase of life as reflected in a clear and luminous intelligence. The one led to Port Royal, the other turned an electric light upon the selfish corruption of courts. Many of the *Pensées* of Pascal were preserved among the records of this salon, and Cousin finds reason for believing that they were first suggested and discussed here; he even thinks it possible, if not probable, that the *Discours sur les Passions de l'Amour*, which pertains to his mundane life, and presents the grave and ascetic recluse in a new light, had a like origin.

But the presiding genius was La Rochefoucauld. He complains that the mode of relaxation is fatiguing, and that the mania for sentences troubles his repose. The subjects were suggested for conversation, and the thoughts were condensed and reduced to writing at leisure. "Here are all the maxims I have," he writes to Mme. de Sablé; "but as one gives nothing for nothing, I demand a *potage aux carottes, un ragoût de mouton*, etc."

"When La Rochefoucauld had composed his sentences," says Cousin, "he talked them over before or after dinner, or he sent them at the end of a letter. They were discussed, examined, and observations were made, by which he profited. One could lessen their faults, but one could lend them no beauty. There was not a delicate and rare turn, a fine and keen touch, which did not come from him."

After availing himself of the general judgment in this way, he took a novel method of forestalling criticism before committing himself to publication. Mme. de Sablé sent a collection of the *Maxims* to her friends, asking for a written opinion. One is tempted to make long extracts from their replies. The men usually indorse the worldly sentiments, the women rarely. The Princesse de Guéméné, who, in the decline of her beauty, was growing devout, and also had apartments for penitential retreat at Port Royal, responds: "I was just going to write to beg you to send me your carriage as soon as you had dined. I have yet seen only the first maxims,

as I had a headache yesterday; but those I have read appear
to me to be founded more upon the disposition of the author
than upon the truth, for he believes neither in generosity without interest, nor in pity; that is, he judges every one by himself.
For the greater number of people, he is right; but surely there
are those who desire only to do good." The Comtesse de
Maure, who does not believe in the absolute depravity of
human nature, and is inclined to an elevated Christian philosophy quite opposed to Jansenism, writes with so much severity
that she begs her friend not to show her letter to the author.
Mme. de Hautefort expresses her disapproval of a theory which
drives honor and goodness out of the world. After many clever
and well-turned criticisms, she says: " But the maxim which is
quite new to me, and which I admire, is that idleness, languid
as it is, destroys all the passions. It is true, and he has
searched his heart well to find a sentiment so hidden, but so
just. . . . I think one ought, at present, to esteem idleness as
the only virtue in the world, since it is that which uproots all
the vices. As I have always had much respect for it, I am glad
it has so much merit." But she adds wisely: " If I were of the
opinion of the author, I would not bring to the light those mysteries which will forever deprive him of all the confidence one
might have in him."

There is one letter, written by the clever and beautiful
Eléonore de Rohan, Abbess de Malnoue, and addressed to the
author, which deserves to be read for its fine and just sentiments. In closing she says:

The maxim upon humility appears to me perfectly beautiful; but I have
been so surprised to find it there, that I had the greatest difficulty in recognizing
it in the midst of all that precedes and follows it. It is assuredly to make this
virtue practised among your own sex, that you have written maxims in which
their self-love is so little flattered. I should be very much humiliated on my
own part, if I did not say to myself what I have already said to you in this note,
that you judge better the hearts of men than those of women, and that perhaps
you do not know yourself the true motive which makes you esteem them less.
If you had always met those whose temperament had been submitted to virtue,
and in whom the senses were less strong than reason, you would think better of
a certain number who distinguish themselves always from the multitude; and it
seems to me that Mme. de La Fayette and myself deserve that you should have
a better opinion of the sex in general.

Mme. de La Fayette writes to the Marquise: "All people of good sense are not so persuaded of the general corruption as is M. de La Rochefoucauld. I return to you a thousand thanks for all you have done for this gentleman." At a later period she said: "La Rochefoucauld stimulated my intellect, but I reformed his heart." It is to be regretted that he had not known her sooner.

ANNE DE ROHAN, PRINCESSE DE GUÉMÉNÉ,
DUCHESSE DE MONTBAZON.
FROM A COPPERPLATE.

At his request Mme. de Sablé wrote a review of the *Maxims*, which she submitted to him for approval. It seems to have been a fair presentation of both sides, but he thought it too severe, and she kindly gave him permission to change it to suit himself. He took her at her word, dropped the adverse criticisms, retained the eulogies, and published it in the *Journal des Savants* as he wished it to go to the world. The diplomatic Marquise saved her conscience and kept her friend.

The *Maxims* of La Rochefoucauld, which are familiar to all, have extended into a literature. That he generalized from his own point of view, and applied to universal humanity the motives of a class bent upon favor and precedence, is certainly true.   But whatever we may think of his sentiments, which were those of a man of the world whose observations were largely in the atmosphere of courts, we are compelled to admit his unrivaled finish and perfection of form.   Similar theories of human nature run through the maxims of Esprit and Saint Evremond, without the exquisite turn which makes each one of La Rochefoucauld's a gem in itself.   His tone was that of a disappointed courtier, with a vein of sadness only half disguised by cold philosophy and bitter cynicism.   La Bruyère, with a broader outlook upon humanity, had much of the same fine analysis, with less conciseness and elegance of expression.   Vauvenargues and Joubert were his legitimate successors.   But how far removed in spirit!

"The body has graces," writes Vauvenargues, "the mind has talents; has the heart only vices?   And man capable of reason, shall he be incapable of virtue?"

With a fine and delicate touch, Joubert says: "Virtue is the health of the soul.   It gives a flavor to the smallest leaves of life."

These sentiments are in the vein of Pascal, who represents the most spiritual element of the little coterie which has left such a legacy of condensed thought to the world.

The crowning act of the life of Mme. de Sablé was her defense of Port Royal.   She united with Mme. de Longueville in protecting the persecuted Jansenists, Nicole and Arnauld, but she had neither the courage, the heroism, nor the partisan spirit of her more ardent companion.   With all her devotion she was something of a sybarite and liked repose. She had the tact, during all the troubles which scattered her little circle, to retain her friends, of whatever religious color, though not without a few temporary clouds.   Her diplomatic moderation did not quite please the *religieuses* of Port Royal, and chilled a little her pleasant relations with d'Andilly.

Toward the close of her life, the Marquise was in the habit of secluding herself for days together, and declining to see even her dearest friends.   The Abbé de la Victoire, piqued at not being received, spoke of her one day as "the late Mme. la

Marquise de Sablé." La Rochefoucauld writes to her, "I know no more inventions for entering your house; I am refused at the door every day." Mme. de La Fayette declares herself offended, and cites this as a proof of her attachment, saying, "There are very few people who could displease me by not wishing to see me." But the friends of the Marquise are disposed to treat her caprices very leniently. As the years went by and the interests of life receded, Mme. de Sablé became reconciled to the thought that had inspired her with so much dread. When she died at the advanced age of seventy-nine, the longed-for transition was only the quiet passing from fevered dreams to peaceful sleep.

It is a singular fact that this refined, exclusive, fastidious woman, in whom the artistic nature was always dominant to the extent of weakness, should have left a request to be buried, without ceremony, in the parish cemetery with the people, remote alike from the tombs of her family and the saints of Port Royal.

CHAPTER VI

MADAME DE SÉVIGNÉ

*Her Genius — Her Youth — Her unworthy Husband — Her
impertinent Cousin — Her Love for her Daughter — Her
Letters — Hôtel de Carnavalet — Mme. Duplessis Guénégaud
— Mme. de Coulanges — The Curtain Falls.*

MONG the brilliant French women of the seventeenth century, no one is so well known to-day as Mme. de Sévigné. She has not only been sung by poets and portrayed by historians, but she has left us a complete record of her own life and her own character. Her letters reflect every shade of her many-sided nature, as well as the events, even the trifling incidents, of the world in which she lived; the lineaments, the experiences, the virtues, and the follies of the people whom she knew. We catch the changeful tints of her mind that readily takes the complexion of those about her, while retaining its independence; we are made familiar with her small joys and sorrows, we laugh with her at her own harmless weaknesses, we feel the inspiration of her sympathy, we hear the innermost throbbings of her heart. No one was ever less consciously a woman of letters. No one would have been more surprised than herself at her own fame. One is instinctively sure that she would never have seated herself deliberately to write a book of any sort whatever. While she was planning a form for her thoughts, they would have flown. She was essentially a woman of the great world, for which she was fitted by her position, her temperament, her *esprit*, her tastes, and her character. She loved its variety, its movement, its gaiety; she judged leniently even its faults and its frailties. If they often furnished a target for her wit, behind her sharpest epigrams one detects an indulgent smile.

The natural outlet for her full mind and heart was in conversation. When she was alone, they found vent in conversation of another sort. She talks on paper. Her letters have the unstudied freedom, the rapidity, the shades, the inflections of spoken words. She gives her thoughts their own course, " with reins upon the neck," as she was fond of saying, and without knowing where they will lead her. But it is the personal element that inspires her. Let her heart be piqued, or touched by a profound affection, and her mind is illuminated; her pen flies. Her nature unveils itself, her emotions chase one another in quick succession, her thoughts crystallize with wonderful brilliancy, and the world is reflected in a thousand varying colors. The sparkling wit, the swift judgment, the subtle insight, the lightness of touch, the indefinable charm of style — these belong to her temperament and her genius. But the clearness, the justness of expression, the precision, the simplicity that was never banal—such qualities nature does not bestow. One must find their source in careful training, in wise criticism, in early familiarity with good models.

Living from 1626 to 1696, Mme. de Sévigné was *en rapport* with the best life of the great century of French letters. She was the granddaughter of the mystical Mme. de Chantal, who was too much occupied with her convents and her devotions to give much attention to the little Marie, left an orphan at the age of six years. The child did not inherit much of her grandmother's spirit of reverence, and at a later period was wont to indulge in many harmless pleasantries about her pious ancestress and "our grandfather, St. François de Sales."   Deprived so early of the care of a mother, she was brought up by an uncle, the good Abbé de Coulanges—the *"Bien-Bon"*—whose life was devoted to her interests.   Though born in the Place Royale, that long-faded center of so much that was brilliant and fascinating two centuries ago, much of her youth was passed in the family chateau at Livry, where she was carefully educated in a far more solid fashion than was usual among the women of her time.   She had an early introduction to the Hôtel de Rambouillet, and readily caught its intellectual tastes, though she always retained a certain bold freedom of speech and manners, quite opposed to its spirit.

Her instructors were Chapelain and Ménage, both honored *habitués* of that famous salon.   The first was a dull poet, a profound scholar, somewhat of a pedant, and notoriously careless in his dress—*le vieux* Chapelain, his irreverent pupil used to call him.   When he died of apoplexy, years afterwards, she wrote to her daughter: "He confesses by pressing the hand; he is like a statue in his chair.   So God confounds the pride of philosophers."   But he taught her Latin, Spanish, and Italian, made her familiar with the beauties of Virgil and Tasso, and gave her a critical taste for letters.

Ménage was younger, and aspired to be a man of the world as well as a *savant*.   Repeating one day the remark of a friend, that out of ten things he knew he had learned nine in conversation, he added, "I could say about the same thing myself"— a confession that savors more of the salon than of the library. He had a good deal of learning, but much pretension, and Molière has given him an undesirable immortality as *Vadius* in *Les Femmes Savantes*, in company with his deadly enemy, the Abbé Cotin, who figures as *Trissotin*.   It appears that the susceptible *savant* lost his heart to his lively pupil, and sighed not only in secret but quite openly.   He wrote her bad verses in several languages, loaded her with eulogies, and followed her persistently.   "The name of Mme. de Sévigné," said the Bishop of Laon, "is in the works of Ménage what Bassan's dog is in his portraits. He cannot help putting it there." She treated him in a sisterly fashion that put to flight all sentimental illusions, but she had often to pacify his wounded vanity. One day, in the presence of several friends, she gave him

MARIE DE RABUTIN–CHANTAL — MARQUISE DE SÉVIGNÉ.

FROM THE OIL PORTRAIT BY HENRI BEAUBRUN.

a greeting rather more cordial than dignified. Noticing the looks of surprise, she turned away laughing and said, " So they kissed in the primitive church." But the wide knowledge and scholarly criticism of Ménage were of great value to the versatile woman, who speedily surpassed her master in style if not in learning. Evidently she appreciated him, since she addresses him in one of her letters as " friend of all friends, the best."

II

At eighteen the gay and unconventional Marie de Rabutin-Chantal was married to the Marquis de Sévigné ; but her period of happiness was a short one. The husband, who was rich, handsome, and agreeable, proved weak and faithless.   He was one of the temporary caprices of the dangerous Ninon, led a dashing, irresponsible life, spent his fortune recklessly, and left his pretty young wife to weep alone at a convenient distance, under the somber skies of Brittany.   Fortunately for her and for posterity, his career was rapid and brief.   For some trifling affair of so-called honor—a quality of which, from our point of view, he does not seem to have possessed enough to be worth the trouble of defending—he had the kindness to get himself killed in a duel, after seven years of marriage.   His spirited wife had loved him sincerely, and first illusions die slowly.   She shed many bitter and natural tears, but she never showed any disposition to repeat the experiment.   Perhaps she was of the opinion of another young widow who thought it "a fine thing to bear the name of a man who can commit no more follies." But it is useless to speculate upon the reasons why a woman does or does not marry.   It is certain that the love of her two children filled the heart of Mme. de Sévigné ; her future life was devoted to their training, and to repairing a fortune upon which her husband's extravagance had made heavy inroads.

But the fascinating widow of twenty-five had a dangerous path to tread.   That she lived in a society so lax and corrupt, unprotected and surrounded by distinguished admirers, without a shadow of suspicion having fallen upon her fair reputation is a strong proof of her good judgment and her discretion.   She was not a great beauty, though the flattering verses of her poet friends might lead one to think so.   A complexion fresh and fair, eyes of remarkable brilliancy, an abundance of blond hair, a face mobile and animated, and a fine figure — these were her visible attractions.   She danced well, sang well, talked well, and had abounding health.   Mme. de La Fayette made a pen-portrait of her, which was thought to be strikingly true.   It was in the form of a letter from an unknown man.   A few extracts will serve to bring her more vividly before us.

Your mind so adorns and embellishes your person, that there is no one in the world so fascinating when you are animated by a conversation from which constraint is banished. All that you say has such a charm, and becomes you so well, that the words attract the Smiles and the Graces around you; the brilliancy of your intellect gives such luster to your complexion and your eyes, that although it seems that wit should touch only the ears, yours dazzles the sight.

Your soul is great and elevated. You are sensitive to glory and to ambition, and not less so to pleasures; you were born for them and they seem to have been made for you. . . In a word, joy is the true state of your soul, and grief is as contrary to it as possible. You are naturally tender and impassioned; there was never a heart so generous, so noble, so faithful. . . You are the most courteous and amiable person that ever lived, and the sweet, frank air which is seen in all your actions makes the simplest compliments of politeness seem from your lips protestations of friendship.

Mlle. de Scudéry sketches her as the *Princesse Clarinte* in *Clélie*, concluding with these words: "I have never seen together so many attractions, so much gaiety, so much coquetry, so much light, so much innocence and virtue. No one ever understood better the art of having grace without affectation, raillery without malice, gaiety without folly, propriety without constraint, and virtue without severity."

Her malicious cousin, Bussy-Rabutin, who was piqued by her indifference, and basely wished to avenge himself, said that her "warmth was in her intellect"; that for a woman of quality she was too *badine*, too economical, too keenly alive to her own interests; that she made too much account of a few trifling words from the queen, and was too evidently flattered when the king danced with her. This opinion of a vain and jealous man is not entitled to great consideration, especially when we recall that he had already spoken of her as "the delight of mankind," and said that antiquity would have dressed altars for her and she would "surely have been goddess of something." The most incomprehensible page in her history is her complaisance towards the persistent impertinences of this perfidious friend. The only solution of it seems to lie in the strength of family ties, and in her unwillingness to be on bad terms with one of her very few near relatives. Bussy-Rabutin was handsome, witty, brilliant, a *bel esprit*, a member of the *Académie Française*, and very much in love with his charming cousin, who clearly appreciated his talents, if not his character. "You are the fagot of my intellect," she says to him; but she forbids him to talk of love. Unfortunately for himself, his vanity got the better of his discretion. He wrote the *Histoire Amoureuse des Gauls*, and raised such a storm about his head by his attack upon many fair reputations, that, after a few months of lonely meditation in the Bastille, he was exiled from Paris for seventeen years. Long afterwards he repented the unkind blow he had given to Mme. de Sévigné, confessed its injustice, apologized, and made his peace. But the world is less forgiving, and wastes little sympathy upon the base but clever and ambitious man who was doomed to wear his restless life away in the uncongenial solitude of his chateau.

Among the numerous adorers of Mme. de Sévigné were the Prince de Conti, the witty Comte de Lude, the poet Segrais, Fouquet, and Turenne. Her friendship for the last two seems to have been the most lively and permanent. We owe to her sympathetic pen the best account of the death of Turenne. Her devotion to the interests of Fouquet and his family lasted through the many years of imprisonment that ended only with his life. There was nothing of the spirit of the courtier in her generous affection for the friends who were out of favor. The loyalty of her character was notably displayed in her unwavering attachment to Cardinal de Retz, during his long period of exile and misfortune, after the Fronde.

But one must go outside the ordinary channels to find the veritable romance of Mme. de Sévigné's life. Her sensibility lent itself with great facility to impressions, and her gracious manners, her amiable character, her inexhaustible fund of gaiety could not fail to bring her a host of admirers. She had doubtless a vein of harmless coquetry, but it was little more than the natural and variable grace of a frank and sympathetic woman who likes to please, and who scatters about her the flowers of a rich mind and heart, without taking violent passions too seriously, if, indeed, she heeds them at all. Friendship, too, has its shades, its subtleties, its half-perceptible and quite unconscious coquetries. But the supreme passion of Mme. de Sévigné was her love for her daughter. It was the exaltation of her mystical grandmother, in another form. "To love as I love you makes all other friendships frivolous," she writes. Whatever her gifts and attractions may have been, she is known to the world mainly through this affection and the letters which have immortalized it. Nowhere in literature has maternal love found such complete and perfect expression. Nowhere do we find a character so clearly self-revealed. Others have professed to unveil their innermost lives, but there is always a suspicion of posing in deliberate revelations. Mme. de Sévigné has portrayed herself unconsciously. It is the experience of yesterday, the thought of to-day, the hope of to-morrow, the love that is at once the joy and sorrow of all the days, that are woven into a thousand varying but living forms. One naturally seeks in the character of the daughter a key to the absorbing sentiment which is the inspiration and soul of these letters; but one does not find it there. More beautiful than her mother, more learned, more accomplished, she lacked her sympathetic charm. Cold, reserved, timid and haughty, without vivacity and apparently without fine sensibility, she was much admired but little loved by the world in which she lived. "When you choose, you are adorable," wrote her mother; but evidently she did not always so choose. Bussy-Rabutin says of her, "This woman has *esprit*, but it is *esprit* soured and of insupportable egotism. She will make as many enemies as her mother makes friends and adorers." He did not like her, and one must again take his opinion with reserve; but she says of herself that she is "of a temperament little communicative." In her mature life she naïvely writes: "At first people thought me amiable enough, but when they knew me better they loved me no more." "The prettiest girl in France," whose beauty was expected to "set the world on fire," created a mild sensation at court; was noticed by the king, who danced with her; received her share of adulation, and finally became the third wife of the Comte de Grignan, who carried her off to Provence, to the lasting grief of her adoring mother, and to the great advantage of posterity, which owes to this fact the series of incomparable letters that made the fame of their writer, and threw so direct and vivid a light upon an entire generation.

The world has been inclined to regard the son of Mme. de
Sévigné as the more lovable of her two children; but she
doubtless recognized in his light and inconsequent character
many of the qualities of her husband which had given her so
much sorrow during the brief years of her marriage. Amiable,
affectionate, and not without talent, he was nevertheless the
source of many anxieties and little pride. He followed in the
footsteps of his father, and became a willing victim to the fascinations of Ninon; he frequented the society of Champmeslé,
where he met habitually Boileau and Racine. He recited well,
had a fine literary taste, much sensibility, and a gracious ease
of manner that made him many friends. "He was almost as
much loved as I am," remarked the brilliant Mme. de Coulanges, after accompanying him on a visit to Versailles. He
appealed to Mme. de La Fayette to use her influence with his
mother to induce her to pay his numerous debts. There is a
touch of satire in the closing line of the note in which she
intercedes for him. "The great friendship you have for Mme.
de Grignan," she writes, "makes it necessary to show some for
her brother." But we have glimpses of his weakness and insta-
bility, in many of his mother's intimate letters. In the end,
however, having exhausted the pleasures of life and felt the
bitterness of its disappointments, he took refuge in devotion,
and died in the odor of sanctity, after the example of his
devout ancestress.

Mme. de Grignan certainly offered a more solid foundation
for her mother's confidence and affection. It is quite possible,
too, that her reserve concealed graces of character only apparent on a close intimacy. But love does not wait for reasons,
and this one had all the shades and intensities of a passion,
with few of its exactions. D'Andilly called the mother a
"pretty pagan," because she made such an idol of her daughter.
She sometimes has her own misgivings on the score of religion.
"I make this a little Trappe," she wrote from Livry, after the
separation. "I wish to pray to God and make a thousand
reflections; but, *ma pauvre chère*, what I do better than all that
is to think of you. . . I see you, you are present to me; I think
and think again of everything; my head and my mind are

racked; but I turn in vain, I seek in vain; the dear child whom
I love with so much passion is two hundred leagues away. I
have her no more. Then I weep without the power to help
myself." She rings the changes upon this inexhaustible theme.
A responsive word delights her; a brief silence terrifies her; a
slight coldness plunges her into despair. "I have an imagination so lively that uncertainty makes me die," she writes. If
a shadow of grief touches her idol, her sympathies are overflowing. "You weep, my very dear child; it is an affair for
you; it is not the same thing for me, it is my temperament."

But though this love pulses and throbs behind all her letters, it does not make up the substance of them. To amuse
her daughter she gathers all the gossip of the court, all the
news of her friends; she keeps her *au courant* with the most
trifling as well as the most important events. Now she entertains her with a witty description of a scene at Versailles, a
tragical adventure, a gracious word about Mme. Scarron, "who
sups with me every evening," a tender message from Mme. de
La Fayette; now it is a serious reflection upon the death of
Turenne, a vivid picture of her own life, a bit of philosophy, a
spicy anecdote about a dying man who takes forty cups of tea
every morning, and is cured. A few touches lay bare a character or sketch a vivid scene. It is this infinite variety of
detail that gives such historic value to her letters. In a correspondence so intimate she has no interest to conciliate, no
ends to gain. She is simply a mirror in which the world about
her is reflected.

But the most interesting thing we read in her letters is the
life and nature of the woman herself. She has a taste for society and for seclusion, for gaiety and for thought, for friendship and for books. For the moment each one seems dominant.
"I am always of the opinion of the one I heard last," she says,
laughing at her own impressibility. It is an amiable admission, but she has very fine and rational ideas of her own, not-
withstanding. In books, for which she had always a passion,
she found unfailing consolation. Corneille and La Fontaine
were her favorite traveling companions. "I am well satisfied
to be a substance that thinks and reads," she says, finding her

good uncle a trifle dull for a *compagnon de voyage.* Her tastes
were catholic. She read Astrée with delight, loved Petrarch,
Ariosto, and Montaigne; Rabelais made her "die of laughter";
she found Plutarch admirable, enjoyed Tacitus as keenly as did
Mme. Roland a century later, read Josephus and Lucian, dipped
into the history of the crusades and of the iconoclasts, of the holy
fathers and of the saints. She preferred the history of France
to that of Rome, because she had "neither relatives nor friends
in the latter place." She finds the music of Lulli celestial and
the preaching of Bourdaloue divine. Racine she did not quite
appreciate. In his youth, she said he wrote tragedies for
Champmeslé and not for posterity. Later she modified her
opinion, but Corneille held always the first place in her affection.
She had a great love for books on morals, read and re-read the
essays of Nicole, which she found a perpetual resource against
the ills of life — even rain and bad weather. St. Augustine
she reads with pleasure, and she is charmed with Bossuet and
Pascal; but she is not very devout, though she often tries to
be. There is a serious *naïveté* in all her efforts in this direction.
She seems to have always one eye upon the world while she
prays, and she mourns over her own lack of devotion. "I
wish my heart were for God, as it is for you," she writes to her
daughter. "I am neither of God nor of the devil," she says
again; "that state troubles me, though, between ourselves, I find
it the most natural in the world." Her reason quickly pierces
to the heart of superstition; sometimes she cannot help a touch
of sarcasm. "I fear that this *Trappe,* which wishes to pass
humanity, may become a lunatic asylum," she says. She believes little in saints and processions. Over the high altar of
her chapel she writes *Soli Deo honor et gloria.* "It is the way
to make no one jealous," she remarks.

She was rather inclined toward Jansenism, but she could not
fathom all the subtleties of her friends the Port Royalists, and
begged them to "have the kindness, out of pity for her, to
thicken their religion a little, as it evaporated in so much reason-
ing." As she grows older the tone of seriousness is more perceptible. ."If I could only live two hundred years," she writes,
"it seems to me that I might be an admirable person." The

rationalistic tendencies of Mme. de Grignan give her some anxiety, and she rallies her often upon the doubtful philosophy of her *père Descartes*. She could not admit a theory which pretended to prove that her dog Marphise had no soul, and she insisted that if the Cartesians had any desire to go to heaven, it was out of curiosity. "Talk to the Cardinal [de Retz] a little of your *machines;* machines that love, machines that have a choice for some one, machines that are jealous, machines that fear. *Allez, allez,* you are jesting! Descartes never intended to make us believe all that."

In her youth Mme. de Sévigné did not like the country, because it was windy and spoiled her beautiful complexion; perhaps, too, because it was lonely. But with her happy gift of adaptation she came to love its tranquillity. She went often to the solitary old family chateau in Brittany, to make economies and to retrieve the fortune which suffered successively from the reckless extravagance of her husband and son, and from the expensive tastes of the Comte de Grignan, who was acting governor of Provence, and lived in a state much too magnificent for his resources. Of her life at The Rocks she has left us many exquisite pictures. "I go out into the pleasant avenues; I have a footman who follows me; I have books, I change place, I vary the direction of my promenade; a book of devotion, a book of history; one changes from one to the other; that gives diversion; one dreams a little of God, of his providence; one possesses one's soul, one thinks of the future."

She embellishes her park, superintends the planting of trees, and "a labyrinth from which one could not extricate one's self without the thread of Ariadne"; she fills her garden with orange-trees and jessamine until the air is so perfumed that she imagines herself in Provence. She sits in the shade and embroiders while her son "reads trifles, comedies which he plays like Molière, verses, romances, tales; he is very amusing, he has *esprit*, he is appreciative, he entertains us." She notes the changing color of the leaves, the budding of the springtime. "It seems to me that in case of need I should know very well how to make a spring," she writes. She loves too the "fine, crystal days of autumn." Sometimes, in the

12

evening, she has "gray-brown thoughts which grow black at night," but she never dwells upon these. Her "habitual thought—that which one must have for God, if one does his duty"—is for her daughter. "My dear child," she writes, "it is only you that I prefer to the tranquil repose I enjoy here."

If her own soul is open to us in all its variable and charming moods, we also catch in her letters many unconscious reflections of her daughter's character. She offers her a little needed worldly advice. "Try, my child," she says, "to adjust yourself to the manners and customs of the people with whom you live; adapt yourself to that which is not bad; do not be disgusted with that which is only mediocre; make a pleasure of that which is not ridiculous." She entreats her to love the little Pauline and not to scold her, nor send her away to the convent as she did her sister Marie-Blanche. With what infinite tenderness she always speaks of this child, smiling at her small outbursts of temper, soothing her little griefs, and giving wise counsels about her education. Evidently she doubted the patience of the mother. "You do not yet too well comprehend maternal love," she writes: "so much the better, my child; it is violent."

Unfortunately this adoring mother could not get on very well with her daughter when they were together. She drowned her with affection, she fatigued her with care for her health, she was hurt by her ungracious manner, she was frozen by her indifference,—in short, they killed each other. It is not a rare thing to make a cult of a distant idol, and to find one's self unequal to the perpetual shock of the small collisions which diversities of taste and temperament render inevitable in daily intercourse. In this instance, one can readily imagine that a love so interwoven with every fiber of the mother's life, must have been a little over-sensitive, a little exacting, a trifle too demonstrative for the colder nature of the daughter; but that it was the less genuine and profound, no one who has at all studied the character of Mme. de Sévigné can for a moment imagine. How she suffers when it becomes necessary for Mme. de Grignan to go back to Provence! How the tears flow! How readily she forgives all, even to denying that there is anything

to forgive. "A word, a sweetness, a return, a caress, a tenderness, disarms me, cures me in a moment," she writes. And
again: "Would to God, my daughter, that I might see you
once more at the Hôtel de Carnavalet, not for eight days, nor to
make there a penitence, but to embrace you and to make you

MARIE LOUISE GONZAGUE–CLÈVES.
FROM AN ENGRAVING.

see clearly that I cannot be happy without you, and that the
chagrins which my friendship for you might give me are more
agreeable than all the false peace of a wearisome absence."
In spite of these little clouds, the old love is never dimmed:
we are constantly bewildered with the inexhaustible riches of a
heart which gives so lavishly and really asks so little for itself.

The Hôtel de Carnavalet was one of the social centers of
the latter part of the century, but it was the source of no spe-

cial literature and of no new diversions.   Mme. de Sévigné
was herself luminous, and her fame owes none of its luster to
the reflection from those about her.   She was original and
spontaneous.   She read because she liked to read, and not because she wished to be learned.   She wrote as she talked, from
the impulse of the moment, without method or aim excepting
to follow where her rapid thought led her.   Her taste for society
was of the same order.   Her variable and sparkling genius
would have broken loose from the formal conversations and
rather studied brilliancy that had charmed her youth at the
Hôtel de Rambouillet.   The onerous duties of a perpetual hostess would not have suited her temperament, which demanded its
hours of solitude and repose.   But she was devoted to her
friends, and there was a delightful freedom in all her intercourse
with them.   She has not chronicled her salon, but she has
chronicled her world, and we gather from her letters the quality
of her guests.   She liked to pass an evening in the literary
coterie at the Luxembourg; to drop in familiarly upon Mme. de
La Fayette, where she found La Rochefoucauld, Cardinal de
Retz, sometimes Segrais, Huet, La Fontaine, Molière, and other
wits of the time; to sup with Mme. de Coulanges and Mme.
Scarron.   She is a constant visitor at the old Hôtel de Nevers,
where Marie de Gonzague and the Princesse Palatine had
charmed an earlier generation, and where Mme. Duplessis Guénégaud, a woman of brilliant intellect, heroic courage, large
heart, and pure character, whom d'Andilly calls one of the great
souls, presided over a new circle of young poets and men of
letters, reviving the fading memories of the Hôtel de Rambouillet.   Mme. de Sévigné, who had fine dramatic talent,
acted here in little comedies.   She heard Boileau read his
satires and Racine his tragedies.   She met the witty Chevalier
de Châtillon, who asked eight days to make an impromptu, and
Pomponne, who wrote to his father that the great world he
found in this salon did not prevent him from appearing in a gray
habit.   In a letter from the country-house of Mme. Duplessis,
at Fresnes, to the same Pomponne, then ambassador to Sweden,
Mme. de Sévigné says: "I have M. d'Andilly at my left, that is,
on the side of my heart; I have Mme. de La Fayette at my right;

Mme. Duplessis before me, daubing little pictures; Mme. de Motteville a little further off, who dreams profoundly; our uncle de Cessac, whom I fear because I do not know him very well."

It is this life of charming informality; this society of lettered tastes, of wit, of talent, of distinction, that she transfers to her own salon. Its continuity is often broken by her long absences in the country or in Provence, but her irresistible magnetism quickly draws the world around her, on her return. In addition to her intimate friends and to men of letters like Racine, Boileau, Benserade, one meets representatives of the most distinguished of the old families of France. Condé, Richelieu, Colbert, Louvois, and Sully are a few among the great names, of which the list might be indefinitely extended. We have many interesting glimpses of the Grande Mademoiselle, the "adorable" Duchesse de Chaulnes, the Duc and Duchesse de Rohan, who were "Germans in the art of *savoir-vivre*," the Abbess de Fontevrault, so celebrated for her *esprit* and her virtue, and a host of others too numerous to mention. The sculptured portals and time-stained walls of the Hôtel de Carnavalet are still alive with the memories of these brilliant reunions and the famous people who shone there two hundred years ago.

Among those who exercised the most important influence upon the life of Mme. de Sévigné was Corbinelli, the wise counselor, who, with a soul untouched by the storms of adversity through which he had passed, devoted his life to letters and the interests of his friends. No one had a finer appreciation of her gifts and her character. He compared her letters to those of Cicero, but he always sought to temper her ardor, and to turn her thoughts toward an elevated Christian philosophy. "In him," said Mme. de Sévigné, "I defend one who does not cease to celebrate the perfections and the existence of God; who never judges his neighbor, who excuses him always; who is insensible to the pleasures and delights of life, and entirely submissive to the will of Providence; in fine, I sustain the faithful admirer of Sainte Thérèse, and of my grandmother, Sainte Chantal." This gentle, learned, and disinterested man, whose friendship deepened with years, was an unfailing resource. In her troubles and perplexities she seeks his advice; in her intellectual tastes she is sustained by his sympathy. She speaks often of the happy days in Provence, when, together with her daughter, they translate Tacitus, read Tasso, and get entangled in endless discussions upon Descartes. Even Mme. de Grignan, who rarely likes her mother's friends, in the end gives due consideration to this loyal confidant, though she does not hesitate to ridicule the mysticism into which he finally drifted.

After Mme. de La Fayette, the woman whose relations with Mme. de Sévigné were the most intimate was Mme. de Coulanges, who merits here more than a passing word. Her wit was proverbial, her popularity universal. The Leaf, the Fly, the Sylph, the Goddess, her friend calls her in turn, with many a light thrust at her volatile but loyal character. This brilliant, *spirituelle*, caustic woman was the wife of a cousin of the Marquis de Sévigné, who was as witty as herself and more inconsequent. Both were amiable, both sparkled with *bons mots* and epigrams, but they failed to entertain each other. The husband goes to Italy or Germany or passes his time in various chateaux, where he is sure of a warm welcome and good cheer. The wife goes to Versailles, visits her cousin Louvois, the Duchesse de Richelieu, and Mme. de Maintenon, who loves her much; or presides at home over a salon that is always well filled. "Ah, Madame," said M. de Barillon, "how much your house pleases me! I shall come here every evening when I am tired of my family." "Monsieur," she replied, "I expect you to-morrow." When she was ill and likely to die, her husband had a sudden access of affection, and nursed her with great tenderness. Mme. de Coulanges dying and her husband in grief, seemed somehow out of the order of things. "A dead vivacity, a weeping gaiety, these are prodigies," wrote Mme de Sévigné. When the wife recovered, however, they took their separate ways as before.

"Your letters are delicious," she wrote once to Mme. de Sévigné, "and you are as delicious as your letters." Her own were as much sought in her time, but she had no profound affection to consecrate them and no children to collect them, so that only a few have been preserved. There is a curious vein of philosophy in one she wrote to her husband, when the

pleasures of life began to fade. "As for myself, I care little
for the world; I find it no longer suited to my age; I have no
engagements, thank God, to retain me there. I have seen all
there is to see. I have only an old face to present to it, nothing new to show nor to discover there. Ah! what avails it to
recommence every day the visits, to trouble one's self always
about things that do not concern us? . . . . My dear sir,
we must think of something more solid." She disappears from
the scene shortly after the death of Mme. de Sévigné. Long
years of silence and seclusion, and another generation heard
one day that she had lived and that she was dead.

The friends of Mme. de Sévigné slip away one after another;
La Rochefoucauld, De Retz, Mme. de La Fayette are gone.
"Alas!" she writes, "how this death goes running about and
striking on all sides." The thought troubles her. "I am em-
barked in life without my consent," she says; "I must go out
of it — that overwhelms me. And how shall I go? whence?
by what door? when will it be? in what disposition? how shall
I be with God? what have I to present to him? what can I
hope? am I worthy of paradise? am I worthy of hell? What
an alternative! What a complication! I would like better to
have died in the arms of my nurse."

The end came to her in the one spot where she would most
have wished it. She died while on a visit to her daughter in
Provence. Strength and resignation came with the moment,
and she faced with calmness and courage the final mystery.
To the last she retained her wit, her vivacity, and that eternal
youth of the spirit which is one of the rarest of God's gifts to
man. "There are no more friends left to me," said Mme. de
Coulanges; and later she wrote to Mme. de Grignan, "The
grief of seeing her no longer is always fresh to me. I miss too
many things at the Hôtel de Carnavalet."

The curtain falls upon this little world which the magical
pen of Mme. de Sévigné has made us know so well. The
familiar faces retreat into the darkness, to be seen no more.
But the picture lives, and the woman who has outlined it so
clearly, and colored it so vividly and so tenderly, smiles upon
us still, out of the shadows of the past, crowned with the white
radiance of immortal genius and immortal love.

The Women
of the
French Salons

CHAPTER VII

MADAME DE LA FAYETTE

*Her Friendship with Mme. de Sévigné — Her Education —
Her Devotion to the Princess Henrietta — Her Salon — La
Rochefoucauld — Talent as a Diplomatist — Comparison with
Mme. de Maintenon — Her Li........ — Sadness of her
Last Days — Woman in Literature.*

"ELIEVE me, my dearest, you are the person in the world whom I have most truly loved," wrote Mme. de La Fayette to Mme. de Sévigné a short time before her death. This friendship of more than forty years, which Mme. de Sévigné said had never suffered the least cloud, was a living tribute to the mind and heart of both women. It may also be cited for the benefit of the cynically disposed who declare that feminine friendships are simply "pretty bows of ribbon" and nothing more. These women were fundamentally unlike, but they supplemented each other. The character of Mme. de La Fayette was of firmer and more serious texture. She had greater precision of thought, more delicacy of sentiment, and affections not less deep.   But her temperament was less sunny, her genius less impulsive, her wit less sparkling, and her manner less demonstrative.   "She has never been without that divine reason which was her dominant trait," wrote her friend.   No praise pleased her so much as to be told that her judgment was superior to her intellect, and that she loved truth in all things.   "She would not have accorded the least favor to any one, if she had not been convinced it was merited," said Segrais; "this is why she was sometimes called hard, though she was really tender."   As an evidence of her candor, he thinks it worth while to record that "she did not even conceal her age, but told freely in what year and place she was born."   But she combined to an eminent degree sweetness with strength, sensibility with reason, and it was the blending of such diverse qualities that gave so rare a flavor to her character.   In this, too, lies the secret of the vast capacity for friendship which was one of her most salient points.   It is through the records which these friendships have left, through the literary work that formed the solace of so many hours of sadness and suffering, and through the letters of Mme. de Sévigné, that we are able to trace the classic outlines of this fine and complex nature, so noble, so poetic, so sweet, and yet so strong.

Mme. de La Fayette was eight years younger than Mme. de Sévigné, and died three years earlier; hence they traversed together the brilliant world of the second half of the century of which they are among the most illustrious representatives. The young Marie-Madeleine Pioche de La Vergne had inherited a taste for letters and was carefully instructed by her father, who was a field-marshal and the governor of Havre, where he died when she was only fifteen.   She had not passed the first flush of youth when her mother contracted a second marriage with the Chevalier Renaud de Sévigné, whose name figures among the *frondeurs* as the ardent friend of Cardinal de Retz, and later among the devout Port Royalists.   It is a fact of more interest to us that he was an uncle of the Marquis de Sévigné, and the best result of the marriage to the young girl, who was not at all pleased and whose fortunes it clouded a little, was to bring her into close relations with the woman to whom we owe the most intimate details of her life.

The rare natural gifts of Mlle. de La Vergne were not left
without due cultivation.   Rapin and Ménage taught her Latin.
" That tiresome Ménage," as she lightly called him, did not fail,
according to his custom, to lose his susceptible heart to the

Mme. de La Fayette.

remarkable pupil who, after three months of study, translated
Virgil and Horace better than her masters.   He put this amiable weakness on record in many Latin and Italian verses, in
which he addresses her as Laverna, a name more musical than
flattering, if one recalls its Latin significance.   She received an
education of another sort, in the salon of her mother, a woman
of much intelligence, as well as a good deal of vanity, who
posed a little as a patroness of letters, gathering about her a

circle of *beaux esprits*, and in other ways signaling the taste which was a heritage from her Provençal ancestry. One can readily imagine the rapidity with which the young girl developed in such an atmosphere. The Abbé Costar, "most gallant of pedants and most pedantic of gallants," who had an equal taste for literature and good dinners, calls her "the incomparable," sends her his books, corresponds with her, and expresses his delight at finding her "so beautiful, so *spirituelle*, so full of reason." The poet Scarron speaks of her as "*toute lumineuse, toute précieuse.*"

The circle she met in the salon of her godmother, the Duchesse d'Aiguillon, had no less influence in determining her future fortunes. With her rare reputation for beauty and *esprit*, as well as learning, she took her place early in this brilliant and distinguished society in which she was to play so graceful and honored a part. She was sought and admired not only by the men of letters who were so cordially welcomed by the favorite niece of Richelieu, but by the gay world that habitually assembled at the Petit Luxembourg. It was here that she perfected the tone of natural elegance which always distinguished her and made her conspicuous even at court, where she passed so many years of her life.

She was not far from twenty-one when she became the wife of the Comte de La Fayette, of whom little is known save that he died early, leaving her with two sons. He is the most shadowy of figures, and whether he made her life happy or sad does not definitely appear, though there is a vague impression that he left something to be desired in the way of devotion. A certain interest attaches to him as the brother of the beautiful Louise de La Fayette, maid of honor to Anne of Austria, who fled from the compromising infatuation of Louis XIII., to hide her youth and fascinations in the cloister, under the black robe and the cherished name of Mère Angélique de Chaillot.

The young, brilliant, and gifted *comtesse* goes to the convent to visit her gently austere sister-in-law, and meets there the Princess Henrietta of England, then a child of eleven years. The attraction is mutual, and ripens into a deep and lasting friendship. When this graceful and light-hearted girl becomes the Duchesse d'Orléans, and sister-in-law of the king, she

attaches her friend to her court and makes her the *confidante*
of her romantic experiences.   " Do you not think," she said
to her one day, " that if all which has happened to me, and
the things relating to it, were told it would make a fine story?
You write well; write; I will furnish you good materials."
The interesting memorial, to which madame herself contributes
many pages, is interrupted by the mysterious death of the gay
and charming woman who had found so sympathetic and so
faithful a chronicler.   She breathed her last sigh in the arms
of this friend.   " It is one of those sorrows for which one never
consoles one's self, and which leave a shadow over the rest of
one's life," wrote Mme. de La Fayette.   She had no heart to
finish the history, and added only the few simple lines that
record the touching incidents which left upon her so melancholy
and lasting an impression.   She did not care to remain longer
at court, where she was constantly reminded of her grief, and
retired permanently from its gaieties; but in these years of
intimacy with one of its central figures, she had gained an insight into its spirit and its intrigues, which was of inestimable
value in the memoirs and romances of her later years.

The natural place of Mme. de La Fayette was in a society
of more serious tone and more lettered tastes.   In her youth
she had been taken by her mother to the Hôtel de Rambouillet,
and she always retained much of its spirit, without any of its
affectations.   We find her sometimes at the *Samedis*, and she
belonged to the exclusive coterie of the Grande Mademoiselle,
at the Luxembourg, where her facile pen was in demand for
the portraits so much in vogue.   She was also a frequent
visitor in the literary salon of Mme. de Sablé, at Port Royal.
It was here that her friendship with La Rochefoucauld glided
imperceptibly into the intimacy which became so important a
feature in her life.   This intimacy was naturally a matter of
some speculation, but the world made up its mind of its perfectly irreproachable character.   " It appears to be only friendship," writes Mme. de Scudéry to Bussy-Rabutin; "in short,
the fear of God on both sides, and perhaps policy, have cut the
wings of love.   She is his favorite and his first friend."   " I do
not believe he has ever been what one calls in love," writes

Mme. de Sévigné. But this friendship was a veritable romance, without any of the storms or exactions or jealousies of a passionate love. "You may imagine the sweetness and charm of an intercourse full of all the friendship and confidence possible between two people whose merit is not ordinary," she says again;

HENRIETTE ANNE D'ANGLETERRE,
DUCHESSE D'ORLÉANS.

FROM A PAINTING ATTRIBUTED TO RIGAUD.

"add to this the circumstance of their bad health, which rendered them almost necessary to each other, and gave them the leisure not to be found in other relations, to enjoy each other's good qualities. It seems to me that at court people have no time for affection; the whirlpool which is so stormy for others was peaceful for them, and left ample time for the pleasures of a friendship so delicious. I do not believe that any passion can surpass the strength of such a tie."

In the earlier stages of this intimacy, Mme. de La Fayette was a little sensitive as to how the world might regard it, as

may be seen in a note to Mme. de Sablé, in which she asks
her to explain it to the young Comte de Saint-Paul, a son of
Mme. de Longueville.

"I beg of you to speak of the matter in such a way as to put
out of his head the idea that it is anything serious," she writes. "I
am not sufficiently sure what you think of it yourself to feel certain
that you will say the right thing, and it may be necessary to begin
by convincing my embassador. However, I must trust to your
tact, which is superior to ordinary rules. Only convince him. I
dislike mortally that people of his age should imagine that I have
affairs of gallantry. It seems to them that every one older than
themselves is a hundred, and they are astonished that such should
be regarded of any account. Besides, he would believe these
things of M. de La Rochefoucauld more readily than of any
one else. In fine, I do not want him to think anything about
it except that the gentleman is one of my friends."

The picture we have of La Rochefoucauld from the pen of
Mme. de Sévigné has small resemblance to the ideal that one
forms of the cynical author of the *Maxims.* He had come out
of the storms of the Fronde a sad and disappointed man. The
fires of his nature seem to have burned out with the passions
of his youth, if they had ever burned with great intensity. "I
have seen love nowhere except in romances," he says, and even
his devotion to Mme. de Longueville savors more of the ambitious courtier than of the lover. His nature was one that
recoiled from all violent commotions of the soul. The cold
philosophy of the *Maxims* marked perhaps the reaction of his
intellect against the disenchanting experiences of his life. In
the tranquil atmosphere of Mme. de Sablé he found a certain
mental equilibrium; but his character was finally tempered
and softened by the gentle influence of Mme. de La Fayette,
whose exquisite poise and delicacy were singularly in harmony
with a nature that liked nothing in exaggeration. "I have
seen him weep with a tenderness that made me adore him,"
writes Mme. de Sévigné, after the death of his mother. "The
heart of M. de La Rochefoucauld for his family is a thing
incomparable." When the news came that his favorite grand-
son had been killed in battle, she says again: "I have seen his

heart laid bare in this cruel misfortune; he ranks first among all I have ever known for courage, fortitude, tenderness, and reason; I count for nothing his *esprit* and his charm." In all the confidences of the two women, La Rochefoucauld makes a third. He seems always to be looking over the shoulder of Mme. de La Fayette while she writes to the one who "satisfies his idea of friendship in all its circumstances and dependences"; adding usually a message, a line or a pretty compliment to Mme. de Grignan that is more amiable than sincere, because he knows it will gladden the heart of her adoring mother.

The side of Mme. de La Fayette which has the most fascination for us is this intimate life of which Mme. de Sévigné gives such charming glimpses. For a moment it was her ambition to establish a popular salon, a rôle for which she had every requisite of position, talent, and influence. " She presumed very much upon her *esprit*," says Gourville, who did not like her, " and proposed to fill the place of the Marquise de Sablé, to whom all the young people were in the habit of paying great deference, because, after she had fashioned them a little, it was a passport for entering the world; but this plan did not succeed, as Mme. de La Fayette was not willing to give her time to a thing so futile." One can readily understand that it would not have suited her tastes or her temperament. Besides, her health was too delicate, and her moods were too variable. " You know how she is weary sometimes of the same thing," wrote Mme. de Sévigné. But she had her coterie, which was brilliant in quality if not in numbers. The fine house with its pretty garden, which may be seen to-day opposite the Petit Luxembourg, was a favorite meeting-place for a distinguished circle. The central figure was La Rochefoucauld. Every day he came in and seated himself in the *fauteuil* reserved for him. One is reminded of the little salon in the Abbaye-aux-Bois, where more than a century later Chateaubriand found the pleasure and the consolation of his last days in the society of Mme. Récamier. They talk, they write, they criticize each other, they receive their friends. The Cardinal de Retz comes in, and they recall the fatal souvenirs of the Fronde. Perhaps he thinks of the time when he found the young Mlle. de La

Vergne pretty and amiable, and she did not smile upon him. The Prince de Condé is there sometimes, and honors her with his confidence, which Mme. de Sévigné thinks very flattering, as he does not often pay such consideration to women. Segrais has transferred his allegiance from the Grande Mademoiselle to Mme. de La Fayette, and is her literary counselor as well as a constant visitor. La Fontaine, "so well known by his fables and tales, and sometimes so heavy in conversation," may be found there. Mme. de Sévigné comes almost every day with her sunny face and her witty story. "The Mist" she calls Mme. de La Fayette, who is so often ill and sad. She might have called herself The Sunbeam, though she, too, has her hours when she can only dine tête-à-tête with her friend, because she is "so gloomy that she cannot support four people together." Mme. de Coulanges adds her graceful, vivacious, and sparkling presence. Mme. Scarron, before her days of grandeur, is frequently of the company, and has lost none of the charm which made the salon of her poet-husband so attractive during his later years. "She has an amiable and marvelously just mind," says Mme. de Sévigné. . . . "It is pleasant to hear her talk. These conversations often lead us very far, from morality to morality, sometimes Christian, sometimes political." This circle was not limited however to a few friends, and included from time to time the learning, the elegance and the aristocracy of Paris.

But Mme. de La Fayette herself is the magnet that quietly draws together this fascinating world. In her youth she had much life and vivacity, perhaps a spice of discreet coquetry, but at this period she was serious, and her fresh beauty had given place to the assured and captivating grace of maturity. She had a face that might have been severe in its strength but for the sensibility expressed in the slight droop of the head to one side, the tender curve of the full lips, and the variable light of the dark, thoughtful eyes. In her last years, when her stately figure had grown attenuated, and her face was pallid with long suffering, the underlying force of her character was more distinctly defined in the clear and noble outlines of her features. Her nature was full of subtle shades. Over her reserved strength, her calm judgment, her wise penetration played the delicate light of a lively imagination, the shifting tints of a tender sensibility. Her sympathy found ready expression in tears, and she could not even bear the emotion of saying good-by to Mme. de Sévigné when she was going away to Provence. But her accents were always tempered, and her manners had the gracious and tranquil ease of a woman superior to circumstances. Her extreme frankness lent her at times a certain sharpness, and she deals many light blows at the small vanities and affectations that come under her notice. "Mon Dieu," said the frivolous Mme. de Marans to her one day, " I must have my hair cut." " Mon Dieu," replied Mme. de La Fayette simply, "do not have it done ; that is becoming only to young persons." Gourville said she was imperious and over-bearing, scolding those she loved best, as well as those she did not love. But this *valet-de-chambre* of La Rochefoucauld, who amassed a fortune and became a man of some note, was jealous of her influence over his former master, and his opinions should be taken with reservation. Her delicate satire may have been sometimes a formidable weapon, but it was directed only against follies, and rarely, if ever, used unkindly. She was a woman for intimacies, and it is to those who knew her best that we must look for a just estimate of her qualities. " You would love her as soon as you had time to be with her, and to become familiar with her *esprit* and her wisdom," wrote Mme. de Sévigné to her daughter, who was disposed to be critical ; " the better one knows her, the more one is attached to her."

One must also take into consideration her bad health. People thought her selfish or indifferent when she was only sad and suffering. For more than twenty years she was ill, consumed by a slow fever which permitted her to go out only at intervals. La Rochefoucauld had the gout, and they consoled each other. Mme. de Sévigné thought it better not to have the genius of a Pascal, than to have so many ailments. "Mme de La Fayette is always languishing, M. de La Rochefoucauld always lame," she writes ; " we have conversations so sad that it seems as if there were nothing more to do but to bury us ; the garden of Mme. de La Fayette is the prettiest spot in

14

the world, everything blooming, everything perfumed; we pass there many evenings, for the poor woman does not dare go out in a carriage." "Her health is never good," she writes again, "nevertheless she sends you word that she should not like death better; *au contraire*." There are times when she can no longer "think, or speak, or answer, or listen; she is tired of saying good-morning and good-evening." Then she goes away to Meudon for a few days, leaving La Rochefoucauld "incredibly sad." She speaks for herself in a letter from the country-house which Gourville has placed at her disposal.

"I am at Saint Maur; I have left all my affairs and all my husbands; I have my children and the fine weather; that suffices. I take the waters of Forges; I look after my health, I see no one. I do not mind at all the privation; every one seems to me so attached to pleasures which depend entirely upon others, that I find my disposition a gift of the fairies.

"I do not know but Mme de Coulanges has already sent you word of our after-dinner conversations at Gourville's about people who have taste above or below their intelligence. Mme. Scarron and the Abbé Têtu were there; we lost ourselves in subtleties until we no longer understood anything. If the air of Provence, which subtilizes things still more, magnifies for you our visions, you will be in the clouds. You have taste below your intelligence; so has M. de La Rochefoucauld; and myself also, but not so much as you two. *Voilà* an example which will guide you."

She disliked writing letters, and usually limited herself to a few plain facts, often in her late years to a simple bulletin of her health. This negligence was the subject of many passages-at-arms between herself and Mme. de Sévigné. "If I had a lover who wished my letters every morning, I would break with him," she writes. "Do not measure our friendship by our letters. I shall love you as much in writing you only a page in a month, as you me in writing ten in eight days." Again she replies to some reproach: "Make up your mind, *ma belle*, to see me sustain, all my life, with the whole force of my eloquence, that I love you still more than you love me. I will make Corbinelli agree with me in a quarter of an hour; your distrust is your sole defect, and the only thing in you that can displease me."

But in spite of a certain apparent indolence, and her constant ill health, there were many threads that connected with the outside world the pleasant room in which Mme. de La Fayette spent so many days of suffering. "She finds herself rich in friends from all sides and all conditions," writes Mme. de Sévigné; "she has a hundred arms; she reaches everywhere. Her children appreciate all this, and thank her every day for possessing a spirit so engaging." She goes to Versailles, on one of her best days, to thank the king for a pension, and receives so many kind words that it "suggests more favors to come." He orders a carriage and accompanies her with other ladies through the park, directing his conversation to her, and seeming greatly pleased with her judicious praise. She spends a few days at Chantilly, where she is invited to all the fêtes, and regrets that Mme. de Sévigné could not be with her in that charming spot, which she is "fitted better than anyone else to enjoy." No one understands so well the extent of her influence and her credit as this devoted friend, who often quotes her to Mme. de Grignan as a model. "Never did any one accomplish so much without leaving her place," she says.

But there was one phase in the life of Mme. de La Fayette which was not fully confided even to Mme. de Sévigné. It concerns a chapter of obscure political history which it is needless to dwell upon here, but which throws much light upon her capacity for managing intricate affairs. Her connection with it was long involved in mystery, and was only unveiled in a correspondence given to the world at a comparatively recent date. It was in the salon of the Grande Mademoiselle that she was thrown into frequent relations with the two daughters of Charles Amédée de Savoie, Duc de Nemours, one of whom became Queen of Portugal, the other, Duchesse de Savoie and, later, Regent during the minority of her son. These relations resulted in one of the ardent friendships which played so important a part in her career. Her intercourse with the beautiful but vain, intriguing, and imperious Duchesse de Savoie assumed the proportion of a delicate diplomatic mission. "Her salon," says Lescure, "was, for the affairs of Savoy, a center of information much more important in the eyes of shrewd politicians than that of the ambassador." She not only looked after the personal matters of Mme. Royale, but was practically entrusted with the entire management of her interests in Paris. From affairs of state and affairs of the heart to the daintiest articles of the toilette her versatile talent is called into requisition. Now it is a message to Louvois or the king, now a turn to be adroitly given to public opinion, now the selection of a perfume or a pair of gloves. "She watches everything, thinks of everything, combines, visits, talks, writes, sends counsels, procures advice, baffles intrigues, is always in the breach, and renders more service by her single efforts than all the envoys avowed or secret whom the Duchesse keeps in France." Nor is the value of these services unrecognized. "Have I told you," wrote Mme. de Sévigné to her daughter, "that Mme. de Savoie has sent a hundred ells of the finest velvet in the world to Mme. de La Fayette, and a hundred ells of satin to line it, and two days ago her portrait, surrounded with diamonds, which is worth three hundred louis?"

This practical side of Mme. de La Fayette's character was remarkable in a woman of so fine a sensibility and so rare a genius. Her friends often sought her counsel; and it was through her familiarity with legal technicalities that La Rochefoucauld was enabled to save his fortune, which he was at one time in danger of losing. In clear insight, profound judgment, and knowledge of affairs, she was scarcely, if at all, surpassed by Mme. de Maintenon, the feminine diplomatist *par excellence* of her time, though her field of action was less broad and conspicuous. But her love of consideration was not so dominant and her ambition not so active. It was one of her theories that people should live without ambition as well as without passion. "It is sufficient to exist," she said. Her energy when occasion called for it does not quite accord with this passive philosophy, and suggests at least a vast reserved force; but if she directed her efforts toward definite ends it was usually to serve other interests than her own. She had been trained in a different school from Mme. de Maintenon, her temperament was modified by her frail health, and the prizes of life had come to her apparently without special exertion. She was a woman, too, of more sentiment and imagination.

Her fastidious delicacy and luxurious tastes were the subject of critical comment on the part of this austere censor, who condemned the gilded decorations of her bed as a useless extravagance, giving the characteristic reason that "the pleasure they afforded was not worth the ridicule they excited." The old friendship that had existed when Mme. Scarron was living in such elegant and mysterious seclusion, devoting herself to the king's children, and finding her main diversion in the little suppers enlivened by the wit of Mme. de Sévigné and Mme. de Coulanges, and the more serious, but not less agreeable, conversation of Mme. de La Fayette, had evidently grown cool. They had their trifling disagreements. "Mme. de La Fayette puts too high a price upon her friendship," wrote Mme. de Maintenon, who had once attached such value to a few approving words from her. In her turn Mme. de La Fayette indulged in a little light satire. Referring to the comedy of Esther, which Racine had written by command for the pupils at Saint Cyr, she said, "It represents the fall of Mme. de Montespan and the rise of Mme. de Maintenon; all the difference is that Esther was rather younger, and less of a *précieuse* in the matter of piety." There was certainly less of the ascetic in Mme. de La Fayette. She had more color and also more sincerity. In symmetry of character, in a certain feminine quality of taste and tenderness, she was superior, and she seems to me to have been of more intrinsic value as a woman. Whether under the same conditions she would have attained the same power may be a question. If not, I think it would have been because she was unwilling to pay the price, not because she lacked the grasp, the tact, or the diplomacy.

It is mainly as a woman of letters that Mme. de La Fayette is known to-day, and it was through her literary work that she made the strongest impression upon her time. Boileau said that she had a finer intellect and wrote better than any other woman in France. But she wrote only for the amusement of idle or lonely hours, and always avoided any display of learning, in order not to attract jealousy as well as from instinctive delicacy of taste. "He who puts himself above others," she said, "whatever talent he may possess, puts himself below his talent." But her natural atmosphere was an intellectual one, and the friend of La Rochefoucauld, who would have "liked Montaigne for a neighbor," had her own message for the world. Her mind was clear and vigorous, her taste critical and severe, and her style had a flexible quality that readily took the tone of her subject. In concise expression she doubtless profited much from the author of the *Maxims*, who rewrote many of his sentences at least thirty times. "A phrase cut out of a book is worth a louis d'or," she said, "and every word twenty sous." Unfortunately her *Mémoires de la Cour de France* is fragmentary, as her son carelessly lent the manuscripts, and many of them were lost. But the part that remains gives ample evidence of the breadth of her intelligence, the penetrating, lucid quality of her mind, and her talent for seizing the salient traits of the life about her. In her romances, which were first published under the name of Segrais, one finds the touch of an artist, and the subtle intuitions of a woman. In the rapid evolution of modern taste and the hopeless piling up of books, these works have fallen somewhat into the shade, but they are written with a vivid naturalness of style, a truth of portraiture, and a delicacy of sentiment, that commend them still to all lovers of imaginative literature. Fontenelle read the *Princesse de Clèves* four times when it appeared. La Harpe said it was "the first romance that offered reasonable adventures written with interest and elegance." It marked an era in the history of the novel. "Before Mme. de La Fayette," said Voltaire, "people wrote in a stilted style of improbable things." We have the rare privilege of reading her own criticism in a letter to the secretary of the Duchesse de Savoie, in which she disowns the authorship, and adds a few lines of discreet eulogy.

"As for myself," she writes, "I am flattered at being suspected of it. I believe I should acknowledge the book, if I were assured the author would never appear to claim it. I find it very agreeable and well written without being excessively polished, full of things of admirable delicacy, which should be read more than once; above all, it seems to be a perfect presentation of the world of the court and the manner of living there. It is not romantic or ambitious; indeed it is not a romance; properly speaking, it is a book of memoirs, and that I am told was its title, but it was changed. *Voilà*, monsieur, my judgment upon *Mme. de Clèves;* I ask yours, for people are divided upon this book to the point of devouring each other. Some condemn what others admire; whatever you may say, do not fear to be alone in your opinion."

Sainte-Beuve, whose portrait of Mme. de La Fayette is so delightful as to make all others seem superfluous, has devoted some exquisite lines to this book. "It is touching to think," he writes, "of the peculiar situation which gave birth to these beings so charming, so pure, these characters so noble and so spotless, these sentiments so fresh, so faultless, so tender; how Mme. de La Fayette put into it all that her loving, poetic soul retained of its first, ever-cherished dreams, and how M. de La Rochefoucauld was pleased doubtless to find once more in *M. de Nemours* that brilliant flower of chivalry which he had too much misused — a sort of flattering mirror in which he lived again his youth. Thus these two old friends renewed in imagination the pristine beauty of that age when they had not known each other, hence could not love each other. The blush so characteristic of *Mme. de Clèves*, and which at first is almost her only language, indicates well the design of the author, which is to paint love in its freshest, purest, vaguest, most adorable, most disturbing, most irresistible — in a word, in its own color. It is constantly a question of that joy which youth joined to beauty gives, of the trouble and embarrassment that love causes in the innocence of early years, in short, of all that is farthest from herself and her friend in their late tie."

But whatever tints her tender and delicate imaginings may have taken from her own soul, Mme. de La Fayette has caught the eternal beauty of a pure and loyal spirit rising above the mists of sense into the serene air of a lofty Christian renunciation.

The sad but triumphant close of her romance foreshadowed the swift breaking up of her own pleasant life. In 1680, not long after the appearance of the *Princesse de Clèves*, La Rochefoucauld died, and the song of her heart was changed to a *miserere*. "Mme. de La Fayette has fallen from the clouds," says Mme. de Sévigné. "Where can she find such a friend, such society, a like sweetness, charm, confidence, consideration for her and her son?" A little later she writes from The Rocks, "Mme. de La Fayette sends me word that she is more deeply affected than she herself believed, being occupied with her health and her children; but these cares have only rendered more sensible the veritable sadness of her heart. She is alone in the world. . . . The poor woman cannot close the ranks so as to fill this place."

The records of the thirteen years that remain to Mme. de La Fayette are somber and melancholy. "Nothing can replace the blessings I have lost," she says. Restlessly she seeks diversion in new plans. She enlarges her house as her horizon diminishes; she finds occupation in the affairs of Mme. Royale and interests herself in the marriage of the daughter of her never forgotten friend, the Princess Henrietta, with the heir to the throne of Savoy. She writes a romance without the old vigor, occupies herself with historic reminiscences, and takes a passing refuge in an ardent affection for the young Mme. de Schomberg, which excites the jealousy of some older friends. But the strongest link that binds her to the world is the son whose career opens so brilliantly as a young officer and for whom she secures an ample fortune and a fine marriage. In this son and the establishment of a family centered all her hopes and ambitions. She was spared the pain of seeing them vanish like the "baseless fabric of a vision." The object of so many cares survived her less than two years; her remaining son and the only person left to represent her was the abbé who had so little care for her manuscripts and her literary fame. A century later, through a collateral branch of the family, the glory of the name was revived by the distinguished general so dear to the American heart. It was in the less tangible realm of the intellect that Mme. de La Fayette was destined to an unlooked-for immortality.

But in spite of these interests, the sense of loneliness and desolation is always present. Her few letters give us occasional flashes of the old spirit, but the burden of them is inexpressibly sad. Her sympathies and associations led her toward a mild form of Jansenism, and as the evening shadows darkened, her thoughts turned to fresh speculations upon the destiny of

FRANÇOISE D'AUBIGNÉ, MARQUISE DE MAINTENON, WIFE OF LOUIS XIV.
FROM A PAINTING BY MIGNARD.

the soul. She went with Mme. de Coulanges to visit Mme. de La Sablière, who was expiating the errors and follies of her life in austere penitence at the *Incurables.* The devotion of this once gay and brilliant woman, who had been so deeply tinged with the philosophy of Descartes, touched her profoundly, and suggested a source of consolation which she had never found. She sought the counsels of her confessor, who did not spare her, and though she was never sustained by the ardor and exaltation of the *religieuse,* her last days were not without peace and a tranquil hope. To the end she remained a gracious, thoughtful, self-poised, calmly-judging woman, whose illusions never blinded her to the simple facts of existence, though sometimes throwing over them a transparent veil woven from the

15

tender colors of her own heart.   Above the weariness and resignation of her last words written to Mme. de Sévigné sounds the refrain of a life that counts among its crowning gifts and graces a genius for friendship.

" Alas, *ma belle*, all I have to tell you of my health is very bad ; in a word, I have repose neither night nor day, neither in body nor in mind.   I am no more a person either by one or the other.   I perish visibly.   I must end when it pleases God, and I am submissive.   *Believe me, my dearest, you are the person in the world whom I have most truly loved.*"

Mme. de La Fayette represents better than any other woman the social and literary life of the last half of the seventeenth century.   Mme. de Sévigné had an individual genius that might have made itself equally felt in any other period.   Mme. de Maintenon, whom Roederer regards as the true successor of Mme. de Rambouillet, was narrowed by personal ambition, and by the limitations of her early life.   Born in a prison, reared in poverty, wife in name, but practically secretary and nurse of a crippled, witty, and licentious poet over whose salon she presided brilliantly ; discreet and penniless widow, governess of the illegitimate children of the king, adviser and finally wife of that king, friend of Ninon, model of virtue, *femme d'esprit*, politician, diplomatist, and *dévote*—no fairy tale can furnish more improbable adventures and more striking contrasts.   But she was the product of exceptional circumstances joined to an exceptional nature.   It is true she put a final touch upon the purity of manners which was so marked a feature of the Hôtel de Rambouillet, and for a long period gave a serious tone to the social life of France.   But she ruled through repression, and one is inclined to accept the opinion of Sainte-Beuve that she does not represent the distinctive social current of the time.   In Mme. de La Fayette we find its delicacy, its courtesy, its elegance, its intelligence, its critical spirit, and its charm.

In considering the great centers in which the fashionable, artistic, literary, and scientific Paris of the seventeenth century found its meeting-ground, one is struck with the practical training given to its versatile, flexible feminine minds.   Women entered intelligently and sympathetically into the interests of men, who, in turn, did not reserve their best thoughts for the club or an after-dinner talk among themselves. There was stimulus as well as diversity in the two modes of thinking and being. Men became more courteous and refined, women more comprehensive and clear. But conversation is the spontaneous overflow of full minds, and the light play of the intellect is only possible on a high level, when the current thought has become a part of the daily life, so that a word suggests infinite perspectives to the swift intelligence. It is not what we know, but the flavor of what we know, that adds "sweetness and light" to social intercourse. With their rapid intuition and instinctive love of pleasing, these French women were quick to see the value of a ready comprehension of the subjects in which clever men are most interested. It was this keen understanding, added to the habit of utilizing what they thought and read, their ready facility in grasping the salient points presented to them, a natural gift of graceful expression, with a delicacy of taste and an exquisite politeness which prevented them from being aggressive, that gave them their unquestioned supremacy in the salons which made Paris for so long a period the social capital of Europe. It was impossible that intellects so plastic should not expand in such an atmosphere, and the result is not difficult to divine. From Mme. de Rambouillet to Mme. de La Fayette and Mme. de Sévigné, from these to Mme. de Staël and George Sand, there is a logical sequence. The Saxon temperament, with a vein of La Bruyère, gives us George Eliot.

This new introduction of the feminine element into literature, which is directly traceable to the salons of the seventeenth century, suggests a point of special interest to the moralist. It may be assumed that, whether through nature or a long process of evolution, the minds of women as a class have a different coloring from the minds of men as a class. Perhaps the best evidence of this lies in the literature of the last two centuries, in which women have been an important factor, not only through what they have done themselves, but through their reflex influence. The books written by them have rapidly multiplied. Doubtless, the excess of feeling is often unbalanced by mental or artistic training; but even in the crude productions, which are by no means confined to one sex, it may be remarked that women deal more with pure affections and men with the coarser passions. A feminine Zola of any grade of ability has not yet appeared.

It is not, however, in literature of pure sentiment that the influence of women has been most felt. It is true that, as a rule, they look at the world from a more emotional standpoint than men, but both have written of love, and for one Sappho there have been many Anacreons. Mlle. de Scudéry and Mme. de La Fayette did not monopolize the sentiment of their time, but they refined and exalted it. The tender and exquisite coloring of Mme. de Staël and George Sand had a worthy counterpart in that of Chateaubriand or Lamartine. But it is in the moral purity, the touch of human sympathy, the divine quality of compassion, the swift insight into the soul pressed down by

> The heavy and the weary weight
> Of all this unintelligible world,

that we trace the minds of women attuned to finer spiritual issues. This broad humanity has vitalized modern literature. It is the penetrating spirit of our century, which has been aptly called the Woman's Century. We do not find it in the great literatures of the past. The Greek poets give us types of tragic passions, of heroic virtues, of motherly and wifely devotion, but woman is not recognized as a profound spiritual force. This masculine literature, so perfect in form and plastic beauty, so vigorous, so statuesque, so calm, and withal so cold, shines across the centuries side by side with the feminine Christian ideal — twin lights which have met in the world of to-day. It may be that from the blending of the two, the crowning of a man's vigor with a woman's finer insight, will spring the perfected flower of human thought.

Robert Browning in his poem *By the Fireside* has said a fitting word :

> Oh, I must feel your brain prompt mine,
> Your heart anticipate my heart.
> You must be just before, in fine,
> See and make me see, for your part,
> New depths of the Divine !

The Women of the French Salons

CHAPTER VIII

SALONS OF THE EIGHTEENTH CENTURY

Characteristics of the Eighteenth Century — Its Epicurean Philosophy — Anecdote of Mme. du Deffand — The Salon an Engine of Political Power — Great Influence of Women — Salons Defined — Literary Dinners — Etiquette of the Salons — An Exotic on American Soil.

HE traits which strike us most forcibly in the lives and characters of the women of the early salons, which colored their minds, ran through their literary pastimes, and gave a distinctive flavor to their conversation, are delicacy and sensibility. It was these qualities, added to a decided taste for pleasures of the intellect, and an innate social genius, that led them to revolt from the gross sensualism of the court, and form, upon a new basis, a society that has given another complexion to the last two centuries. The natural result was, at first, a reign of sentiment that was often overstrained, but which represented on the whole a reaction of morality and refinement.   The wits and beauties of the *salon bleu* may have committed a thousand follies, but their chivalrous codes of honor and of manners, their fastidious tastes, even their prudish affectations, were open though sometimes rather bizarre tributes to the virtues that lie at the very foundation of a well-ordered society.   They had exalted ideas of the dignity of womanhood, of purity, of loyalty, of devotion.   The heroines of Mlle. de Scudéry, with their endless discourses upon the metaphysics of love, were no doubt tiresome sometimes to the *blasé* courtiers, as well as to the critics ; but they had their originals in living women who reversed the common traditions of a Gabrielle and a Marion Delorme, who combined with the intellectual brilliancy and fine courtesy of the Greek Aspasia the moral graces that give so poetic a fascination to the Christian and medieval types.   Mme. de La Fayette painted with rare delicacy the old struggle between passion and duty, but character triumphs over passion, and duty is the final victor.   In spite of the low standards of the age, the ideal woman of society, as of literature, was noble, tender, modest, pure, and loyal.

But the eighteenth century brings new types to the surface. The *précieuses*, with their sentimental theories and naïve reserves, have had their day.   It is no longer the world of Mme. de Rambouillet that confronts us with its chivalrous models, its refined platonism, and its flavor of literature, but rather that of the epicurean Ninon, brilliant, versatile, free, lax, skeptical, full of intrigue and wit, but without moral sense or spiritual aspiration.   Literary portraits and ethical maxims have given place to a spicy mixture of scandal and philosophy, humanitarian speculations and equivocal *bons mots*.   It is piquant and amusing, this light play of intellect, seasoned with clever and sparkling wit, but the note of delicacy and sensibility is quite gone. Society has divested itself of many crudities and affectations perhaps, but it has grown as artificial and self-conscious as its rouged and befeathered leaders.

The women who presided over these centers of fashion and intelligence represent to us the genius of social sovereignty. We fall under the glamour of the luminous but factitious atmosphere that surrounded them.   We are dazzled by the subtlety and clearness of their intellect, the brilliancy of their wit. Their faults are veiled by the smoke of the incense we burn before them, or lost in the dim perspective. It is fortunate, perhaps, for many of our illusions, that the golden age, which is always receding, is seen at such long range that only the softly colored outlines are visible. Men and women are trans-figured in the rosy light that rests on historic heights as on far-off mountain-tops. But if we bring them into closer view, and turn on the pitiless light of truth, the aureole vanishes, a thousand hidden defects are exposed, and our idol stands out hard and bare, too often divested of its divinity and its charm.

To do justice to these women, we must take the point of view of an age that was corrupt to the core. It is needless to discuss here the merits of the stormy, disenchanting eighteenth century, which was the mother of our own, and upon which the world is likely to remain hopelessly divided. But whatever we may think of its final outcome, it can hardly be denied that this period, which in France was so powerful in ideas, so active in thought, so teeming with intelligence, so rich in philosophy, was poor in faith, bankrupt in morals, without religion, with-out poetry, and without imagination. The divine ideals of virtue and renunciation were drowned in a sea of selfishness and materialism. The austere devotion of Pascal was out of fashion. The spiritual teachings of Bossuet and Fénelon represented the out-worn creeds of an age that was dead. It was Voltaire who gave the tone, and even Voltaire was not radical enough for many of these iconoclasts. " He is a bigot and a deist," exclaimed a feminine disciple of d'Holbach's atheism. The gay, witty, pleasure-loving abbé, who derided piety, defied morality, was the pet of the salon, and figured in the worst scandals, was a fair representative of the fashionable clergy who had no attribute of priesthood but the name, and clearly justified the sneers of the philosophers. Tradition had given place to private judgment, and in its first reaction private judgment knew no law but its own caprices. The watchword of intellectual freedom was made to cover universal license, and clever sophists constructed theories to justify the mad carnival of vice and frivolity. " As soon as one does a bad action, one never fails to make a bad maxim," said the clever Marquise de Créqui. "As soon as a school-boy has his love affairs, he wishes no more to say his prayers; and when a woman wrongs her husband, she tries to believe no more in God."

The fact that this brilliant but heartless and epicurean world was tempered with intellect and taste changed its color but not its moral quality. Talent turned to intrigue, and character was the toy of the scheming and flexible brain. The maxims of La Rochefoucauld were the rule of life. Wit counted for everything, the heart for nothing. The only sins that could not be pardoned were stupidity and awkwardness. "Bah! he has only revealed every one's secret," said Mme. du Deffand to an acquaintance who censured Helvétius for making selfishness the basis of all human actions. To some one who met this typical woman of her time, in the gay salon of Mme. de Marchais, and condoled with her upon the death of her lifelong friend and lover, Pont de Veyle, she quietly replied, "Alas! he died this evening at six o'clock; otherwise you would not see me here." "My friend fell ill, I attended him; he died, and I dissected him" was the remark of a wit on reading her satirical pen-portrait of the Marquise du Châtelet. This cold skepticism, keen analysis, and undisguised heartlessness strike the keynote of the century which was socially so brilliant, intellectually so fruitful, and morally so weak.

The liberty and complaisance of the domestic relations were complete. It is true there were examples of conjugal devotion, for the gentle human affections never quite disappear in any atmosphere; but the fact that they were considered worthy of note sufficiently indicates the drift of the age. In the world of fashion and of form there was not even a pretense of preserving the sanctity of marriage, if the chronicles of the time are to be credited. It was simply a commercial affair which united names and fortunes, continued the glory of families, replenished exhausted purses, and gave freedom to women. If love entered into it at all, it was by accident. This superfluous sentiment was ridiculed, or relegated to the *bourgeoisie*, to whom it was left to preserve the tradition of household virtues. Every one seems to have accepted the philosophy of the irrepressible

Ninon, who "returned thanks to God every evening for her *esprit,* and prayed him every morning to be preserved from follies of the heart." If a young wife was modest or shy, she was the object of unflattering *persiflage.* If she betrayed her

MARIE FRANÇOISE CATHERINE,
MARQUISE DE BOUFFLERS.

innocent love for her husband, she was not of the charmed circle of wit and good tone which frowned upon so vulgar a weakness, and laughed at inconvenient scruples.

"Indeed," says a typical husband of the period, "I cannot conceive how, in the barbarous ages, one had the courage to wed. The ties of marriage were a chain. To-day you see kindness, liberty, peace reign in the bosom of families. If

16

husband and wife love each other, very well; they live together; they are happy.   If they cease to love, they say so
honestly, and return to each other the promise of fidelity.
They cease to be lovers; they are friends.   That is what I call
social manners, gentle manners."   This reign of the senses is
aptly illustrated by the epitaph which the gay, voluptuous, and
spirituelle Marquise de Boufflers wrote for herself:

> Ci-gît dans une paix profonde
> Cette Dame de Volupté
> Qui, pour plus grande sûreté,
> Fit son paradis de ce monde.

"*Courte et bonne,*" said the favorite daughter of the Regent, in
the same spirit.

It is against such a background that the women who figure
so prominently in the salons are outlined.   Such was the air
they breathed, the spirit they imbibed.   That it was fatal to the
finer graces of character goes without saying.   Doubtless, in
quiet and secluded nooks, there were many human wild-flowers
that had not lost their primitive freshness and delicacy, but
they did not flourish in the withering atmosphere of the great
world.   The type in vogue savored of the hothouse.   With its
striking beauty of form and tropical richness of color, it had
no sweetness, no fragrance.   Many of these women we can
only consider on the worldly and intellectual side.   Sydney
Smith has aptly characterized them as "women who violated
the common duties of life, and gave very pleasant little suppers."   But standing on the level of a time in which their
faults were mildly censured, if at all, their characteristic gifts
shine out with marvelous splendor.   It is from this standpoint
alone that we can present them, drawing the friendly mantle of
silence over grave weaknesses and fatal errors.

In this century, in which women have so much wider scope,
when they may paint, carve, act, sing, write, enter professional
life, or do whatever talent and inclination dictate, without loss
of dignity or prestige, unless they do it ill,— and perhaps even
this exception is a trifle superfluous,— it is difficult to understand fully, or estimate correctly, a society in which the best

feminine intellect was centered upon the art of entertaining and of wielding an indirect power through the minds of men. These Frenchwomen had all the vanity that lies at the bottom of the Gallic character, but when the triumphs of youth were over, the only legitimate path to individual distinction was that of social influence. This was attained through personal charm, supplemented by more or less cleverness, or through the gift of creating a society that cast about them an illusion of talent of which they were often only the reflection. To these two classes belong the queens of the salons. But the most famous of them only carried to the point of genius a talent that was universal.

In its best estate a brilliant social life is essentially an external one. Its charm lies largely in the superficial graces, in the facile and winning manners, the ready tact, the quick intelligence, the rare and perishable gifts of conversation—in the nameless trifles which are elusive as shadows and potent as light. It is the way of putting things that tells, rather than the value of the things themselves. This world of draperies and amenities, of dinners and *conversaziones*, of epigrams, coquetries, and sparkling trivialities is the Frenchwoman's *milieu*. It has little in common with the inner world that surges forever behind and beneath it; little sympathy with inconvenient ideals and exalted sentiments. The serious and earnest soul to which divine messages have been whispered in hours of solitude finds its treasures unheeded, its language unspoken here. The cares, the burdens, the griefs that weigh so heavily on the great heart of humanity are banished from this social Eden. The Frenchman has as little love for the somber side of life as the Athenian, who veiled every expression of suffering. "Joy marks the force of the intellect," said the pleasure-loving Ninon. It is this peculiar gift of projecting themselves into a joyous atmosphere, of treating even serious subjects in a piquant and lively fashion, of dwelling upon the pleasant surface of things, that has made the French the artists, above all others, of social life. The Parisienne selects her company, as a skilful leader forms his orchestra, with a fine instinct of harmony; no single instrument dominates, but every member is an artist in his way, adding his touch of melody or color in the fitting place. She aims, perhaps unconsciously, at a poetic ideal which shall express the best in life and thought, divested of the rude and commonplace, untouched by sorrow or passion, and free from personality.

But the representative salons, which have left a permanent mark upon their time, and a memory that does not seem likely to die, were no longer simply centers of refined and intellectual amusement. The moral and literary reaction of the seventeenth century was one of the great social and political forces of the eighteenth. The salon had become a vast engine of power, an organ of public opinion, like the modern press. Clever and ambitious women had found their instrument and their opportunity. They had long since learned that the homage paid to weakness is illusory; that the power of beauty is short-lived. With none of the devotion which had made the convent the time-honored refuge of tender and exalted souls, finding little solace in the domestic affections which played so small a rôle in their lives, they turned the whole force of their clear and flexible minds to this new species of sovereignty. Their keenness of vision, their consummate skill in the adaptation of means to ends, their knowledge of the world, their practical intelligence, their instinct of pleasing, all fitted them for the part they assumed. They distinctly illustrated the truth that "our ideal is not out of ourselves, but in ourselves wisely modified." The intellect of these women was rarely the dupe of the emotions. Their clearness was not befogged by sentiment, nor, it may be added, were their characters enriched by it. "The women of the eighteenth century loved with their minds and not with their hearts," said the Abbé Galiani. The very absence of the qualities so essential to the highest womanly character, according to the old poetic types, added to their success. To be simple and true is to forget often to consider effects. Spontaneity is not apt to be discriminating, and the emotions are not safe guides to worldly distinction. It is not the artist who feels the most keenly, who sways men the most powerfully; it is the one who has most perfectly mastered the art of swaying men. Self-sacrifice and a lofty sense of duty find their rewards in the intangible realm of the spirit, but they do not find them in a brilliant society whose foundations are laid in vanity and sensualism. "The virtues, though superior to the sentiments, are not so agreeable," said Mme. du Deffand; and she echoed the spirit of an age of which she was one of the most striking representatives. To be agreeable was the cardinal aim in the lives of these women. To this end they knew how to use their talents, and they studied, to the minutest shade, their own limitations. They had the gift of the general who marshals his forces with a swift eye for combination and availability. To this quality was added more or less mental brilliancy, or, what is equally essential, the faculty of calling out the brilliancy of others; but their education was rarely profound or even accurate. To an abbé who wished to dedicate a grammar to Mme. Geoffrin she replied: "To me? Dedicate a grammar to me! Why, I do not even know how to spell." Even Mme. du Deffand, whom Sainte-Beuve ranks next to Voltaire as the purest classic of the epoch in prose, says of herself, "I do not know a word of grammar; my manner of expressing myself is always the result of chance, independent of all rule and all art."

But it is not to be supposed that women who were the daily and lifelong companions and *confidantes* of men like Fontenelle, d'Alembert, Montesquieu, Helvétius, and Marmontel were deficient in a knowledge of books, though this was always subservient to a knowledge of life. It was a means, not an end. When the salon was at the height of its power, it was not yet time for Mme. de Staël; and, with rare exceptions, those who wrote were not marked, or their literary talent was so overshadowed by their social gifts as to be unnoted. Their writings were no measure of their abilities. Those who wrote for amusement were careful to disclaim the title of *bel esprit*, and their works usually reached the public through accidental channels. Mme. de Lambert herself had too keen an eye for consideration to pose as an author, but it is with an accent of regret at the popular prejudice that she says of Mme. Dacier, "She knows how to associate learning with the amenities: for

at present modesty is out of fashion ; there is no more shame
for vices, and women blush only for knowledge."

But if they did not write, they presided over the mint in
which books were coined.   They were familiar with theories
and ideas at their fountain source.
Indeed the whole literature of the
period pays its tribute to their intelligence and critical taste.   " He
who will write with precision, energy, and vigor only," said Marmontel, "may live with men alone;
but he who wishes for suppleness
in his style, for amenity, and for
that something which charms and
enchants, will, I believe, do well
to live with women.   When I
read that Pericles sacrificed every
morning to the Graces, I understand by it that every day Pericles
breakfasted with Aspasia."   This
same author was in the habit of
reading his tales in the salon, and
noting their effect.   He found a
happy inspiration in " the most
beautiful eyes in the world, swim-
ming in tears"; but he adds, "I
well perceived the cold and feeble
passages, which they passed over
in silence, as well as those where
I had mistaken the word, the tone of nature, or the just shade
of truth."   He refers to the beautiful, witty, but erring and
unfortunate Mme. de la Popelinière, to whom he read his
tragedy, as the best of all his critics.   " Her corrections," he
said, " struck me as so many rays of light."   " A point of
morals will be no better discussed in a society of philosophers
than in that of a pretty woman of Paris," said Rousseau.   This
constant habit of reducing thoughts to a clear and salient form
was the best school for aptness and ready expression.   To

CORNER OF A SALON, TIME OF LOUIS XV.

talk wittily and well, or to lead others to talk wittily and well, was the crowning gift of these women. This evanescent art was the life and soul of the salons, the magnet which attracted the most brilliant of the French men of letters, who were glad to discuss safely and at their ease many subjects which the public censorship made it impossible to write about. They found companions and advisers in women, consulted their tastes, sought their criticism, courted their patronage, and established a sort of intellectual comradeship that exists to the same extent in no country outside of France. Its model may be found in the limited circle that gathered about Aspasia in the old Athenian days.

It is perhaps this habit of intellectual companionship that, more than any other single thing, accounts for the practical cleverness of the Frenchwomen, and the conspicuous part they have played in the political as well as social life of France. Nowhere else are women linked to the same degree with the success of men. There are few distinguished Frenchmen with whose fame some more or less gifted woman is not closely allied. Montaigne and Mlle. de Gournay, La Rochefoucauld and Mme. de La Fayette, d'Alembert and Mlle. de Lespinasse, Chateaubriand and Mme. Récamier, Joubert and Mme. de Beaumont—these are only a few of the well-known and unsullied friendships that suggest themselves out of a list that might be extended indefinitely. The social instincts of the French, and the fact that men and women met on a common plane of intellectual life, made these friendships natural; that they excited little comment and less criticism made them possible.

The result was that from the quiet and thoughtful Marquise de Lambert, who was admitted to have made half of the Academicians, to the clever but less scrupulous Mme. de Pompadour, who had to be reckoned with in every political change in Europe, women were everywhere the power behind the throne. No movement was carried through without them. "They form a kind of republic," said Montesquieu, "whose members, always active, aid and serve one another. It is a new state within a state; and whoever observes the action of those in power, if he does not know the women who govern them, is like a man who sees the action of a machine but does not know its secret springs." Mme. de Tencin advised Marmontel, before all things, to cultivate the society of women, if he wished to succeed. It is said that both Diderot and Thomas, two of the most brilliant thinkers of their time, failed of the fame they merited, through their neglect to court the favor of women. Bolingbroke, then an exile in Paris, with a few others, formed a club of men for the discussion of literary and political questions. While it lasted it was never mentioned by women. It was quietly ignored. Cardinal Fleury considered it dangerous to the State, and suppressed it. At the same time, in the salon of Mme. de Tencin, the leaders of French thought were safely maturing the theories which Montesquieu set forth in his *Esprit des Lois,* the first open attack on absolute monarchy, the forerunner of Rousseau, and the germ of the Revolution.

But the salons were far from being centers of " plain living and high thinking." " Supper is one of the four ends of man," said Mme. du Deffand; and it must be admitted that the great doctrine of human equality was rather luxuriously cradled. The supreme science of the Frenchwomen was a knowledge of men. Understanding their tastes, their ambitions, their interests, their vanities, and their weaknesses, they played upon this complicated human instrument with the skill of an artist who knows how to touch the lightest note, to give the finest shade of expression, to bring out the fullest harmony. In their efforts to raise social life to the most perfect and symmetrical proportions, the pleasures of sense and the delicate illusions of color were not forgotten. They were as noted for their good cheer, for their attention to the elegances that strike the eye, the accessories that charm the taste, as for their intelligence, their tact, and their conversation.

But one must look for the power and the fascination of the French salons in their essential spirit and the characteristics of the Gallic race, rather than in any definite and tangible form. The word simply suggests habitual and informal gatherings of men and women of intelligence and good breeding in the drawing-room, for conversation and amusement.

JEANNE-ANTOINETTE POISSON, MARQUISE DE POMPADOUR.

FROM THE OIL PORTRAIT BY NATTIER.

The hostess who opened her house for these assemblies selected her guests with discrimination, and those who had once gained an *entrée* were always welcome.   In studying the character of the noted salons, one is struck with a certain unity that could result only from natural growth about a nucleus of people bound together by many ties of congeniality and friendship.   Society, in its best sense, does not signify a multitude, nor can a salon be created on commercial principles.   This spirit of commercialism, so fatal to modern social life, was here conspicuously absent.   It was not at all a question of debit and credit, of formal invitations to be given and returned.   Personal values were regarded.   The distinctions of wealth were ignored, and talent, combined with the requisite tact, was, to a certain point, the equivalent of rank.   If rivalries existed, they were based upon the quality of the guests rather than upon material display.   But the modes of entertainment were as varied as the tastes and abilities of the women who presided.   Many of the well-known salons were open daily.   Sometimes there were suppers, which came very much into vogue after the *petits soupers* of the regent.   The Duchesse de Choiseul, during the ministry of her husband, gave a supper every evening excepting on Friday and Sunday.   At a quarter before ten the steward glanced through the crowded rooms, and prepared the table for all who were present.   The Monday suppers at the Temple were thronged.   On other days a more intimate circle gathered round the tables, and the ladies served tea after the English fashion.   A few women of rank and fortune imitated these princely hospitalities, but it was the smaller coteries which presented the most charming and distinctive side of French society.   It was not the luxurious salon of the Duchesse du Maine, with its whirl of festivities and passion for *esprit*, nor that of the Temple, with its brilliant and courtly, but more or less intellectual, atmosphere ; nor that of the clever and critical Maréchale de Luxembourg, so elegant, so witty, so noted in its day—which left the most permanent traces and the widest fame.   It was those presided over by women of lesser rank and more catholic sympathies, of whom Voltaire aptly said that "the decline of their beauty revealed the dawn of their intellect"; women who had the talent, tact, and address to gather about them a circle of distinguished men who have crowned them with a luminous ray from their own immortality. The names of Mme. de Lambert, Mme. de Tencin, Mme. Geoffrin, Mme. du Deffand, Mme. Necker, Mme. de Staël, and others of lesser note, call up visions of a society which the world is not likely to see repeated.

Not the least among the attractions of this society was its charming informality. A favorite custom in the literary and philosophical salons was to give dinners, at an early hour, two or three times a week. In the evening a larger company assembled without ceremony. A popular man of letters, so inclined, might dine Monday and Wednesday with Mme. Geoffrin, Tuesday with Mme. Helvétius, Friday with Mme. Necker, Sunday and Thursday with Mme. d'Holbach, and have ample time to drop into other salons afterward, passing an hour or so, perhaps, before going to the theater, in the brilliant company that surrounded Mlle. de Lespinasse, and, very likely, supping elsewhere later. At many of these gatherings he would be certain to find readings, recitations, comedies, music, games, or some other form of extemporized amusement. The popular mania for *esprit*, for literary lions, for intellectual diversions ran through the social world, as the craze for clubs and culture, poets and parlor readings, musicales and amateur theatricals, runs through the society of to-day. It had numberless shades and gradations, with the usual train of pretentious follies which in every age furnish ample material for the pen of the satirist, but it was a spontaneous expression of the marvelously quickened taste for things of the intellect. The woman who improvised a witty verse, invented a proverb, narrated a story, sang a popular air, or acted a part in a comedy entered with the same easy grace into the discussion of the last political problem, or listened with the subtlest flattery to the new poem, essay, or tale of the aspiring young author, whose fame and fortune perhaps hung upon her smile. In the musical and artistic salon of Mme. de la Popelinière the succession of *fêtes*, concerts, and receptions seems to have been continuous. On Sunday there was a mass in the morning, afterward a grand dinner, at five o'clock a light repast, at nine a supper, and later a musicale.   One is inclined to wonder if there was ever any retirement, any domesticity in this life so full of movement and variety.

But it was really the freedom, wit, and brilliancy of the conversation that constituted the chief attraction of the salons. Men were in the habit of making the daily round of certain drawing-rooms, just as they drop into clubs in our time, sure of more or less pleasant discussion on whatever subject was uppermost at the moment, whether it was literature, philosophy, art, politics, music, the last play, or the latest word of their friends.   The talk was simple, natural, without heat, without aggressive egotism, animated with wit and repartee, glancing upon the surface of many things, and treating all topics, grave or gay, with the lightness of touch, the quick responsiveness that make the charm of social intercourse.

The unwritten laws that governed this brilliant world were drawn from the old ideas of chivalry, upon which the etiquette of the early salons was founded.   The fine morality and gentle virtues which were the bases of these laws had lost their force in the eighteenth century, but the manners which grew out of them had passed into a tradition.   If morals were in reality not pure, nor principles severe, there was at least the vanity of posing as models of good breeding.   Honor was a religion ; politeness and courtesy were the current, though by no means always genuine, coin of unselfishness and amiability ; the amenities stood in the place of an ethical code.   Egotism, ill temper, disloyalty, ingratitude, and scandal were sins against taste, and spoiled the general harmony.   Evil passions might exist, but it was agreeable to hide them, and enmities slept under a gracious smile.   *Noblesse oblige* was the motto of these censors of manners ; and as it is perhaps a Gallic trait to attach greater importance to reputation than to character, this sentiment was far more potent than conscience.   Vice in many veiled forms might be tolerated, but that which called itself good society barred its doors against those who violated the canons of good taste, which recognize at least the outward semblance of many amiable virtues.   Sincerity certainly was not one of these virtues; but no one was deceived, as it was perfectly well understood that courteous forms meant little more than the dress which may or may not conceal a physical defect, but is fit and becoming. It was not best to inquire too closely into character and motives, so long as appearances were fair and decorous. How far the individual may be affected by putting on the garb of qualities and feelings that do not exist may be a question for the moralist; but this conventional untruth has its advantages, not only in reducing to a minimum the friction of social machinery, and subjecting the impulses to the control of the will, but in the subtle influence of an ideal that is good and true, however far one may in reality fall short of it.

Imagine a society composed of a leisure class with more or less intellectual tastes : men eminent in science and letters; men less eminent, whose success depended largely upon their social gifts, and clever women supremely versed in the art of pleasing, who were the intelligent complements of these men ; add a universal talent for conversation, a genius for the amenities of social life, habits of daily intercourse, and manners formed upon an ideal of generosity, amiability, loyalty, and urbanity ; consider, also, the fact that the journals and the magazines, which are so conspicuous a feature of modern life, were practically unknown ; that the salons were centers in which the affairs of the world were discussed, its passing events noted—and the power of these salons may be to some extent comprehended.

The reason, too, why it is idle to dream of reproducing them to-day on American soil will be readily seen. The forms may be repeated, but the vitalizing spirit is not there. We have no leisure class that finds its occupation in this pleasant daily converse. Our feverish civilization has no time for it. We sit in our libraries and scan the news of the world, instead of gathering it in the drawing-rooms of our friends. Perhaps we read and think more, but we talk less, and conversation is a relaxation rather than an art. The ability to think aloud, easily and gracefully, is not eminently an Anglo-Saxon gift, though there are many individual exceptions to this limitation.   Our social life is largely a form, a whirl, a commercial relation, a display, a duty, the result of external accretion, not of internal growth.   It is not in any sense a unity, nor an expression of our best intellectual life ; this seeks other channels.   Men are immersed in business and politics, and prefer the easy, less exacting atmosphere of the club.   The woman who aspires to hold a salon is confronted at the outset by this formidable rival.   She is a queen without a kingdom, presiding over a fluctuating circle without homogeneity, and composed largely of women—a fact in itself fatal to the true *esprit de société.*   It is true we have our literary coteries, but they are apt to savor too much of the library ; we take them too seriously, and bring into them too strong a flavor of personality.   We find in them, as a rule, little trace of the spontaneity, the variety, the wit, the originality, the urbanity, the polish, that distinguished the French literary salons of the last century. Even in their own native atmosphere, the salons exist no longer as recognized institutions.   This perfected flower of a past civilization has faded and fallen, as have all others.   The salon in its widest sense, and in some modified form, may always constitute a feature of French life, but the type has changed, and its old glory has forever departed.   In a foreign air, even in its best days, it could only have been an exotic, flourishing feebly, and lacking both color and fragrance.   As a copy of past models it is still less likely to be a living force. Society, like government, takes its spirit and its vitality from its own soil.

The Women
of the
French Salons

CHAPTER IX

AN ANTECHAMBER OF THE ACADÉMIE FRANÇAISE

The Marquise de Lambert — Her "Bureau d'Esprit" — Fontenelle — Advice to her Son — Wise Thoughts on the Education of Women — Her Love of Consideration — Her Generosity — Influence of Women upon the Academy.

HILE the gay suppers of the regent were giving a new but by no means desirable tone to the great world of Paris, and chasing away the last vestiges of the stately decorum that marked the closing days of Louis XIV. and Mme. de Maintenon, there was one quiet drawing-room which still preserved the old traditions. The Marquise de Lambert forms a connecting link between the salons of the seventeenth and eighteenth centuries, leaning to the side of the latter, intellectually, but retaining much of the finer morality that distinguished the best life of the former. Her attitude towards the disorders of the regency was similar to that which Mme. de Rambouillet had held towards the profligate court of

Henry IV., though her salon never attained the vogue of its model. It lacked a certain charm of youth and freshness perhaps, but it was one of the few in which gambling was not permitted, and in which conversation had not lost its serious and critical flavor.

If Mme. de Lambert were living to-day she would doubtless figure openly as an author. Her early tastes pointed clearly in that direction. She was inclined to withdraw from the amusements of her age, and to pass her time in reading,

MME. DE LAMBERT.
FROM AN ENGRAVING FROM THE OIL PORTRAIT BY MIGNARD.

or in noting down the thoughts that pleased her. The natural bent of her mind was towards moral reflections. In this quality she resembled Mme. de Sablé, but she was a woman of greater breadth and originality, though less fine and exclusive. She wrote much in later life on educational themes, for the benefit of her children and for her own diversion ; but she yielded to the prejudices of her age against the woman author, and her works were given to the world only through the medium of friends to whom she had read or lent them. "Women," she said, "should have towards the sciences a modesty almost as sensitive as towards vices." But in spite of her studied observance of the conventional limits which tradition still assigned to her sex, her writings suggest much more care than is usually bestowed upon the amusement of an idle hour. If, like many other women of her time, she wrote only for her friends, she evidently doubted their discretion in the matter of secrecy.

As the child who inherited the rather formidable name of Anne Thérèse de Marguenat de Courcelles was born during the last days of the Hôtel de Rambouillet, she doubtless cherished many illusions regarding this famous salon. Its influence was more or less apparent when the time came to open one of her own. Her father was a man of feeble intellect, who died early ; but her mother, a woman more noted for beauty than for decorum, was afterward married to Bachaumont, a well-known *bel esprit*, who appreciated the gifts of the young girl, and brought her within a circle of wits who did far more towards forming her impressible mind than her light and frivolous mother had done. She was still very young when she became the wife of the Marquis de Lambert, an officer of distinction, to whose interests she devoted her talents and her ample fortune. The exquisitely decorated Hôtel Lambert, on the Ile Saint Louis, still retains much of its old splendor, though the finest masterpieces of Lebrun and Lesueur which ornamented its walls have found their way to the Louvre. "It is a home made for a sovereign who would be a philosopher," wrote Voltaire to Frederick the Great. In these magnificent salons, Mme. de Lambert, surrounded by every luxury that wealth and taste could furnish, entertained a distinguished company. She carried her lavish hospitalities also to Luxembourg, where she adorned the position of her husband, who was governor of that province for a short period before his death in 1686. After this event, she was absorbed for some years in settling his affairs, which were left in great disorder, and in protecting the fortunes of her two children. This involved her in long and vexatious lawsuits which she seems to have conducted with admirable ability. "There are so few great fortunes that are innocent," she writes to her son, "that I pardon your ancestors for not leaving you one. I have done what I could to put in order our affairs, in which there is left

18

to women only the glory of economy." It was not until the closing years of her life, from 1710 to 1733, that her social influence was at its height. She was past sixty, at an age when the powers of most women are on the wane, when her real career began. She fitted up luxurious apartments in the Palais Mazarin, employing artists like Watteau upon the decorations, and expending money as lavishly as if she had been in the full springtide of life, instead of the golden autumn. Then she gathered about her a choice and lettered society, which seemed to be a world apart, a last revival of the genius of the seventeenth century, and quite out of the main drift of the period. "She was born with much talent," writes one of her friends; "she cultivated it by assiduous reading; but the most beautiful flower in her crown was a noble and luminous simplicity, of which, at sixty years, she took it into her head to divest herself. She lent herself to the public, associated with the Academicians, and established at her house a *bureau d'esprit.*" Twice a week she gave dinners, which were as noted for the *cuisine* as for the company, and included, among others, the best of the Forty Immortals. Here new works were read or discussed, authors talked of their plans, and candidates were proposed for vacant chairs in the Academy. "The learned and the lettered formed the dominant element," says a critic of the time. "They dined at noon, and the rest of the day was passed in conversations, in readings, in literary and scientific discussions. No card tables : it was in ready wit that each one paid his contribution." *Ennui* never came to shed its torpors over these reunions, of which the Academy furnished the most distinguished guests, in company with *grands seigneurs* eager to show themselves as worthy by intelligence as by rank to play a rôle in these gatherings of the intellectual *élite.* Fontenelle was the presiding genius of this salon, and added to its critical and literary spirit a tinge of philosophy. This gallant *savant,* who was adored in society as "a man of rare and exquisite conversation," has left many traces of himself here. No one was so sparkling in epigram; no one talked so beautifully of love, of which he knew nothing; and no one talked so delightfully of science, of which he knew a great deal. But he thought that knowledge needed a seasoning of sentiment to make it palatable to women. In his *Pluralité des Mondes*, a singular *mélange* of science and sentiment, which he had written some years before and dedicated to a daughter of the gay and learned Mme. de La Sablière, he talks about the stars, to *la belle Marquise*, like a lover ; but his delicate flatteries are the seasoning of serious truths. It was the first attempt to offer science sugar-coated, and suggests the character of this coterie, which prided itself upon a discreet mingling of elevated thought with decorous gaiety. The world moves. Imagine a female undergraduate of Harvard or Columbia taking her astronomy diluted with sentiment!

President Hénault, the life-long friend of Mme. du Deffand, whose light criticism of a pure-minded woman might be regarded as rather flattering than otherwise, says : " It was apparent that Mme. de Lambert touched upon the time of the Hôtel de Rambouillet : she was a little affected, and had not the force to overstep the limits of the prude and the *précieuse*. Her salon was the rendezvous of celebrated men. . . . . In the evening the scenery changed as well as the actors. A more elegant world assembled at the suppers. The Marquise took pleasure in receiving people who were agreeable to each other. Her tone, however, did not vary, and she preached *la belle galanterie* to some who went a little beyond it. I was of the two parties : I dogmatized in the morning and sang in the evening." The two eminent Greek scholars, La Motte and Mme. Dacier, held spirited discussions on the merits of Homer, which came near ending in permanent ill-feeling, but the amiable hostess gave a dinner for them, " they drank to the health of the poet, and all was forgotten." The war between the partizans of the old and the new was as lively then as it is to-day. " La Motte and Fontenelle prefer the moderns," said the caustic Mme. du Deffand ; " but the ancients are dead, and the moderns are themselves." The names of Sainte-Aulaire, de Sacy, Mairan, President Hénault, and others equally scholarly and witty, suffice to indicate the quality of the conversation, which treated lightly and gracefully of the most serious things. The Duchesse du Maine and her clever

companion Mlle. de Launay were often among the guests ; also
the beautiful and brilliant Mme. de Caylus, a niece of Mme.
de Maintenon, whom some poetical critic has styled "the last
flower of the seventeenth century." Sainte-Aulaire, tired of
the perpetual excitement at Sceaux, characterized this salon by
a witty quatrain :

> Je suis las de l'esprit, il me met en courroux,
>   Il me renverse la cervelle :
> Lambert, je viens chercher un asile chez vous,
>   Entre La Motte et Fontenelle.

The wits of the day launched many a shaft of satire against
it, as they had against the Hôtel de Rambouillet a century
earlier ; but it was an intellectual center of great influence, and
was regarded as the sanctuary of old manners as well as the
asylum of new liberties. Its decorous character gave it the
epithet of "very respectable"; but this eminently respectable
company, which represented the purest taste of the time, often
included Adrienne Lecouvreur, who was much more remarkable for talent than for respectability. We have a direct
glimpse of it through the pen of d'Argenson :

I have just met with a very grievous loss in the death of the Marquise de
Lambert [he writes in 1733]. For fifteen years I have been one of her special
friends, and she has done me the favor of inviting me to her house, where it is
an honor to be received. I dined there regularly on Wednesday, which was one
of her days. . . . . She was rich, and made a good and amiable use of her
wealth, for the benefit of her friends, and above all for the unfortunate. A pupil
of Bachaumont, having frequented only the society of people of the world, and
of the highest intelligence, she knew no other passion than a constant and platonic tenderness.

The quality of character and intellect which gave Mme. de
Lambert so marked an influence, we find in her own thoughts
on a great variety of subjects. She gives us the impression of
a woman altogether sensible and judicious, but not without a
certain artificial tone. Her well-considered philosophy of life
had an evident groundwork of ambition and worldly wisdom,
which appears always in her advice to her children. She
counsels her son to aim high and believe himself capable of
great things. "Too much modesty," she says, "is a languor

of the soul, which prevents it from taking flight and carrying itself rapidly towards glory"—a suggestion that would be rather superfluous in this generation. Again, she advises him to seek the society of his superiors, in order to accustom himself to respect and politeness. "With equals one grows negligent; the mind falls asleep." But she does not regard superiority as an external thing, and says very wisely, "It is merit which should separate you from people, not dignity or

MME. DE STAAL, NÉE DE LAUNAY.
FROM AN ENGRAVING FROM THE OIL PORTRAIT BY MIGNARD.

pride." By "people" she indicates all those who think meanly and commonly. "The court is full of them," she adds. Her standards of honor are high, and her sentiments of humanity quite in the vein of the coming age. She urges her daughter to treat her servants with kindness. "One of the ancients says they should be regarded as unfortunate friends. Think that humanity and Christianity equalize all."

Her criticisms on the education of women are of especial interest. Behind her conventional tastes and her love of consideration she has a clear perception of facts and an appreciation of unfashionable truths.   She recognizes the superiority of her sex in matters of taste and in the enjoyment of "serious pleasures which make only the *mind laugh* and do not trouble the heart."   She reproaches men with "spoiling the disposi- tions nature has given to women, neglecting their education, filling their minds with nothing solid, and destining them solely to please, and to please only by their graces or their vices." But she had not always the courage of her convictions, and it was doubtless quite as much her dislike of giving voice to un- popular opinions as her aversion to the publicity of authorship, that led her to buy the entire edition of her *Réflexions sur les Femmes*, which was published without her consent.

One of her marked traits was moderation.   "The taste is spoiled by amusements," she writes.   "One becomes so accus- tomed to ardent pleasures that one cannot fall back upon simple ones.   We should fear great commotions of the soul, which prepare *ennui* and disgust."   This wise thought suggests the influence of Fontenelle, who impressed himself strongly upon the salons of the first half of the century.   His calm philosophy is distinctly reflected in the character of Mme. de Lambert, also in that of Mme. Geoffrin, with whom he was on very intimate terms.   It is said that this poet, critic, *bel esprit*, and courtly favorite, whom Rousseau calls "the daintiest pedant in the world," was never swayed by any emotion whatever.   He never laughed, only smiled ; never wept ; never praised warmly, though he did say pretty things to women ; never hurried ; was never angry ; never suffered, and was never moved by suf- fering.   "He had the gout," says one of his critics, "but no pain ; only a foot wrapped in cotton.   He put it on a foot- stool ; that was all."   It is perhaps fair to present, as the other side of the medallion, the portrait drawn by the friendly hand of Adrienne Lecouvreur.   "The charms of his intellect often veiled its essential qualities.   Unique of his kind, he combines all that wins regard and respect.   Integrity, rectitude, equity compose his character ; an imagination lively and brilliant, turns fine and delicate, expressions new and always happy ornament it.   A heart pure, actions clear, conduct uniform, and everywhere principles. . . . Exact in friendship, scrupulous in love; nowhere failing in the attributes of a gentleman. Suited to intercourse the most delicate, though the delight of *savants;* modest in his conversation, simple in his actions, his superiority is evident, but he never makes one feel it." He lived a century, apparently because it was too much trouble to die. When the weight of years made it too much trouble to live, he simply stopped. "I do not suffer, my friends, but I feel a certain difficulty in existing," were his last words. With this model of serene tranquillity, who analyzed the emotions as he would a problem in mathematics, and reduced life to a debit and credit account, it is easy to understand the worldly philosophy of the women who came under his influence.

But while Mme. de Lambert had a calm and equable temperament, and loved to surround herself with an atmosphere of repose, she was not without a fine quality of sentiment. "I exhort you much more to cultivate your heart," she writes to her son, "than to perfect your mind; the true greatness of the man is in the heart." "She was not only eager to serve her friends without waiting for their prayers or the humiliating exposure of their needs," said Fontenelle, "but a good action to be done in favor of indifferent people always tempted her warmly. . . . . The ill success of some acts of generosity did not correct the habit; she was always equally ready to do a kindness." She has written very delicately and beautifully of friendships between men and women; and she had her own intimacies that verged upon tenderness, but were free from any shadow of reproach. Long after her death, d'Alembert, in his academic eulogy upon de Sacy, refers touchingly to the devoted friendship that linked this elegant *savant* with Mme. de Lambert. "It is believed," says President Hénault, "that she was married to the Marquis de Sainte-Aulaire. He was a man of *esprit*, who only bethought himself, after more than sixty years, of his talent for poetry; and Mme. de Lambert, whose house was filled with Academicians, gained him entrance into the Academy, not without strong opposition on the part of Boileau and some others." Whether the report of this alliance was true or not, the families were closely united, as the daughter of Mme. de Lambert was married to a son of Sainte-

Aulaire : it is certain that the enduring affection of this ancient friend lighted the closing years of her life.

Though tinged with the new philosophy, Mme. de Lambert regarded religion as a part of a respectable, well-ordered life. " Devotion is a becoming sentiment in women, and befitting in both sexes," she writes.   But she clearly looked upon it as an external form, rather than an internal flame.   When about to die, at the age of eighty-six, she declined the services of a friendly confessor, and sent for an *abbé* who had a great reputation for *esprit.*   Perhaps she thought he would give her a more brilliant introduction into the next world ; this points to one of her weaknesses, which was a love of consideration that carried her sometimes to the verge of affectation.   It savors a little of the hypercritical spirit that is very well illustrated by an anecdote of the witty Duchesse de Luxembourg.   One morning she took up a prayer-book that was lying upon the table and began to criticize severely the bad taste of the prayers. A friend ventured to remark that if they were said reverently and piously, God surely would pay no attention to their good or bad form.   "Indeed," exclaimed the fastidious Maréchale, whose religion was evidently a becoming phase of estheticism, "do not believe that."

The thoughts of Mme. de Lambert, so elevated in tone, so fine in moral quality, so rich in worldly wisdom, and often so felicitous in expression, tempt one to multiply quotations, especially as they show us an intimate side of her life, of which otherwise we know very little.   Her personality is veiled.   Her human experiences, her loves, her antipathies, her mistakes, and her errors are a sealed book to us, excepting as they may be dimly revealed in the complexion of her mind.   Of her influence we need no better evidence than the fact that her salon was called the antechamber to the Académie Française.

The precise effect of this influence of women over the most powerful critical body of the century, or of any century, perhaps, we can hardly measure.   In the fact that the Academy became for a time philosophical rather than critical, and dealt with theories rather than with pure literature, we trace the finger of the more radical thinkers who made themselves so strongly felt in the salons. Sainte-Beuve tells us that Fontenelle, with other friends of Mme. de Lambert, first gave it this tendency; but his mission was apparently an unconscious one, and strikingly illustrates the accidental character of the sources of the intellectual currents which sometimes change the face of the world. "If I had a handful of truths, I should take good care not to open it," said this sybarite, who would do nothing that was likely to cause him trouble. But the truths escaped in spite of him, and these first words of the new philosophy were perhaps the more dangerous because veiled and insidious. "You have written the *Histoire des Oracles*," said a philosopher to him, after he had been appointed the royal censor, "and you refuse me your approbation." "Monsieur," replied Fontenelle, "if I had been censor when I wrote the *Histoire des Oracles*, I should have carefully avoided giving it my approbation." But if the philosophers finally determined the drift of this learned body, it was undoubtedly the tact and diplomacy of women which constituted the most potent factor in the elections which placed them there. The mantle of authority, so gracefully worn by Mme. de Lambert, fell upon her successors, Mme. Geoffrin and Mlle. de Lespinasse, losing none of its prestige. As a rule, the best men in France were sooner or later enrolled among the Academicians. If a few missed the honor through failure to enlist the favor of women, as has been said, and a few better courtiers of less merit attained it, the modern press has not proved a more judicious tribunal.

A CARD-PARTY, TIME OF LOUIS XV.

CHAPTER X

THE DUCHESSE DU MAINE

*Her Capricious Character— Her Esprit— Mlle. de Launay—
Clever Portrait of Her Mistress— Perpetual Fêtes at Sceaux
— Voltaire and the " Divine Emilie"— Dilettante Character
of this Salon.*

HE life of the eighteenth century, with its restlessness, its love of amusements, its ferment of activities, and its essential frivolity, finds a more fitting representative in the Duchesse du Maine, granddaughter of the Grand Condé, and wife of the favorite son of Louis XIV. and Mme. de Montespan. The transition from the serene and thoughtful atmosphere which surrounded Mme. de Lambert, to the tumultuous whirl of existence at Sceaux, was like passing from the soft light and tranquillity of a summer evening to the glare and confusion of perpetual fireworks. Of all the unique figures of a masquerading age this small and ambitious princess was perhaps the most striking, the most pervading. It was by no means her aim to take her place in the world as queen of a salon. Louise-Bénédicte de Bourbon belonged to the royal race, and this was by far the most vivid fact in her life. She was but a few steps from the throne, and political intrigues played a conspicuous part in her singular career. But while she waited for the supreme power to which she aspired, and later, when the feverish dream of her life was ended, she must be amused, and her diversions must have an intellectual and imaginative flavor. Wits, artists, literary men, and *savants* were alike welcome at Sceaux, if they amused her and entertained her guests. " One lived there by *esprit*, and *esprit* is my God," said Mme. du Deffand, who was among the brightest ornaments of this circle.

Born in 1676, the Duchesse du Maine lived through the first half of the next century, of which her little court was one of the most notable features. Scarcely above the stature of a child of ten years, slightly deformed, with a fair face lighted by fine eyes ; classically though superficially educated ; gifted in conversation, witty, brilliant, adoring talent, but cherishing all the prejudices of the old *noblesse* — she represented in a superlative degree the passion for *esprit* which lent such exceptional brilliancy to the social life of the time.

In character the duchess was capricious and passionate. " If she were as good as she is wicked," said the sharp-tongued Palatine, " there would be nothing to say against her. She is tranquil during the day and passes it playing at cards, but at its close the extravagances and fits of passion begin ; she torments her husband, her children, her servants, to such a point that they do not know which way to turn." Her will brooked no opposition. When forced to leave the Tuileries after the collapse of her little bubble of political power, she deliberately broke every article of value in her apartments, consigning mirrors, vases, statues, porcelains alike to a common ruin, that no one else might enjoy them after her. This fiery scion of a powerful family, who had inherited its pride, its ambition, its uncontrollable passions, and its colossal will, had little patience with the serene temperament and *dilettante* tastes of her amiable husband, and it is said she did not scruple to make him feel the force of her small hands. " You will waken some morning to find yourself in the Académie Française, and the Duc d'Orléans regent," she said to him one day when he showed her a song he had translated.   Her device was a bee, with this motto: "I am small, but I make deep wounds."   Doubtless its fitness was fully realized by those who belonged to the *Ordre de la Mouche-à-miel* which she had instituted, and whose members were obliged to swear, by Mount Hymettus, fidelity and obedience to

THE DUCHESSE DU MAINE AT THE TUILERIES.

their perpetual dictator.   But what pains and chagrins were not compensated by the bit of lemon-colored ribbon and its small meed of distinction !

The little princess worked valiantly for political power, but she worked in vain.   The conspiracy against the regent, which seemed to threaten another Fronde, came to nothing, and this ardent *intrigante*, who had the disposition to "set the four corners of the kingdom on fire" to attain her ends, found her party dispersed and herself in prison.   But this was only an episode, and though it gave a death-blow to her dreams of power, it did not quench her irrepressible ardor.   If she could not rule in one way, she would in another. As soon as she regained her freedom, her little court was again her kingdom, and no sovereign ever reigned more imperiously. "I am fond of company," she said, "for I listen to no one, and every one listens to me." It was an incessant thirst for power, a perpetual need of the sweet incense of flattery, that was at the bottom of this "passion for a multitude." "She believed in herself," writes Mlle. de Launay, afterward Baronne de Staal, "as she believed in God or Descartes, without examination and without discussion."

This lady's maid, who loved mathematics and anatomy, was familiar with Malebranche and Descartes, and left some literary reputation as a writer of gossipy memoirs, was a prominent figure in the lively court at Sceaux for more than forty years, and has given us some vivid pictures of her capricious mistress. A young girl of clear intellect and good education, but without rank, friends, or fortune, she was forced to accept the humiliating position of *femme de chambre* with the Duchesse du Maine, who had been attracted by her talents. She was brought into notice through a letter to Fontenelle, which was thought witty enough to be copied and circulated. If she had taken this cool dissector of human motives as a model, she certainly did credit to his teaching. Her curiously analytical mind is aptly illustrated by her novel method of measuring her lover's passion. He was in the habit of accompanying her home from the house of a friend. When he began to cross the square, instead of going round it, she concluded that his love had diminished in the exact proportion of two sides of a square to the diagonal. Promoted to the position of a companion, she devoted herself to the interests of her restless mistress, read to her, talked with her, wrote plays for her, and was the animating spirit of the famous *Nuits Blanches*. While the duchess was in exile she shared her disgrace, refused to betray her, and was sent to the Bastille for her loyalty. She resigned herself to her imprisonment with admirable philosophy, amused herself in the study of Latin, in watching the gambols of a cat and kitten, and in carrying on a safe and sentimental flirtation with the fascinating Duc de Richelieu, who occupied an adjoining cell and passed the hours in singing with her popular airs from *Iphigénie*. "Senti-

mental" is hardly a fitting word to apply to the coquetries of
this remarkably clear and calculating young woman. She returned with her patroness to Sceaux, found many admirers,
but married finally with an eye to her best worldly interests,
and, it appears, in the main happily — at least, not unhappily.
The shade of difference implies much. She had a keen, penetrating intellect which nothing escaped, and as it had the peculiar clearness in which people and events are reflected as in a
mirror, her observations are of great value. "Aside from the
prose of Voltaire, I know of none more agreeable than that of
Mme. de Staal de Launay," said Grimm. Her portrait of her
mistress serves to paint herself as well.

"Mme. la Duchesse du Maine, at the age of sixty years, has
yet learned nothing from experience; she is a child of much
talent; she has its defects and its charms. Curious and credu-
lous, she wishes to be instructed in all the different branches of
knowledge; but she is contented with their surface. The decisions of those who educated her have become for her principles and rules upon which her mind has never formed the least
doubt; she submits once for all. Her provision of ideas is
made; she rejects the best demonstrated truths and resists the
best reasonings, if they are contrary to the first impressions she
has received. All examination is impossible to her lightness,
and doubt is a state which her weakness cannot support. Her
catechism and the philosophy of Descartes are two systems
which she understands equally well. . . . . Her mirror cannot
make her doubt the charms of her face; the testimony of her
eyes is more questionable than the judgment of those who have
decided that she is beautiful and well-formed. Her vanity is of
a singular kind, but seems the less offensive because it is not
reflective, though in reality it is the more ridiculous. Intercourse with her is a slavery; her tyranny is open: she does not
deign to color it with the appearance of friendship. She says
frankly that she has the misfortune of not being able to do without people for whom she does not care. She proves it effectu-
ally. One sees her learn with indifference the death of those
who would call forth torrents of tears if they were a quarter of
an hour too late for a card party or a promenade."

ANNE-LOUISE-BÉNÉDICTE DE BOURBON, DUCHESSE DU MAINE.

But this vain and self-willed woman read Virgil and Terence in the original, was devoted to Greek tragedies, dipped into philosophy, traversed the surface of many sciences, turned a madrigal with facility, and talked brilliantly. "The language is perfect only when you speak it or when one speaks of you," wrote Mme. de Lambert, in a tone of discreet flattery. "No one has ever spoken with more correctness, clearness, and rapidity, neither in a manner more noble or more natural," said Mlle. de Launay.

Through this feminine La Bruyère, as Sainte-Beuve has styled her, we are introduced to the life at Sceaux. It was the habit of the guests to assemble at eight, listen to music or plays, improvise verses for popular airs, relate racy anecdotes, or amuse themselves with proverbs. "Write verses for me," said the insatiable duchess when ill; "I feel that verses only can give me relief." The quality does not seem to have been essential, provided they were sufficiently flattering. Sainte-Aulaire wrote madrigals for her. Malézieu, the learned and versatile preceptor of the Duc du Maine, read Sophocles and Euripides. Mme. du Maine herself acted the rôles of *Athalie* and *Iphigénie* with the famous Baron. They played at science, contemplated the heavens through a telescope and the earth through a microscope. In their eager search for novelty they improvised *fêtes* that rivaled in magnificence the Arabian Nights; they posed as gods and goddesses, or, affecting simplicity, assumed rustic and pastoral characters, even to their small economies and romantic platitudes. Mythology, the chivalry of the Middle Ages, costumes, illuminations, scenic effects, the triumphs of the artists, the wit of the *bel esprit* — all that ingenuity could devise or money could buy was brought into service. It was the life that Watteau painted, with its quaint and grotesque fancies, its sylvan divinities, and its sighing lovers wandering in endless masquerade, or whispering tender nothings on banks of soft verdure, amid the rustle of leaves, the sparkle of fountains, the glitter of lights, and the perfume of innumerable flowers. It was a perpetual carnival, inspired by imagination, animated by genius, and combining everything that could charm the taste, distract the mind, and intoxicate the senses. The presiding genius of this fairy scene was the irrepressible duchess, who reigned as a goddess and demanded the homage due to one. Well might the weary courtiers cry out against *les Galères du Bel-Esprit.*

But this fantastic princess who carried on a sentimental correspondence with the blind La Motte, and posed as the

tender shepherdess of the adoring but octogenarian Sainte-
Aulaire, had no really democratic notions. There was no question in her mind of the divine right of kings or of princesses.
She welcomed Voltaire because he flattered her vanity and
amused her guests, but she was far enough from the theories
which were slowly fanning the sparks of the Revolution. Her
rather imperious patronage of literary and scientific men set a
fashion which all her world tried to follow. It added doubtless
to the prestige of those who were insidiously preparing the
destruction of the very foundations on which this luxurious and
pleasure-loving society rested. But, after all, the bond between
this restless, frivolous, heartless coterie and the genuine men
of letters was very slight. There was no seriousness, no earnestness, no sincerity, no solid foundation.

The literary men, however, who figured most conspicuously
in the intimate circle of the Duchesse du Maine were not of
the first order. Malézieu was learned, a member of two
Academies, faintly eulogized by Fontenelle, warmly so by
Voltaire, and not at all by Mlle. de Launay ; but twenty-five
years devoted to humoring the caprices and flattering the
tastes of a vain and exacting patroness were not likely to
develop his highest possibilities. There is a point where the
stimulating atmosphere of the salon begins to enervate. His
clever assistant, the Abbé Genest, poet and Academician, was
a sort of Voiture, witty, versatile, and available. He tried
to put Descartes into verse, which suggests the quality of
his poetry. Sainte-Aulaire, who, like his friend Fontenelle,
lived a century, frequented this society more or less for forty
years, but his poems are sufficiently light, if one may judge
from a few samples, and his genius doubtless caught more
reflections in the salon than in a larger world. He owed his
admission to the Academy partly to a tender quatrain which
he improvised in praise of his lively patroness. It is true
we have occasional glimpses of Voltaire. Once he sought
an asylum here for two months, after one of his numerous indiscretions, writing tales during the day, which he read
to the duchess at night. Again he came with his " divine
Emilie," the learned Marquise du Châtelet, who upset the

20

household with her eccentric ways.   "Our ghosts do not show themselves by day," writes Mlle. de Launay ; "they appeared yesterday at ten o'clock in the evening.   I do not think we shall see them earlier to-day ; one is writing high facts, the other, comments upon Newton.   They wish neither to play nor to promenade ; they are very useless in a society where their learned writings are of no account."   But Voltaire was a courtier, and, in spite of his frequent revolts against patronage, was not at all averse to the incense of the salons and the favors of the great.   It was another round in the ladder that led him towards glory.

The cleverest women in France were found at Sceaux, but the dominant spirit was the princess herself.   It was amusement she wanted, and even men of talent were valued far less for what they were intrinsically than for what they could contribute to her vanity or to her diversion.   "She is a predestined soul," wrote Voltaire.   "She will love comedy to the last moment, and when she is ill I counsel you to administer some beautiful poem in the place of extreme unction.   One dies as one has lived."

Mme. du Maine represented the conservative side of French society in spite of the fact that her abounding mental vitality often broke through the stiff boundaries of old traditions.   It was not because she did not still respect them, but she had the defiant attitude of a princess whose will is an unwritten law superior to all traditions.   The tone of her salon was in the main *dilettante,* as is apt to be the case with any circle that plumes itself most upon something quite apart from intellectual distinction.   It reflected the spirit of an old aristocracy, with its pride, its exclusiveness, its worship of forms, but faintly tinged with the new thought that was rapidly but unconsciously encroaching upon time-honored institutions.   Beyond the clever pastimes of a brilliant coterie, it had no marked literary influence.   This ferment of intellectual life was one of the signs of the times, but it led to no more definite and tangible results than the turning of a madrigal or the sparkle of an epigram.

CHAPTER XI

MADAME DE TENCIN AND MADAME DU CHÂTELET

*An Intriguing Chanoinesse — Her Singular Fascination —
Her Salon — Its Philosophical Character — Mlle. Aïssé —
Romances of Mme. de Tencin — D'Alembert — La Belle
Emilie — Voltaire — The Two Women Compared.*

T was not in the restless searchings of an old
society for new sensations, new diversions, nor
in the fleeting expressions of individual taste or
caprice, which were often little more than the
play of small vanities, that the most potent
forces in the political as well as in the intellectual life of France were found. It was in the coteries which
attracted the best representatives of modern thought, men and
women who took the world on a more serious side, and mingled
more or less of earnestness even in their amusements. While
the Duchesse du Maine was playing her little comedy, which
began and ended in herself, another woman, of far different
type, and without rank or riches, was scheming for her friends,
and nursing the germs of the philosophic party in one of the

most notable salons of the first half of the century.   Mme. de
Tencin is not an interesting figure to contemplate from a moral
standpoint.   " She was born with the most fascinating qualities
and the most abominable defects that God ever gave to one of
his creatures," said Mme. du Deffand, who was far from being
able to pose, herself, as a model of virtue or decorum.   But sin
has its degrees, and the woman who errs within the limits of
conventionality considers herself entitled to sit in judgment
upon her sister who wanders outside of the fold.   Measured
even by the complaisant standards of her own time, there can
be but one verdict upon the character of Mme. de Tencin,
though it is to be hoped that the scandal-loving chroniclers
have painted her more darkly than she deserved.   But whatever her faults may have been, her talent and her influence
were unquestioned.   She posed in turn as a saint, an *intrigante*,
and a *femme d'esprit*, with marked success in every one of these
rôles.   But it was not a comedy she was playing for the amusement of the hour.   Beneath the velvet softness of her manner
there was a definite aim, an inflexible purpose.   With the tact
and facility of a Frenchwoman, she had a strong, active intellect, boundless ambition, indomitable energy, and the subtlety
of an Italian.

An incident of her early life, related by Mme. du Deffand,
furnishes a key to her complex character, and reveals one
secret of her influence.   Born of a poor and proud family in
Grenoble, in 1681, Claudine Alexandrine Guérin de Tencin
was destined from childhood for the cloister.   Her strong
aversion to the life of a nun was unavailing, and she was sent
to a convent at Montfleury.   This prison does not seem to have
been a very austere one, and the discipline was far from rigid.
The young novice was so devout that the archbishop prophe-
sied a new light for the Church, and she easily persuaded him
of the necessity of occupying the minds of the *religieuses*
by suitable diversions.   Though not yet sixteen, this pretty,
attractive, vivacious girl was fertile in resources, and won her
way so far into the good graces of her superiors as to be permitted to organize reunions, and to have little comedies played
which called together the provincial society.   She transformed

the convent, but her secret disaffection was unchanged. She took the final vows under the compulsion of her inflexible father, then continued her rôle of *dévote* to admirable purpose.

Claudine Alexandrine Guerin

DE TENCIN

Née en 1681 Morte en 1749.

FROM AN OLD PRINT.

By the zeal of her piety, the severity of her penance, and the ardor of her prayers, she gained the full sympathy of her ascetic young confessor, to whom she confided her feeling of unfitness for a religious life, and her earnest desire to be freed from the vows which sat so uneasily upon her sensitive conscience. He exhorted her to steadfastness, but finally she wrote him a letter in which she confessed her hopeless struggle against a consuming passion, and urged the necessity of immediate release. The conclusion was obvious. The Abbé Fleuret was horrified by the conviction that this pretty young nun was in love with himself, and used his influence to secure her transference to a secular order at Neuville, where, as *chanoinesse*, she had many privileges and few restrictions. Here she became at once a favorite, as before, charming by her modest devotion, and amusing by her brilliant wit. Artfully, and by degrees, she convinced those in authority of the need of a representative in Paris. This office she was chosen to fill. Playing her pious part to the last, protesting with tears her pain at leaving a life she loved, and her unfitness for so great an honor, she set out upon her easy mission. There are many tales of a scandalous life behind all this sanctity and humility, but her new position gave her consideration, influence, and a good revenue. "Young, beautiful, clever, with an adorable talent," this "nun unhooded" fascinated the regent, and was his favorite for a few days. But her ambition got the better of her prudence. She ventured upon political ground, and he saw her no more. With his minister, the infamous Dubois, she was more successful, and he served her purpose admirably well. Through her notorious relations with him she enriched her brother and secured him a cardinal's hat. The intrigues of this unscrupulous trio form an important episode in the history of the period. When Dubois died, within a few months of the regent, she wept, as she said, "that fools might believe she regretted him."

Her clear, incisive intellect and conversational charm would have assured the success of any woman at a time when these things counted for so much. "At thirty-six," wrote Mme. du Deffand, "she was beautiful and fresh as a woman of twenty; her eyes sparkled, her lips had a smile at the same time sweet and perfidious; she wished to be good, and gave herself great trouble to seem so, without succeeding." Indolent and languid, with flashes of witty vivacity, insinuating and facile, unconscious of herself, interested in everyone with whom she talked, she combined the tact, the *finesse*, the subtle penetration of a

woman with the grasp, the comprehensiveness, and the knowledge of political machinery which are traditionally accorded to
a man. " If she wanted to poison you, she would use the mild-
est poison," said the Abbé Trublet.

"I cannot express the illusion which her air of *nonchalance*
and easy grace left with me," says Marmontel. "Mme. de
Tencin, the woman in the kingdom who moved the most
political springs, both in the city and at court, was for me only
an *indolente*. Ah, what finesse, what suppleness, what activity
were concealed beneath this naïve air, this appearance of calm
and leisure ! " But he confesses that she aided him greatly with
her counsel, and that he owed to her much of his knowledge of
the world.

"Unhappy those who depend upon the pen," she said to
him ; "nothing is more chimerical. The man who makes shoes
is sure of his wages ; the man who makes a book or a tragedy
is never sure of anything." She advises him to make friends of
women rather than of men. " By means of women, one attains
all that one wishes from men, of whom some are too pleasure-
loving, others too much preoccupied with their personal interests not to neglect yours ; whereas women think of you, if only
from idleness. Speak this evening to one of them of some
affair that concerns you ; to-morrow at her wheel, at her tapes-
try, you will find her dreaming of it, and searching in her head
for some means of serving you."

Prominent among her friends were Bolingbroke and Fontenelle. " It is not a heart which you have there," she said to the
latter, laying her hand on the spot usually occupied by that
organ, "but a second brain." She had enlisted what stood in
the place of it, however, and he interested himself so far as
to procure her final release from her vows, through Benedict
XIV., who, as Cardinal Lambertini, had frequented her salon,
and who sent her his portrait as a souvenir, after his election
to the papacy.

Through her intimacy with the Duc de Richelieu, Mme. de
Tencin made herself felt even in the secret councils of Louis XV.
Her practical mind comprehended more clearly than many
of the statesmen the forces at work and the weakness that

coped with them. "Unless God visibly interferes," she said, "it is physically impossible that the state should not fall in pieces." It was her influence that inspired Mme. de Château-roux with the idea of sending her royal lover to revive the spirits of the army in Flanders. "It is not, between ourselves, that he is in a state to command a company of grenadiers," she wrote to her brother, "but his presence will avail much. The troops will do their duty better, and the generals will not dare to fail them so openly. . . . A king, whatever he may be, is for the soldiers and people what the ark of the covenant was for the Hebrews; his presence alone promises success."

Her devotion to her friends was the single redeeming trait in her character, and she hesitated at nothing to advance the interests of her brother, over whose house she gracefully pre-sided. But she failed in her ultimate ambition to elevate him to the ministry, and her intrigues were so much feared that Cardinal Fleury sent her away from Paris for a short time. Her disappointments, which it is not the purpose to trace here, left her one of the disaffected party, and on her return her draw-ing-room became a rallying-point for the radical thinkers of France.

Such was the woman who courted, flattered, petted, and patronized the literary and scientific men of Paris, called them her *ménagerie*, put them into a sort of uniform, gave them two suppers a week, and sent them two ells of velvet for small-clothes at New Year's. Of her salon, Marmontel gives us an interest-ing glimpse. He had been invited to read one of his tragedies, and it was his first introduction.

"I saw assembled there Montesquieu, Fontenelle, Mairan, Marivaux, the young Helvétius, Astruc, and others, all men of science or letters, and, in the midst of them, a woman of brilliant intellect and profound judgment, who, with her kind and simple exterior, had rather the appearance of the housekeeper than the mistress. This was Mme. de Tencin. . . . I soon perceived that the guests came there prepared to play their parts, and that their wish to shine did not leave the conversation always free to follow its easy and natural course. Every one tried to seize quickly and on the wing the moment to bring in his word, his story, his anecdote, his maxim, or to add his dash of light and sparkling wit; and, in order to do this opportunely, it was often rather far-fetched.   In Marivaux, the impatience to display his *finesse* and sagacity was quite apparent.   Montesquieu, with more calmness, waited for the ball to come to him, but he waited.   Mairan watched his opportunity. Astruc did not deign to wait.   Fontenelle alone let it come to him without seeking it, and he used so discreetly the attention given him, that his witty sayings and his clever stories never occupied more than a moment.   Alert and reserved, Helvétius listened and gathered material for the future."

Mme. de Tencin loved literature and philosophy for their own sake, and received men of letters at their intrinsic value. She encouraged, too, the freedom of thought and expression at that time so rare and so dangerous.   It was her influence that gave its first impulse to the success of Montesquieu's *Esprit des Lois*, of which she personally bought and distributed many copies.   If she talked well, she knew also how to listen, to attract by her sympathy, to aid by her generosity, to inspire by her intelligence, to charm by her versatility.

Another figure flits in and out of this salon, whose fine qualities of soul shine so brightly in this morally stifling atmosphere that one forgets her errors in a mastering impulse of love and pity.   There is no more pathetic history in this arid and heartless age than that of Mlle. Aïssé, the beautiful Circassian, with the "lustrous, dark, Oriental eyes," who was brought from Constantinople in infancy by the French envoy, and left as a precious heritage to Mme. de Ferriol, the intriguing sister of Mme. de Tencin, and her worthy counterpart, if not in talent, in the faults that darkened their common womanhood.   This delicate young girl, surrounded by worldly and profligate friends, and drawn in spite of herself into the errors of her time, redeemed her character by her romantic heroism, her unselfish devotion, and her final revolt against what seemed to be an inexorable fate.   The struggle between her self-forgetful love for the knightly Chevalier d'Aydie and her sensitive conscience, her refusal to cloud his future by a portionless marriage, and her firmness in severing an unholy tie,

21

knowing that the sacrifice would cost her life, as it did, form an episode as rare as it is tragical. But her exquisite personality, her rich gifts of mind and soul, her fine intelligence, her passionate love, almost consecrated by her pious but fatal re-

MLLE. AÏSSÉ.

nunciation, call up one of the loveliest visions of the century — a vision that lingers in the memory like a medieval poem.

Mme. de Tencin amused her later years by writing sentimental tales, which were found among her papers after her death. These were classed with the romances of Mme. de La Fayette. Speaking of the latter, La Harpe said, "Only one other woman succeeded, a century later, in painting with equal power the struggles of love and virtue." It is one of the curious inconsistencies of her character, that her creations contained an element which her life seems wholly to have lacked. Behind all her faults of conduct there was clearly an ideal of purity and goodness. Her stories are marked by a vividness and an ardor of passion rarely found in the insipid and colorless romances of the preceding age. Her pictures of love and intrigue and crime are touched with the religious enthusiasm of the cloister, the poetry of devotion, the heroism of self-sacrifice. Perhaps the dark and mysterious facts of her own history shaped themselves in her imagination. Did the tragedy of La Fresnaye, the despairing lover who blew out his brains at her feet, leaving the shadow of a crime hanging over her, with haunting memories of the Bastille, recall the innocence of her own early convent days? Did she remember some long-buried love, and the child left to perish upon the steps of St. Jean le Rond, but grown up to be her secret pride in the person of the great mathematician and philosopher d'Alembert? What was the subtle link between this worldly woman and the eternal passion, the tender self-sacrifice of Adelaïde, the loyal heroine who breathes out her solitary and devoted soul on the ashes of La Trappe, unknown to her faithful and monastic lover, until the last sigh? The fate of Adelaïde has become a legend. It has furnished a theme for the poet and the artist, an inspiration for the divine strains of Beethoven, another leaf in the annals of pure and heroic love. But the woman who conceived it toyed with the human heart as with a beautiful flower, to be tossed aside when its first fragrance was gone. She apparently knew neither the virtue, nor the honor, nor the purity, nor the truth of which she had so exquisite a perception in the realm of the imagination. Or were some of the episodes which darken the story of her life simply the myths of a gossiping age, born of the incidents of an idle tale, to live forever on the pages of history?

But it was not as a literary woman that Mme. de Tencin held her position and won her fame. Her gifts were eminently those of her age and race, and it may be of interest to compare her with a woman of larger talent of a purely intellectual order, who belonged more or less to the world of the salons, without aspiring to leadership, and who, though much younger, died in the same year.

Mme. du Châtelet was essentially a woman of letters.   She loved the exact sciences, expounded Leibnitz, translated Newton, gave valuable aid to Voltaire in introducing English thought into France, and was one of the first women among the nobility to accept the principles of philosophic deism.   " I confess that she is tyrannical," said Voltaire: " one must talk about metaphysics, when the temptation is to talk of love.   Ovid was formerly my master; it is now the turn of .Locke."   She has been clearly but by no means pleasantly painted for us in the familiar letters of Mme. de Graffigny, in the rather malicious sketches of the Marquise de Créqui, and in the still more strongly outlined portrait of Mme. du Deffand, as a veritable *bas bleu*, learned, pedantic, eccentric, and without grace or beauty. "Imagine a woman tall and hard, with florid complexion, face sharp, nose pointed — *voilà la belle Emilie*," writes the latter; "a face with which she was so contented that she spared nothing to set it off; curls, topknots, precious stones, all are in profusion. . . . She was born with much *esprit;* the desire of appearing to have more made her prefer the study of the abstract sciences to agreeable branches of knowledge; she thought by this singularity to attain a greater reputation and a decided superiority over all other women.   Madame worked with so much care to seem what she was not, that no one knew exactly what she was; even her defects were not natural."   "She talks like an angel " — "she sings divinely " — "our sex ought to erect altars to her," wrote Mme. de Graffigny during a visit at her *château*.   A few weeks later her tone changed.   They had quarreled.   Of such stuff is history made.   But she had already given a charming picture of the life at Cirey.

Mme. du Châtelet plunged into abstractions during the day. In the evening she was no more the *savante*, but gave herself up to the pleasures of society with the ardor of a nature that was extreme in everything.   Voltaire read his poetry and his dramas, told stories that made them weep and then laugh at their tears, improvised verses, and amused them with marionettes, or the magic lantern.   *La belle Emilie* criticized the poems, sang, and played prominent parts in the comedies and tragedies of the philosopher-poet, which were first given in her

MME. DU CHÂTELET.

little private theater. Among the guests were the eminent scientist, Maupertuis, her life-long friend and teacher; the Italian *savant*, Algarotti, President Hénault, Helvétius, the poet, Saint-Lambert, and many others of equal distinction. "Of what do we not talk!" writes Mme. de Graffigny. "Poetry, science, art, everything, in a tone of graceful badinage. I should like to be able to send you these charming conversations, these enchanting conversations, but it is not in me."

Mme. du Châtelet owned for several years the celebrated Hôtel Lambert, and a choice company of *savants* assembled there as in the days when Mme. de Lambert presided in those stately apartments. But this learned salon had only a limited vogue. The thinking was high, but the dinners were too plain. The real life of Mme. du Châtelet was an intimate one. "I confess that in love and friendship lies all my happiness," said this astronomer, metaphysician, and mathematician, who wrote against revelation and went to mass with her free-thinking lover. Her learning and eccentricities made her the target for many shafts of ridicule, but she counted for much with Voltaire, and her chief title to fame lies in his long and devoted friendship. He found the "sublime and respectable Emilie" the incarnation of all the virtues, though a trifle ill-tempered. The contrast between his kindly portrait and those of her feminine friends is striking and rather suggestive.

"She joined to the taste for glory a simplicity which does not always accompany it, but which is often the fruit of serious studies. No woman was ever so learned, and no one deserves less to be called a *femme savante*. Born with a singular eloquence, this eloquence manifested itself only when she found subjects worthy of it. . . . The fitting word, precision, justness, and force were the characteristics of her style. She would rather write like Pascal and Nicole than like Mme. de Sévigné ; but this severe strength and this vigorous temper of her mind did not render her inaccessible to the beauties of sentiment. The charms of poetry and eloquence penetrated her, and no one was ever more sensitive to harmony. . . . She gave herself to the great world as to study. Everything that occupies society was in her province except scandal. She was never known to repeat an idle story. She had neither time nor disposition to give attention to such things, and when told that some one had done her an injustice, she replied that she did not wish to hear about it."

"She led him a life a little hard," said Mme. de Graffigny, after her quarrel ; but he seems to have found it agreeable, and broke his heart — for a short time — when she died. "I have lost half of my being," he wrote — "a soul for which mine was made." To Marmontel he says : "Come and share my sorrow. I have lost my illustrious friend. I am in despair. I am inconsolable." One cannot believe that so clear-sighted a man, even though a poet, could live for twenty years under the spell of a pure illusion. What heart revelations, what pictures of contemporary life, were lost in the eight large volumes of his letters which were destroyed at her death !

While Mme. de Tencin studied men and affairs, Mme. du Châtelet studied books. One was mistress of the arts of diplomacy, gentle but intriguing, ambitious, always courting society and shunning solitude. The other was violent and imperious, hated *finesse*, and preferred burying herself among the rare treasures of her library at Cirey.

The influence of Mme. de Tencin was felt, not only in the social and intellectual, but in the political life of the century. The traditions of her salon lingered in those which followed, modified by the changes that time and personal taste always bring. Mme. du Châtelet was more learned, but she lacked the tact and charm which give wide personal ascendancy. Her influence was largely individual, and her books have been mostly forgotten. These women were alike defiant of morality, but taken all in all, the character of Mme. du Châtelet has more redeeming points, though little respect can be accorded to either. With the wily intellect of a Talleyrand, Mme. de Tencin represents the social genius, the intelligence, the *esprit*, and the worst vices of the century on which she has left such conspicuous traces.

" She knew my tastes and always offered me those dishes I preferred," said Fontenelle when she died, in 1749. " It is an irreparable loss." Perhaps his hundred years should excuse his not going to her funeral for fear of catching cold.

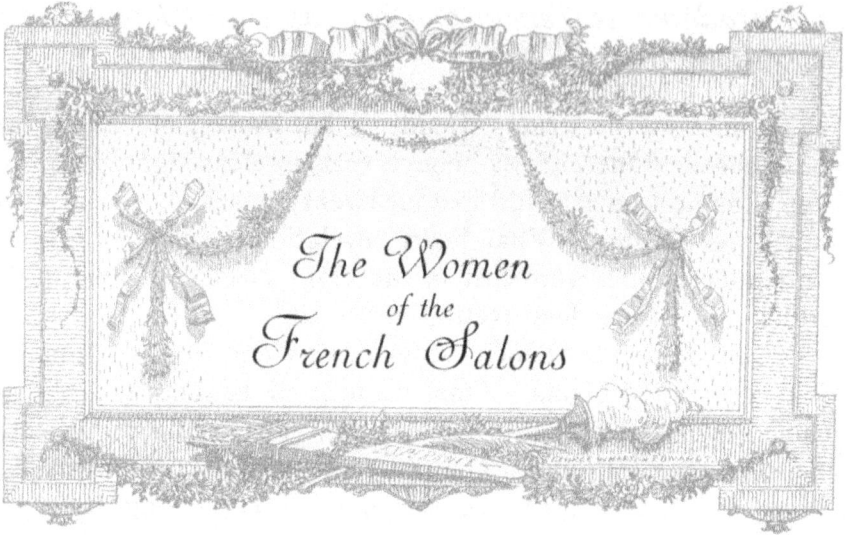

The Women
of the
French Salons

CHAPTER XII

MADAME GEOFFRIN AND THE PHILOSOPHERS

Cradles of the New Philosophy — Noted Salons of this Period — Character of Mme. Geoffrin — Her Practical Education — Anecdotes of her Husband — Composition of her Salon — Its Insidious Influence — Her Journey to Warsaw — Her Death.

DURING the latter half of the eighteenth century the center of social life was no longer the court, but the salons. They had multiplied indefinitely, and, representing every shade of taste and thought, had reached the climax of their power as schools of public opinion, as well as their highest perfection in the arts and amenities of a brilliant and complex society. There was a slight reaction from the reckless vices and follies of the regency. If morals were not much better, manners were a trifle more decorous. Though the great world did not take the tone of stately elegance and rigid propriety which it had assumed under the rule of Mme. de Maintenon, it was superficially polished, and a note of thoughtfulness was added. Affairs in France had taken too serious an aspect to be ignored, and the theories of the philosophers were among the staple topics of conversation; indeed, it was the great vogue of the philosophers that gave many of the most noted social centers their prestige and their fame. It is not the salons of the high nobility that suggest themselves as the typical ones of this age. It is those which were animated by the habitual presence of the radical leaders of French thought. Economic questions and the rights of man were discussed as earnestly in these brilliant coteries as matters of faith and sentiment, of etiquette and morals, had been a hundred years before. Such subjects were forced upon them by the inexorable logic of events; and fashion, which must needs adapt itself in some measure to the world over which it rules, took them up. If the drawing-rooms of the seventeenth century were the cradles of refined manners and a new literature, those of the eighteenth were literally the cradles of a new philosophy.

The practical growth and spread of French philosophy was too closely interwoven with the history of the salons not to call for a word here. Its innovations were faintly prefigured in the coterie of Mme. de Lambert, where it colored almost imperceptibly the literary and critical discussions. But its foundations were more firmly laid in the drawing-room of Mme. de Tencin, where the brilliant wit and radical theories of Montesquieu, as well as the pronounced materialism of Helvétius, found a congenial atmosphere. Though the mingled romance and satire of the *Persian Letters*, with their covert attack upon the state and society, raised a storm of antagonism, they called out a burst of admiration as well. The original and aggressive thought of men like Voltaire, Rousseau, d'Alembert, and Diderot, with its diversity of shading, but with the cardinal doctrine of freedom and equality pervading it all, had found a rapidly growing audience. It no longer needed careful nursing, in the second half of the century. It had invaded the salons of the *haute noblesse*, and was discussed even in the anterooms of the court. Mme. de Pompadour herself stole away from her tiresome lover-king to the freethinking coterie that met in her physician's apartments in the *entresol* at Versailles, and included the greatest iconoclasts of the age. If she had

any misgivings as to the outcome of these discussions, they
were fearlessly cast aside with "*Après nous le déluge.*"   "In
the depth of her heart she was with us," said Voltaire when
she died.

There were clairvoyant spirits who traced the new theories
to their logical results.   Mme. du Deffand speaks with prophetic vision of the reasoners and *beaux esprits* "who direct
the age and lead it to its ruin."   There were conservative
women, too, who used their powerful influence against them.
It was in the salon of the delicate but ardent young Princesse
de Robecq that Palissot was inspired to write the satirical
comedy of *The Philosophers*, in which Rousseau was represented as entering on all fours, browsing a lettuce, and the
Encyclopedists were so mercilessly ridiculed.   This spirited
and heroic daughter-in-law of the Duchesse de Luxembourg,
the powerful patroness of Rousseau, was hopelessly ill at the
time, and, in a caustic reply to the clever satire, the Abbé
Morellet did not spare the beautiful invalid who desired for
her final consolation only to see its first performance and be
able to say, "Now, Lord, thou lettest thy servant depart in
peace, for mine eyes have seen vengeance."   The cruel attack
was thought to have hastened her death, and the witty abbé
was sent to the Bastille; but he came out in two months, went
away for a time, and returned a greater hero than ever.   There
is a picture, full of pathetic significance, which represents the
dying princess on her pillow, crowned with a halo of sanctity,
as she devotes her last hours to the defense of the faith she
loves.   One is reminded of the sweet and earnest souls of Port
Royal; but her vigorous protest, which furnished only a
momentary target for the wit of the philosophers, was lost in
the oncoming wave of skepticism.

The vogue of these men received its final stamp in the
admiring patronage of the greatest sovereigns in Europe.
Voltaire had his well-known day of power at the court of
Frederick the Great.   Grimm and Diderot, too, were honored
guests of that most liberal of despots, and discussed their novel
theories in familiar fashion with Catherine II. at St. Petersburg.
The reply of this astute and clear-sighted empress to the

MME. GEOFFRIN.

FROM A PORTRAIT BY CHARDIN.

eloquent plea of Diderot may be commended for its wisdom to the dreamers and theorists of to-day.

"I have heard, with the greatest pleasure, all that your brilliant intellect has inspired you to say; but with all your grand principles, which I comprehend very well, one makes fine books and bad business. You forget in all your plans of reform the difference of our two positions. You work only on paper, which permits everything: it is quite smooth and pliant, and opposes no obstacles to your imagination nor to your pen; while I, poor empress, I work upon the human cuticle, which is quite sensitive and irritable."

It is needless to say that the men so honored by sovereigns were petted in the salons, in spite of their disfavor with the Government. They dined, talked, posed as lions or as martyrs, and calmly bided their time. The persecution of the Encyclopedists availed little more than satire had done, in stemming the slowly rising tide of public opinion. Utopian theories took form in the ultra circles, were insidiously disseminated in the moderate ones, and were lightly discussed in the fashionable ones. Men who talked, and women who added enthusiasm, were alike unconscious of the dynamic force of the material with which they were playing.

Of the salons which at this period had a European reputation, the most noted were those of Mme. du Deffand, Mlle. de Lespinasse, and Mme. Geoffrin. The first was the resort of the more intellectual of the *noblesse,* as well as the more famous of the men of letters. The two worlds mingled here; the tone was spiced with wit and animated with thought, but it was essentially aristocratic. The second was the rallying-point of the Encyclopedists and much frequented by political reformers, but the rare gifts of its hostess attracted many from the great world. The last was moderate in tone, though philosophical and thoroughly cosmopolitan. Sainte-Beuve pronounced it "the most complete, the best organized, and best conducted of its time; the best established since the foundation of the salons; that is, since the Hôtel de Rambouillet."

"Do you know why *la Geoffrin* comes here? It is to see what she can gather from my inventory," remarked Mme. de

Tencin on her death-bed. She understood thoroughly her world, and knew that her friend wished to capture the celebrities who were in the habit of meeting in her salon. But she does not seem to have borne her any ill-will for her rather premature schemes, as she gave her a characteristic piece of advice: "Never refuse any advance of friendship," she said; "for, if nine out of ten bring you nothing, one alone may repay you. Everything is of service in a *ménage* if one knows how to use his tools." Mme. Geoffrin was an apt pupil in the arts of diplomacy, and the key to her remarkable social success may be found in her ready assimilation of the worldly wisdom of her sage counselor. But to this she added a far kinder heart and a more estimable character.

Of all the women who presided over famous salons, Mme. Geoffrin had perhaps the least claim to intellectual preëminence. The secret of her power must have lain in some intangible quality that has failed to be perpetuated in any of her sayings or doings. A few commonplace and ill-spelled letters, a few wise or witty words, are all the direct record she has left of herself. Without rank, beauty, youth, education, or remarkable mental gifts of a sort that leave permanent traces, she was the best representative of the women of her time who held their place in the world solely through their skill in organizing and conducting a salon. She was in no sense a luminary; and conscious that she could not shine by her own light, she was bent upon shining by that of others. But, in a social era so brilliant, even this implied talent of a high order. A letter to the Empress of Russia, in reply to a question concerning her early education, throws a ray of light upon her youth and her peculiar training.

"I lost my father and mother," she writes, "in the cradle. I was brought up by an aged grandmother, who had much intelligence and a well-balanced head. She had very little education; but her mind was so clear, so ready, so active, that it never failed her; it served always in the place of knowledge. She spoke so agreeably of the things she did not know that no one wished her to understand them better; and when her ignorance was too visible, she got out of it by pleasantries which baffled the pedants who tried to humiliate her. She was so contented with her lot that she looked upon knowledge as a very useless thing for a woman. She said: 'I have done without it so well that I have never felt the need of it. If my grand-daughter is stupid, learning will make her conceited and in-supportable; if she has talent and sensibility, she will do as I have done — supply by address and with sentiment what she does not know; when she becomes more reasonable, she will learn that for which she has the most aptitude, and she will learn it very quickly.' She taught me in my childhood simply to read, but she made me read much; she taught me to think by making me reason; she taught me to know men by making me say what I thought of them, and telling me also the opinion she had formed. She required me to render her an account of all my movements and all my feelings, correcting them with so much sweetness and grace that I never concealed from her any-thing that I thought or felt; my internal life was as visible as my external. My education was continual."

The daughter of a *valet de chambre* of the Duchess of Bur-gundy, who gave her a handsome dowry, Marie Thérèse Rodet became, at fourteen, the wife of a lieutenant-colonel of the National Guard and a rich manufacturer of glass. Her husband did not count for much among the distinguished guests who in later years frequented her salon, and his part in her life seems to have consisted mainly in furnishing the money so essential to her success, and in looking carefully after the interests of the *ménage*. It is related that some one gave him a history to read, and when he called for the successive volumes the same one was always returned to him. Not observing this, he found the work interesting, but "thought the author repeated a little." He read across the page a book printed in two columns, re-marking that "it seemed to be very good, but a trifle abstract." One day a visitor inquired for the white-haired old gentleman who was in the habit of sitting at the head of the table. "That was my husband," replied Mme. Geoffrin; "he is dead."

But if her marriage was not an ideal one, it does not appear that it was unhappy. Perhaps her *bourgeois* birth and associa-tions saved her youth from the domestic complications which were so far the rule in the great world as to have, in a measure, its sanction. At all events her life was apparently free from the shadows that rested upon many of her contemporaries.

" Her character was a singular one," writes Marmontel, who lived for ten years in her house, " and difficult to understand or paint, because it was all in half-tints and shades ; very decided, nevertheless, but without the striking traits by which one's nature distinguishes and defines itself. She was kind, but had little sensibility; charitable, without any of the charms of benevolence; eager to aid the unhappy, but without seeing them, for fear of being moved; a sure, faithful, even officious friend, but timid and anxious in serving others, lest she should compromise her credit or her repose. She was simple in her taste, her dress, and her furniture, but choice in her simplicity, having the refinements and delicacies of luxury, but nothing of its ostentation nor its vanity; modest in her air, carriage, and manners, but with a touch of pride, and even a little vainglory. Nothing flattered her more than her intercourse with the great. At their houses she rarely saw them,— indeed she was not at her ease there,— but she knew how to attract them to her own by a coquetry subtly flattering; and in the easy, natural, half-respectful and half-familiar air with which she received them, I thought I saw remarkable address."

In a woman of less tact and penetration, this curious vein of hidden vanity would have led to pretension. But Mme. Geoffrin was preëminently gifted with that fine social sense which is apt to be only the fruit of generations of culture. With her it was innate genius. She was mistress of the amiable art of suppressing herself, and her vanity assumed the form of a gracious modesty. "I remain humble, but with dignity," she writes to a friend ; "that is, in depreciating myself I do not suffer others to depreciate me." She had the instinct of the artist who knows how to offset the lack of brilliant gifts by the perfection of details, the modesty that disarms criticism, and a rare facility in the art of pleasing.

There was an air of refinement and simple elegance in her personality that commanded respect. Tall and dignified, with her silvery hair concealed by her coif, she combined a noble

CATHERINE II. IN RUSSIAN COSTUME.

presence with great kindliness of manner. She usually wore
somber colors and fine laces, for which she had great fondness.
Her youth was long past when she came before the world, and
that sense of fitness which always distinguished her led her to
accept her age seriously and to put on its hues. The "dead-
leaf mantle" of Mme. de Maintenon was worn less severely

perhaps, but it was worn without affectation.   Diderot gives us a pleasant glimpse of her at Grandval, where they were din- ing with Baron d'Holbach.   "Mme. Geoffrin was admirable," he wrote to Mlle. Volland.   "I remark always the noble and quiet taste with which this woman dresses.   She wore to-day a simple stuff of austere color, with large sleeves, the smoothest and finest linen, and the most elegant simplicity throughout."

In her equanimity and love of repose she was a worthy disciple of Fontenelle.   She carefully avoided all violent pas- sions and all controversies.   To her lawyer, who was conduct- ing a suit that worried her, she said, "Wind up my case.   Do they want my money?   I have some, and what can I do with money better than to buy tranquillity with it?"   This aversion to annoyance often reached the proportions of a very amiable selfishness.   "She has the habit of detesting those who are unhappy," said the witty Abbé Galiani, "for she does not wish to be so, even by the sight of the unhappiness of others.   She has an impressionable heart; she is old; she is well; she wishes to preserve her health and her tranquillity.   As soon as she learns that I am happy she will love me to folly."

But her generosity was exceptional.   "*Donner et pardon- ner*" was her device.   Many anecdotes are related of her charitable temper.   She had ordered two marble vases of Bouchardon.   One was broken before reaching her.   Learn- ing that the man who broke it would lose his place if it were known, and that he had a family of four children, she immedi- ately sent word to the atelier that the sculptor was not to be told of the loss, adding a gift of twelve francs to console the culprit for his fright.   She often surprised her impecunious friends with the present of some bit of furniture she thought they needed, or an annuity delicately bestowed.   "I have assigned to you fifteen thousand francs," she said one day to the Abbé Morellet; "do not speak of it and do not thank me."   "Economy is the source of independence and liberty" was one of her mottoes, and she denied herself the lux- uries of life that she might have more to spend in charities. But she never permitted any one to compromise her, and often withheld her approbation where she was free with her purse.   To do all the good possible and to respect all the *con-venances* were her cardinal principles.   Marmontel was sent to the Bastille under circumstances that were rather creditable than otherwise ; but it was a false note, and she was never quite the same to him afterwards.   She wept at her own injustice, schemed for his election to the Academy, and scolded him for his lack of diplomacy ; but the little cloud was there. When the Sorbonne censured his *Belisarius* her friendship could no longer bear the strain, and, though still received at her dinners, he ceased to live in her house.

Her dominant passion seems to have been love of consider-ation, if a calm and serene, but steadily persistent, purpose can be called a passion.   No trained diplomatist ever understood better the world with which he had to deal, or managed more adroitly to avoid small antagonisms.   It was her maxim not to create jealousy by praising people, nor irritation by defend-ing them.   If she wished to say a kind word, she dwelt upon good qualities that were not contested.   She prided herself upon ruling her life by reason.   Sainte-Beuve calls her the Fontenelle of women, but it was Fontenelle tempered with a heart.

This " foster-mother of philosophers " evidently wished to make sure of her own safety, however matters might turn out in the next world.   She had a devotional vein, went to mass privately, had a seat at the Church of the Capucins, and an apartment for retreat in a convent.   During her last illness the Marquise de la Ferté-Imbault, who did not love her mother's freethinking friends, excluded them, and sent for a confessor.   Mme. Geoffrin submitted amiably, and said, smil-ing, " My daughter is like Godfrey of Bouillon ; she wishes to defend my tomb against the infidels."

Into the composition of her salon she brought the talent of an artist.   We have a glimpse of her in 1748 through a letter from Montesquieu.   She was then about fifty, and had gathered about her a more or less distinguished company, which was enlarged after the death of Mme. de Tencin, in the following year.   She gave dinners twice a week — one on Monday for artists, among whom were Vanloo, Vernet, and Boucher ; and one on Wednesday for men of letters. As she believed that women were apt to distract the conversation, only one was usually invited to dine with them. Mlle. de Lespinasse, the intellectual peer and friend of these men, sat opposite her, and aided in conducting the conversation into agreeable channels. The talent of Mme. Geoffrin seems to have consisted in telling a story well, in a profound knowledge of people, ready tact, and the happy art of putting every one at ease. She did not like heated discussions nor a too pronounced expression of opinion. "She was willing that the philosophers should remodel the world," says one of her critics, "on condition that the kingdom of Diderot should come without disorder or confusion." But though she liked and admired this very free and eloquent Diderot, he was too bold and outspoken to have a place at her table. Helvétius, too, fell into disfavor after the censure which his atheistic *De l'Esprit* brought upon him; and Baron d'Holbach was too apt to overstep the limits at which the hostess interfered with her inevitable "*Voilà qui est bien.*" Indeed, she assumed the privilege of her years to scold her guests if they interfered with the general harmony or forgot any of the amenities. But her scoldings were very graciously received as a slight penalty for her favor, and more or less a measure of her friendship. She graded her courtesies with fine discrimination, and her friends found the reflection of their success or failure in her manner of receiving them. Her keen, practical mind pierced every illusion with merciless precision. She defined a popular abbé who posed for a *bel esprit*, as a "fool rubbed all over with wit." Rulhière had read in her salon a work on Russia, which she feared might compromise him, and she offered him a large sum of money to throw it into the fire. The author was indignant at such a reflection upon his courage and honor, and grew warmly eloquent upon the subject. She listened until he had finished, then said quietly, "How much more do you want, M. Rulhière?"

The serene poise of a character without enthusiasms and without illusions is very well illustrated by a letter to Mme. Necker. After playfully charging her with being always infatuated, never cool and reserved, she continues:

"Do you know, my pretty one, that your exaggerated praises confound me, instead of pleasing and flattering me? I am always afraid that your giddiness will evaporate. You will then judge me to be so different from your preconceived opinion that you will punish me for your own mistake, and allow me no merit at all. I have my virtues and my good qualities, but I have also many faults. Of these I am perfectly well aware, and every day I try to correct them.

"My dear friend, I beg of you to lessen your excessive admiration. I assure you that you humiliate me; and that is certainly not your intention. The angels think very little about me, and I do not trouble myself about them. Their praise or their blame is indifferent to me, for I shall not come in their way; but what I do desire is that you should love me, and that you should take me as you find me."

Again she assumes her position of mentor and writes: "How is it possible not to answer the kind and charming letter I have received from you? But still I reply only to tell you that it made me a little angry. I see that it is impossible to change anything in your uneasy, restless, and at the same time weak character."

Horace Walpole, who met her during his first visit to Paris, and before his intimacy with Mme. du Deffand had colored his opinions, has left a valuable pen-portrait of Mme. Geoffrin. In a letter to Gray, in 1766, he writes:

"Mme. Geoffrin, of whom you have heard much, is an extraordinary woman, with more common sense than I almost ever met with, great quickness in discovering characters, penetrating and going to the bottom of them, and a pencil that never fails in a likeness, seldom a favorable one. She exacts and preserves, spite of her birth and their nonsensical prejudices about nobility, great court and attention. This she acquires by a thousand little arts and offices of friendship, and by a freedom and severity which seem to be her sole end for drawing a concourse to her. She has little taste and less knowledge, but protects artisans and authors, and courts a few people to have the credit of serving her dependents. In short, she is an epitome of empire, subsisting by rewards and punishments."

Later, when he was less disinterested, perhaps, he writes to another friend : " Mme. du Deffand hates the philosophers, so you must give them up to her. She and Mme. Geoffrin are no friends ; so if you go thither, don't tell her of it. Indeed, you would be sick of that house whither all the pretended *beaux esprits* and false *savants* go, and where they are very impertinent and dogmatic."

The real power of this woman may be difficult to define, but a glance at her society reveals, at least partly, its secret. Nowhere has the glamour of a great name more influence than at Paris. A few celebrities form a nucleus of sufficient attraction to draw all the world, if they are selected with taste and discrimination. After the death of Fontenelle, d'Alembert, always witty, vivacious, and original, in spite of the serious and exact nature of his scientific studies, was perhaps the leading spirit of this salon. Among its constant *habitués* were Helvétius, who put his selfishness into his books, reserving for his friends the most amiable and generous of tempers ; Marivaux, the novelist and dramatist, whose vanity rivaled his genius, but who represented only the literary spirit, and did not hesitate to ridicule his companions the philosophers ; the caustic but brilliant and accomplished Abbé Morellet, who had " his heart in his head and his head in his heart"; the severe and cheerful Mairan, mathematician, astronomer, physician, musical amateur, and member of two academies, whose versatile gifts and courtly manners gave him as cordial a welcome in the exclusive salon at the Temple as among his philosophical friends ; the gay young Marmontel, who has left so clear and simple a picture of this famous circle and its gentle hostess ; Grimm, who combined the *savant* and the courtier ; Saint-Lambert, the delicate and scholarly poet ; Thomas, grave and thoughtful, shining by his character and intellect, but forgetting the graces which were at that time so essential to brilliant success ; the eloquent Abbé Raynal ; and the Chevalier de Chastellux, so genial, so sympathetic, and so animated. To these we may add Galiani, the smallest, the wittiest, and the most delightful of abbés, whose piercing insight and Machiavellian subtlety lent a piquant charm to the stories with which for hours he used to enliven this choice company ; Caraccioli, gay, simple, ingenuous, full of Neapolitan humor, rich in knowledge and observation, luminous with intelligence and sparkling with wit ; and the Comte de Creutz, the learned and versatile Swedish minister, to whom nature had "granted the gift of expressing and painting in touches of fire all that had struck his imagination or vividly seized his soul." Hume, Gibbon, Walpole, indeed every foreigner of distinction who visited Paris, lent to this salon the éclat of their fame, the charm of their wit, or the prestige of their rank. It was such men as these who gave it so rare a fascination and so lasting a fame.

A strong vein of philosophy was inevitable, though in this circle of diplomats and *littérateurs* there were many countercurrents of opinion. It was her consummate skill in blending these diverse but powerful elements, and holding them within harmonious limits, that made the reputation of the autocratic hostess. The friend of *savants* and philosophers, she had neither read nor studied books, but she had studied life to good purpose. Though superficial herself, she had the delicate art of putting every one in the most advantageous light by a few simple questions or words. It was one of her maxims that "the way not to get tired of people is to talk to them of themselves ; at the same time, it is the best way to prevent them from getting tired of you." Perhaps Mme. Necker was thinking of her when she compared certain women in conversation to "light layers of cotton-wool in a box packed with porcelain ; we do not pay much attention to them, but if they were taken away everything would be broken."

Mme. Geoffrin was always at home in the evening, and there were simple little suppers to which a few women were invited. The fare was usually little more than "a chicken, some spinach, and omelet." Among the most frequent guests were the charming, witty, and *spirituelle* Comtesse d'Egmont, daughter of the Duc de Richelieu, who added to the vivacious and elegant manners of her father an indefinable grace of her own, and vein of sentiment that was doubtless deepened by her sad romance ; the Marquise de Duras, more dignified and dis and the beautiful Comtesse de Brionne, "a Venus who resem

Minerva." These women, with others who came there, were intellectual complements of the men ; some of them gay and not without serious faults, but adding beauty, rank, elegance, and the delicate tone of *esprit* which made this circle so famous that it was thought worth while to have its sayings and doings chronicled at Berlin and St. Petersburg. Perhaps its influence was the more insidious and far-reaching because of its polished moderation. The "let us be agreeable" of Mme. Geoffrin was a potent talisman.

Among the guests at one time was Stanislas Poniatowski, afterwards King of Poland. Hearing that he was about to be imprisoned by his creditors, Mme. Geoffrin came forward and paid his debts. "When I make a statue of friendship, I shall give it your features," he said to her; "this divinity is the mother of charity." On his elevation to the throne he wrote to her, "Maman, your son is king. Come and see him." This led to her famous journey when nearly seventy years of age. It was a series of triumphs at which no one was more surprised than herself, and they were all due, she modestly says, "to a few mediocre dinners and some *petits soupers*." One can readily pardon her for feeling flattered, when the emperor alights from his carriage on the public promenade at Vienna and pays her some pretty compliments, "just as if he had been at one of our little Wednesday suppers." There is a charm in the simple *naïveté* with which she tells her friends how cordially Maria Theresa receives her at Schönbrunn, and she does not forget to add that the empress said she had the most beautiful complexion in the world. She repeats quite naturally, and with a slight touch of vanity perhaps, the fine speeches made to her by the "adorable Prince Galitzin" and Prince Kaunitz, "the first minister in Europe," both of whom entertained her. But she would have been more than a woman to have met all this honor with indifference. No wonder she believes herself to be dreaming. "I am known here much better than in the Rue St. Honoré," she writes, "and in a fashion the most flattering. My journey has made an incredible sensation for the last fifteen days." To be sure, she spells badly for a woman who poses as the friend of *littérateurs* and *savants*, and says very little about anything that does not concern her own fame and glory. But she does not cease to remember her friends, whom she "loves, if possible, better than ever." Nor does she forget to send a thousand caresses to her kitten.

A messenger from Warsaw meets her with everything imaginable that can add to the comfort and luxury of her journey, and on reaching there she finds a room fitted up for her like her own boudoir in the Rue St. Honoré. She accepts all this consideration with great modesty and admirable good sense. "This tour finished," she writes to d'Alembert, "I feel that I shall have seen enough of men and things to be convinced that they are everywhere about the same. I have my storehouse of reflections and comparisons well furnished for the rest of my life. All that I have seen since leaving my Penates makes me thank God for having been born French and a private person."

The peculiar charm which attracted such rare and marked attentions to a woman not received at her own court, and at a time when social distinctions were very sharply defined, eludes analysis, but it seems to have lain largely in her exquisite sense of fitness, her excellent judgment, her administrative talent, the fine tact and penetration which enabled her to avoid antagonism, an instinctive knowledge of the art of pleasing, and a kind but not too sensitive heart. These qualities are not those which appeal to the imagination or inspire enthusiasm. We find in her no spark of that celestial flame which gives intellectual distinction. In her amiability there seems to be a certain languor of the heart. Her kindness has a trace of calculation, and her friendship of self-consciousness. Of spontaneity she has none. "She loved nothing passionately, not even virtue," says one of her critics. There was a certain method in her simplicity. She carried to perfection the art of *savoir vivre*, and though she claimed freedom of thought and action, it was always strictly within conventional limits.

She suffered the fate of all celebrities in being occasionally attacked. The rôle assigned to her in the comedy of *The Philosophers* was not a flattering one, and some criticisms of Montesquieu wounded her so deeply that she succeeded in having them suppressed. She did not escape the shafts of envy, nor the sneers of the *grandes dames* who did not relish her popularity. But these were only spots on the surface of a singularly brilliant career. Calm, reposeful, charitable, without affectation or pretension, but not untouched by ennui, the malady of her time, she held her position to the end of a long life which closed in 1777.

"Alas," said d'Alembert, who had been in the habit of spending his mornings with Mlle. de Lespinasse until her death, and his evenings with Mme. Geoffrin, "I have neither evenings nor mornings left."

"She has made for fifty years the charm of her society," said the Abbé Morellet. "She has been constantly, habitually virtuous and benevolent." Her salon brought authors and artists into direct relation with distinguished patrons, especially foreigners, and thus contributed largely to the spread of French art and letters. It was counted among "the institutions of the eighteenth century."

The Women
of the
French Salons

CHAPTER XIII

ULTRA-PHILOSOPHICAL SALONS — MADAME D'EPINAY

Mme. de Graffigny — Baron d'Holbach — Mme. d'Epinay's Portrait of Herself — Mlle. Quinault — Rousseau — La Chevrette — Grimm — Diderot — The Abbé Galiani — Estimate of Mme. d'Epinay.

A FEW of the more radical and earnest of the philosophers rarely, if ever, appeared at the table of Mme. Geoffrin. They would have brought too much heat to this company, which discussed everything in a light and agreeable fashion. Perhaps, too, these free and brilliant spirits objected to the leading-strings which there held every one within prescribed limits. They could talk more at their ease at the weekly dinners of Baron d'Holbach, in the salons of Mme. Helvétius, Mme. de Marchais, or Mme. de Graffigny, in the Encyclopedist coterie of Mlle. de Lespinasse, or in the liberal drawing-room of Mme. d'Epinay, who held a more questionable place in the social world, but received much good company, Mme. Geoffrin herself included.

Mme. de Graffigny is known mainly as a woman of letters whose life had in it many elements of tragedy. Her youth was passed in the brilliant society of the little court at Lunéville.

FRANÇOISE D'ISSEMBOURG D'HAPPONCOURT, DAME DE GRAFFIGNY.

She was distantly related to Mme. du Châtelet, and finally took refuge from the cruelties of a violent and brutal husband in the "terrestrial paradise" at Cirey. *La belle Emilie* was moved to sympathy, and Voltaire wept at the tale of her sorrows. A little later she became a victim to the poet's sensitive vanity. He accused her of sending to a friend a copy of his *Pucelle*, an unfinished poem which was kept under triple lock, though parts of it had been read to her. Her letters were opened, her innocent praises were turned against her, there was a scene, and Cirey was a paradise no more. She came to Paris, ill, sad, and penniless. She wrote *Les Lettres d'une Péruvienne* and found herself famous. She wrote *Cénie*, which was played at the Comédie Française, and her success was established. Then she wrote another drama. "She read it to me," says one of her friends; "I found it bad; she found me ill-natured. It was played; the public died of *ennui* and the author of chagrin." "I am convinced that misfortune will follow me into paradise," she said. At all events, it seems to have followed her to the entrance.

Her salon was more or less celebrated. The freedom of the conversations may be inferred from the fact that Helvétius gathered there the materials for his *De l'Esprit*, a book condemned by the Pope, the Parliament, and the Sorbonne. It was here also that he found his charming wife, a niece of Mme. de Graffigny, and the light of her house as afterwards of his own.

A more permanent interest is attached to the famous dinners of Baron d'Holbach, where twice a week men like Diderot, Helvétius, Grimm, Marmontel, Duclos, the Abbé Galiani, and for a time Buffon and Rousseau, met in an informal way to enjoy the good cheer and good wines of this "*maître d'hôtel* of philosophy," and discuss the affairs of the universe. The learned and free-thinking baron was agreeable, kind, rich, and lavish in his hospitality, but without pretension. "He was a man simply simple," said Mme. Geoffrin. We have many pleasant glimpses of his country place at Grandval, with its rich and rare collections, its library, its pictures, its designs, and of the beautiful wife who turned the heads of some of the philosophers, whom, as a rule, she did not like overmuch, though she received them so graciously. "We dine well and a long time," wrote Diderot. "We talk of art, of poetry, of philosophy, and of love, of the greatness and vanity of our own enterprises, . . . of gods and kings, of space and time, of death and of life."

"They say things to make a thunderbolt strike the house a hundred times, if it struck for that," said the Abbé Morellet.

Among the few women admitted to these dinners was Mme. d'Epinay, for whom d'Holbach, as well as his amiable wife, always entertained the warmest friendship. This woman, whose position was not assured enough to make people overlook her peculiar and unfortunate domestic complications, has told the story of her own life in her long and confidential correspondence with Grimm, Galiani, and Voltaire. The senseless follies of a cruel and worthless husband, who plunged her from great wealth into extreme poverty, and of whom Diderot said that "he had squandered two millions without saying a good word or doing a good action," threw her into intimate relations with Grimm; this brought her into the center of a famous circle. Her letters give us a clear but far from flattering reflection of the manners of the time. She unveils the bare and hard facts of her own experience, the secret workings of her own soul. The picture is not a pleasant one, but it is full of significance to the moralist, and furnishes abundant matter for psychological study.

The young girl, who had entered upon the scene about 1725, under the name of Louise Florence-Pétronille-Tardieu d'Esclavelles, was married at twenty to her cousin. It seems to have been really a marriage of love; but the weak and faithless M. d'Epinay was clearly incapable of truth or honor, and the torturing process by which the confiding young wife was disillusioned, the insidious counsels of a false and profligate friend, with the final betrayal of a tender and desolate heart, form a chapter as revolting as it is pathetic. The fresh, lively, pureminded, sensitive girl, whose intellect had been fed on Rollin's history and books of devotion, who feared the dissipations of the gay world and shrank with horror from the rouge which her frivolous husband compelled her to put on, learned her lesson rapidly in the school of suffering.

At thirty she writes of herself, after the fashion of the pen-portraits of the previous century:

"I am not pretty; yet I am not plain. I am small, thin, very well formed. I have the air of youth, without freshness, but noble, sweet, lively, *spirituelle*, and interesting. My imagination is tranquil. My mind is slow, just, reflective, and inconsequent. I have vivacity, courage, firmness, elevation, and excessive timidity. I am true without being frank. Timidity

MME. D'EPINAY.

often gives me the appearance of dissimulation and duplicity;
but I have always had the courage to confess my weakness, in
order to destroy the suspicion of a vice which I have not.   I
have the *finesse* to attain my end and to remove obstacles; but
I have none to penetrate the purposes of others.   I was born
tender and sensible, constant and no coquette.   I love retirement, a life simple and private; nevertheless, I have almost

always led one contrary to my taste. Bad health, and sorrows sharp and repeated, have given a serious cast to my character, which is naturally very gay."

Her first entrance into the world in which wit reigned supreme was in the free but elegant salon of Mlle. Quinault, an actress of the Comédie Française, who had left the stage, and, taking the rôle of a *femme d'esprit,* had gathered around her a distinguished and fashionable coterie. This woman, who had received a decoration for a fine motet she had composed for the queen's chapel, who was loved and consulted by Voltaire, and who was the best friend of d'Alembert after the death of Mlle. de Lespinasse, represented the genius of *esprit* and *finesse.* She was the companion of princes, the adoration of princesses, the oracle of artists and *littérateurs,* the model of elegance, and the embodiment of social success. It did not matter much that the tone of her salon was lax; it was fashionable. "It distilled dignity, *la convenance,* and formality," says the Marquise de Créqui, who relates an anecdote that aptly illustrates the glamour which surrounded talent at that time. She was taken by her grandmother to see Mlle. Quinault, and by some chance mistook for her Mlle. de Vertus, who was so much flattered by her innocent error that she left her forty thousand francs, when she died a few months later.

Mme. d'Epinay was delighted to find herself in so brilliant a world, and was greatly fascinated by its wit, though she was not sure that those who met there did not "feel too much the obligation of having it." But she caught the spirit, and transferred it, in some degree, to her own salon, which was more literary than fashionable. Here Francueil presents "a sorry devil of an author who is as poor as Job, but has wit and vanity enough for four." This is Rousseau, the most conspicuous figure in the famous coterie. "He is a man to whom one should raise altars," wrote Mme. d'Epinay. "And the simplicity with which he relates his misfortunes! I have still a pitying soul. It is frightful to imagine such a man in misery." She fitted up for him the Hermitage, and did a thousand kind things which entitled her to a better return than he gave. There is a pleasant moment when we find him the center of an admiring circle at La Chevrette, falling madly in love with her clever and beautiful sister-in-law the Comtesse d'Houdetot, writing *La Nouvelle Héloïse* under the inspiration of this passion, and dreaming in the lovely promenades at Montmorency, quite at peace with the world.   But the weeping philosopher, who said such fine things and did such base ones, turned against his benefactress and friend for some imaginary offense, and revenged himself by false and malicious attacks upon her character.   The final result was a violent quarrel with the whole circle of philosophers, who espoused the cause of Mme. d'Epinay.   This little history is interesting, as it throws so much light upon the intimate relations of some of the greatest men of the century.   Behind the perpetual round of comedies, readings, dinners, music, and conversation, there is a real comedy of passion, intrigue, jealousy, and hidden misery that destroys many illusions.

Mme. d'Epinay has been made familiar to us by Grimm, Galiani, Diderot, Rousseau, and Voltaire.   Perhaps, on the whole, Voltaire has given us the most agreeable impression. She was ill of grief and trouble, and had gone to Geneva to consult the famous Tronchin when she was thrown into more or less intimacy with the Sage of Ferney.   He invited her to dinner immediately upon her arrival.   "I was much fatigued, besides having confessed and received communion the evening before.   I did not find it fitting to dine with Voltaire two days afterward," writes this curiously sensitive friend of the free-thinkers.   He addresses her as *ma belle philosophe*, speaks of her as "an eagle in a cage of gauze," and praises in verse her philosophy, her *esprit*, her heart, and her "two great black eyes."   He weeps at her departure, tells her she is "adored at Délices, adored at Paris, adored present and absent."   But "the tears of a poet do not always signify grief," says Mme. d'Epinay.

There is a second period in her life, when she introduces us again to the old friends who always sustained her, and to many new ones.   The world that meets in her salon later is much the same as that which dines with Baron d'Holbach. To measure its attractions one must recall the brilliancy and eloquence of Diderot; the wit, the taste, the learning, the courtly accomplishments of Grimm; the gaiety and originality of d'Holbach, who had "read everything and forgotten nothing interesting"; the sparkling conversation of the most finished

ELISABETH FRANÇOISE, COMTESSE D'HOUDETOT.

and scholarly diplomats in Europe, many of whom we have already met at the dinners of Mme. Geoffrin. They discuss economic questions, politics, religion, art, literature, with equal freedom and ardor. They are as much divided on the merits of Glück's *Armida* and Piccini's *Roland* as upon taxes, grains, and the policy of the government. The gay little Abbé Galiani brings perennial sunshine with the inexhaustible wit and vivacity that lights his clear and subtle intellect. "He is a treasure on rainy days," says Diderot. "If they made him at the toy shops everybody would want one for the country." "He was

25

the nicest little harlequin that Italy has produced," says Marmontel, "but upon the shoulders of this harlequin was the
head of a Machiavelli. Epicurean in his philosophy and with
a melancholy soul, seeing everything on the ridiculous side,
there was nothing either in politics or morals apropos of which
he had not a good story to tell, and these stories were always
apt and had the salt of an unexpected and ingenious allusion."
He did not accept the theories of his friends, which he believed
would "cause the bankruptcy of knowledge, of pleasure, and
of the human intellect." "*Messieurs les philosophes*, you go
too fast," he said. "I begin by saying that if I were pope I
would put you in the Inquisition, and if I were king of France,
into the Bastille." He saw the drift of events; but if he
reasoned like a philosopher he laughed like a Neapolitan.
What matters to-morrow if we are happy to-day !

The familiar notes and letters of these clever people picture
for us a little world with its small interests, its piques, its loves,
its friendships, its quarrels, and its hatreds. Diderot, who
refused for a long time to meet Mme. d'Epinay, but finally
became an intimate and lasting friend, touches often, in his
letters to Sophie, upon the pleasant informality of La Chevrette,
with its curious social episodes and its emotional undercurrents.
He does not forget even the pigeons, the geese, the ducks, and
the chickens, which he calls his own. Pouf, the dog, has his
place here too, and flits often across the scene, a tiny bit of reflected immortality. These letters represent the bold icono-
clast on his best side, kind, simple in his tastes, and loyal to his
friends. He was never at home in the great world. He was
seen sometimes in the salons of Mme. Geoffrin, Mme. Necker,
and others, but he made his stay as brief as possible. Mme.
d'Epinay succeeded better in attaching him to her coterie.
There was more freedom, and he probably had a more sympathetic audience. "Four lines of this man make me dream
more and occupy me more," she said, "than a complete work of
our pretended *beaux esprits*." Grimm, too, was a central figure
here, and Grimm was his friend. But over his genius, as over
that of Rousseau, there was the trail of the serpent. The breadth
of his thought, the brilliancy of his criticisms, the eloquence of
his style, were clouded with sensualism. "When you see on his

forehead the reflection of a ray from Plato," says Sainte-Beuve, " do not trust it; look well, there is always the foot of a satyr."

It was to the clear and penetrating intellect of Grimm, with its vein of German romanticism, that Mme. d'Epinay was indebted for the finest appreciation and the most genuine sympathy. " *Bon Dieu,*" he writes to Diderot, " how this woman is to be pitied! I should not be troubled about her if she were as strong as she is courageous. She is sweet and trusting; she is peaceful, and loves repose above all; but her situation exacts unceasingly a conduct forced and out of her character: nothing so wears and destroys a machine naturally frail." She aided him in his *Correspondance Littéraire;* wrote a treatise on education, which had the honor of being crowned by the Academy; and, among other things of more or less value, a novel, which was not published until long after her death. With many gifts and attractions, kind, amiable, forgiving, and essentially emotional, Mme. d'Epinay seems to have been a woman of weak and undecided character, without sufficient strength of moral fiber to sustain herself with dignity under the unfortunate circumstances which surrounded her. " It depends only upon yourself," said Grimm, " to be the happiest and most adorable creature in the world, provided that you do not put the opinions of others before your own, and that you know how to suffice for yourself." Her education had not given her the worldly tact and address of Mme. Geoffrin, and her salon never had a wide celebrity; but it was a meeting-place of brilliant and radical thinkers, of the men who have perhaps done the most to change the face of the modern world. In a quiet and intimate way, it was one among the numberless forces which were gathering and gaining momentum to culminate in the great tragedy of the century. Mme. d'Epinay did not live to see the catastrophe. Worn out by a life of suffering and ill health, she died in 1783.

Whatever her faults and weaknesses may have been, the woman who could retain the devoted affection of so brilliant and versatile a man as Grimm for twenty-seven years, who was the lifelong friend and correspondent of Galiani and Voltaire, and the valued *confidante* of Diderot, must have had some rare attractions of mind, heart, or character.

Chapter XIV

SALONS OF THE NOBLESSE — MADAME DU DEFFAND

*La Maréchale de Luxembourg — The Temple — Comtesse de
Boufflers — Mme. du Deffand — Her Convent Salon —
Rupture with Mlle. de Lespinasse — Her Friendship with
Horace Walpole — Her Brilliancy and Her Ennui.*

HILE the group of iconoclasts who formed the
nucleus of the philosophical salons was airing
its theories and enjoying its increasing vogue,
there was another circle which played with the
new ideas more or less as a sort of intellectual
pastime, but was aristocratic *au fond*, and carefully preserved all the traditions of the old *noblesse*. One met
here the philosophers and men of letters, but they did not
dominate; they simply flavored these coteries of rank and
fashion. In this age of *esprit* no salon was complete without
its sprinkling of literary men. We meet the shy and awkward
Rousseau even in the exclusive drawing-room of the clever and
witty but critical Maréchale de Luxembourg, who presides over
a world in which the graces rule — a world of elegant manners,
of etiquette, and of forms. This model of the amenities, whose

gay and faulty youth ripened into a pious and charitable age, was at the head of that tribunal which pronounced judgment upon all matters relating to society. She was learned in genealogy, analyzed and traced to their source the laws of etiquette, possessed a remarkable memory, and, without profound education, had learned much from conversation with the *savants* and illustrious men who frequented her house. Her wit was proverbial, and she was never at a loss for a ready repartee or a spicy anecdote. She gave two grand suppers a week. Mme. de Genlis, who was often there, took notes, according to her custom, and has left an interesting record of conversations that were remarkable not only for brilliancy, but for the thoughtful wisdom of the comments upon men and things. La Harpe read a great part of his works in this salon. Rousseau entertained the princely guests at Montmorency with *La Nouvelle Heloïse* and *Emile*, and though never quite at ease, his democratic theories did not prevent him from feeling greatly honored by their friendly courtesies; indeed, he loses his usual bitterness when speaking of this noble patroness. He says that her conversation was marked by an exquisite delicacy that always pleased, and her flatteries were intoxicating because they were simple and seemed to escape without intention.

Mme. de Luxembourg was an autocrat, and did not hesitate to punish errors in taste by social ostracism. " Erase the name of Monsieur ———— from my list," she said, as a gentleman left after relating a scandalous story reflecting upon some one's honor. It was one of her theories that " society should punish what the law cannot attack." She maintained that good manners are based upon noble and delicate sentiments, that mutual consideration, deference, politeness, gentleness, and respect to age are essential to civilization. The disloyal, the ungrateful, bad sons, bad brothers, bad husbands, and bad wives, whose offenses were serious enough to be made public, she banished from that circle which called itself *la bonne compagnie.* It must be admitted, however, that it was *les convenances* rather than morality which she guarded.

A rival of this brilliant salon, and among the most celebrated of its day, was the one at the Temple. The animating spirit here was the amiable and vivacious Comtesse de Boufflers, celebrated in youth for her charms, and later for her talent. She was *dame d'honneur* to the Princesse de Conti, wife of the Duc d'Orléans, who was noted for her caustic wit, as well as for her beauty.   It was in the salon of his clever and rather capricious sister that the learned Prince de Conti met her and formed the intimacy that ended only with his life.   She was called the *Idole* of the Temple, and her taste for letters gave her also the title of *Minerve Savante.*   She wrote a tragedy which was said to be good, though she would never let it go out of her hands, and has been immortalized by Rousseau, with whom she corresponded for sixteen years. Hume also exchanged frequent letters with her, and she tried in vain to reconcile these two friends after their quarrel.   President Hénault said he had never met a woman of so much *esprit*, adding that "outside all her charms she had character."   For society she had a veritable passion.   She said that when she loved England the best she could not think of staying there without "taking twenty-four or twenty-five intimate friends, and sixty or eighty others who were absolutely necessary to her."   Her conversation was full of fire and brilliancy, and her gaiety of heart, her gracious manners, and her frank appreciation of the talent of others added greatly to her piquant fascination.   She delighted in original turns of expression, which were sometimes far-fetched and artificial.   One of her friends said that "she made herself the victim of consideration, and lost it by running after it."   Her rule of life may be offered as a model.   "In conduct, simplicity and reason; in manners, propriety and decorum; in actions, justice and generosity; in the use of wealth, economy and liberality; in conversation, clearness, truth, precision; in adversity, courage and pride; in prosperity, modesty and moderation."   Unfortunately she did not put all this wisdom into practice, if we judge her by present standards.   We have a glimpse of the famous circle over which she presided in an interesting picture formerly at Versailles, now at the Louvre.   The figures are supposed to be portraits.   Among others are Mme. de Luxembourg, the Comtesse de Boufflers, and the lovely but ill-fated

DUCHESSE DE LUXEMBOURG.

young stepdaughter, Amélie, Comtesse de Lauzun, to whom she is so devoted; the beautiful Comtesse d'Egmont, Mme. de Beauvau, President Hénault, the witty Pont de Veyle, Mairan, the versatile scientist, and the Prince de Conti. In the midst of this group the little Mozart, whose genius was then delighting Europe, sits at the harpsichord. The chronicles of the time give us pleasant descriptions of the literary diversions of this society, which met by turns at the Temple and Ile-Adam. But the Prince as well as the clever Comtesse had a strong leaning towards philosophy, and the amusements were interspersed with much conversation of a serious character that has a peculiar interest to-day when read by the light of after events.

Among the numerous salons of the *noblesse* there was one which calls for more than a passing word, both on account of its world-wide fame and the exceptional brilliancy of its hostess. Though far less democratic and cosmopolitan than that of Mme. Geoffrin, with which it was cotemporary, its character was equally distinct and original. Linked by birth with the oldest of the nobility, allied by intellect with the most distinguished in the world of letters, Mme. du Deffand appropriated the best in thought, while retaining the spirit of an elegant and refined social life. She was exclusive by nature and instinct, as well as by tradition, and could not dispense with the arts and amenities which are the fruit of generations of ease; but the energy and force of her intellect could as little tolerate shallowness and pretension, however disguised beneath the graceful tyranny of forms. Her salon offers a sort of compromise between the freedom of the philosophical coteries and the frivolities of the purely fashionable ones. It included the most noted of the men of letters —those who belonged to the old aristocracy and a few to whom nature had given a prescriptive title of nobility—as well as the flower of the great world. Her sarcastic wit, her clear intelligence, and her rare conversational gifts added a tone of individuality that placed her salon at the head of the social centers of the time in brilliancy and in *esprit*. In this group of wits, *littérateurs*, philosophers, statesmen, churchmen, diplomats, and men of rank, Mme. du Deffand herself is always the most striking figure. The art of self-suppression she clearly did not possess. But the art of so blending a choice society that her own vivid personality was a pervading note of harmony she had to an eminent degree. She could easily have made a mark upon her time through her intellectual gifts, without the factitious aid of the men with whom her name is associated. But society was her passion—society animated by intellect, sparkling with wit, and expressing in all its forms the art instincts of her race. She never aspired to authorship, but she has left a voluminous correspondence in which one reads the varying phases of a singularly capricious character. In her old age she found refuge from a devouring *ennui* in writing her own memoirs. Merciless to herself as to others, she veils nothing, revealing her frailties with a freedom that reminds one of Rousseau.

It is not the portrait of an estimable woman that we can paint from these records; but in her intellectual force, her social gifts, and her moral weakness she is one of the best exponents of an age that trampled upon the finest flowers of the soul in the blind pursuit of pleasure and the cynical worship of a hard and unpitying realism. Living from 1697 to 1780, she saw the train laid for the Revolution, and died in time to escape its horrors. She traversed the whole experience of the women of her world with the independence and *abandon* of a nature that was moderate in nothing. It is true she felt the emptiness of this arid existence, and had an intellectual perception of its errors, but she saw nothing better. "All conditions appear to me equally unhappy, from the angel to the oyster," is the burden of her hopeless refrain.

She reveals herself to us as two distinct characters. The one best known is hard, bitter, coldly analytic, and mocks at everything bordering upon sentiment or feeling. The other, which underlies this, and of which we have rare glimpses, is frank, tender, loving even to weakness, and forever at war with the barrenness of a period whose worst faults she seems to have embodied, and whose keenest penalties she certainly suffered.

Voltaire, the lifelong friend whom she loved, but critically measured, was three years old when she was born; Mme. de Sévigné had been dead nearly a year. Of a noble family in Burgundy, Marie de Vichy-Chamroud was brought to Paris at six years of age and placed in the convent of St. Madeleine de Traisnel, where she was educated after the superficial fashion which she so much regrets in later years. She speaks of herself as a romantic, imaginative child, but she began very early to shock the pious sisters by her dawning skepticism. One of the nuns had a wax figure of the infant Jesus, which she discovered to have been a doll formerly dressed to represent the Spanish fashions to Anne of Austria. This was the first blow to her illusions, and had a very perceptible influence upon her life. She pronounced it a deception. Eight days of solitude with a diet of bread and water failed to restore her reverence. "It does not depend upon me to believe or disbelieve," she said. The eloquent and insinuating Massillon was called in to talk with her. "She is charming," was his remark, as he left her after two hours of conversation; adding thoughtfully, "Give her a five-cent catechism."

Skeptical by nature and saturated with the free-thinking spirit of the time, she reasoned that all religion was, *au fond,*

26

only paganism disguised. In later years, when her isolated soul longed for some tangible support, she spoke regretfully of the philosophic age which destroyed beliefs by explaining and analyzing everything.

But a beautiful, clever, high-spirited girl of sixteen is apt to feel her youth all-sufficing. It is certain that she had no inclination towards the life of a *religieuse*, and the country quickly became insupportable after her return to its provincial society. *Ennui* took possession of her. She was glad even to go to confessional, for the sake of telling her thoughts to some one. She complained bitterly that the life of women compelled dependence upon the conduct of others, submission to all ills and all consequences. Long afterwards she said that she would have married the devil if he had been clothed as a gentleman and assured her a moderate life. But a husband was at last found for her, and, merely to escape the monotony of her secluded existence, she was glad, at twenty-one, to become the wife of the Marquis du Deffand — a good but uninteresting man, much older than herself.

Brilliant, fascinating, restless, eager to see and to learn, she felt herself in her element in the gay world of Paris. She confessed that, for the moment, she almost loved her husband for bringing her there. But the moment was a short one. They did not even settle down to what a witty Frenchman calls the "politeness of two indifferences." It is a curious commentary upon the times, that the beautiful but notorious Mme. de Parabère, who introduced her at once into her own unscrupulous world and the *petits soupers* of the Regent, condoled with the young bride upon her marriage, regretting that she had not taken the easy vows of a *chanoinesse*, as Mme. de Tencin had done. "In that case," she said, "you would have been free; well placed everywhere; with the stability of a married woman; a revenue which permits one to live and accept aid from others; the independence of a widow, without the ties which a family imposes; unquestioned rank, which you would owe to no one; indulgence, and impunity. For these advantages there is only the trouble of wearing a cross, which is becoming; black or gray habits, which can be made as magnificent as one likes; a little imperceptible veil, and a knitting sheath."

Under such teaching she was not long in taking her own free and independent course, which was reckless even in that age of laxity. At her first supper at the Palais Royal she met

MARIE DE VICHY-CHAMROUD, MARQUISE DU DEFFAND.

Voltaire and fascinated the Regent, though her reign lasted but a few days. The counsels of her aunt, the dignified Duchesse de Luynes, availed nothing. Her husband was speedily sent off on some mission to the provinces, and she plunged into the current. Once afterwards, in a fit of *ennui*, she recalled him, frankly stating her position. But she quickly wearied of him again; grew dull, silent, lost her vivacity, and fell into a pro-

found melancholy.   Her friend Mme. de Parabère took it upon
herself to explain to him the facts, and he kindly relieved her
forever of his presence, leaving a touching and pathetic letter
which gave her a moment of remorse in spite of her lightened
heart.   This sin against good taste the Parisian world could
not forgive, and even her friends turned against her for a time.
But the Duchesse du Maine came to her aid with an all-power-
ful influence, and restored her finally to her old position.   For
some years she passed the greater part of her time at Sceaux,
and was a favorite at this lively little court.

It is needless to trace here the details of a career which
gives us little to admire and much to condemn.   It was about
1740 when her salon became noted as a center for the fashionable and literary world of Paris.   Montesquieu and d'Alembert
were then among her intimate friends.   Of the latter she says:
"The simplicity of his manners, the purity of his morals,
the air of youth, the frankness of character, joined to all his
talents, astonished at first those who saw him."   It is said to
have been through her zeal that he was admitted to the
Academy so young.   Among others who formed her familiar
circle were her devoted friend Pont de Veyle ; the Chevalier
d'Aydie ; Formont, the *"spirituel* idler and amiable egotist,"
who was one of the three whom she confesses really to have
loved ; and President Hénault, who brought always a fund of
lively anecdote and agreeable conversation.   This world of
fashion and letters, slightly seasoned with philosophy, is also
the world of Mme. de Luxembourg, of the brilliant Mme. de
Mirepoix, of the Prince and Princesse de Beauvau, and of the
lovely Duchesse de Choiseul, a *femme d'esprit* and "mistress
of all the elegances," whose gentle virtues fall like a ray of
sunlight across the dark pages of this period.   It is the world
of elegant forms, the world in which a sin against taste is
worse than a sin against morals, the world which hedges itself
in by a thousand unwritten laws that save it from boredom.

After the death of the Duchesse du Maine, Mme. du Deffand
retired to the little convent of St. Joseph, where, after the manner of many women of rank with small fortunes, she had her
ménage and received her friends.   "I have a very pretty apart-

ment," she writes to Voltaire; "very convenient; I only go out
for supper. I do not sleep elsewhere, and I make no visits. My
society is not numerous, but I am sure it will please you; and
if you were here you would make it yours. I have seen for
some time many *savants* and men of letters; I have not found
their society delightful." The good nuns objected a little to
Voltaire at first, but seem to have been finally reconciled to the
visits of the arch-heretic. At this time Mme. du Deffand had
supposably reformed her conduct, if not her belief.

She continued to entertain the flower of the nobility and the
stars of the literary and scientific world. But while the most
famous of the men of letters were welcome in her salon, the
tone was far from pedantic or even earnest. It was a society
of conventional people, the *élite* of fashion and intelligence,
who amused themselves in an intellectual but not too serious
way. Montesquieu, who liked those houses in which he could
pass with his every-day wit, said, "I love this woman with all
my heart; she pleases and amuses me; it is impossible to feel
a moment's *ennui* in her company." Mme. de Genlis, who
did not love her, expressed her surprise at finding her so natural and so kindly. Her conversation was simple and without
pretension. When she was pleased, her manners were even
affectionate. She never entered into a discussion, confessing
that she was not sufficiently attached to any opinion to defend
it. She disliked the enthusiasm of the philosophers unless it
was hidden behind the arts of the courtier, as in Voltaire, whose
delicate satire charmed her. Diderot came once, "eyed her
epicurean friends," and came no more. The air was not free
enough. When at home she had three or four at supper every
day, often a dozen, and, once a week, a grand supper. All the
intellectual fashions of the time are found here. La Harpe
reads a translation from Sophocles and his own tragedy.
Clairon, the actress in vogue, recites the rôles of *Phèdre* and
Agrippine, Lekain reads Voltaire, and Goldoni a comedy of
his own, which the hostess finds tiresome. New books, new
plays, the last song, the latest word of the philosophers —
all are talked about, eulogized, or dismissed with a sarcasm.
The wit of Mme. du Deffand is feared, but it fascinates.

She delights in clever repartees and sparkling epigrams. A shaft of wit silences the most complacent of monologues. "What tiresome book are you reading?" she said one day to a friend who talked too earnestly and too long — saving herself from the charge of rudeness by an easy refuge in her blindness.

TEA AT THE TEMPLE.

CENTRAL GROUP FROM THE PAINTING "LE THÉ À L'ANGLAISE CHEZ LE PRINCE DE CONTI."

Her criticisms are always severe. "There are only two pleasures for me in the world — society and reading," she writes. "What society does one find? Imbeciles, who utter only commonplaces, who know nothing, feel nothing, think nothing; a few people of talent, full of themselves, jealous, envious, wicked, whom one must hate or scorn." To some one who was eulogizing a mediocre man, adding that all the world was of the same opinion, she replied, "I make small account of the world, Monsieur, since I perceive that one can divide

it into three parts, *les trompeurs, les trompés, et les trompettes.*"
Still it is life alone that interests her. Though she is not satisfied with people, she has always the hope that she will be. In
literature she likes only letters and memoirs, because they are
purely human; but the age has nothing that pleases her. " It
is cynical or pedantic," she writes to Voltaire; "there is no
grace, no facility, no imagination. Everything is *à la glace,*
hardness without force, license without gaiety; no talent, much
presumption."

As age came on, and she felt the approach of blindness, she
found a companion in Mlle. de Lespinasse, a young girl of
remarkable gifts, who had an obscure and unacknowledged
connection with her family. For ten years the young woman
was a slave to the caprices of her exacting mistress, reading to
her through long nights of wakeful restlessness, and assisting
to entertain her guests. The one thing upon which Mme. du
Deffand most prided herself was frankness. She hated *finesse,*
and had stipulated that she would not tolerate artifice in any
form. It was her habit to lie awake all night and sleep all
day, and as she did not receive her guests until six o'clock,
Mlle. de Lespinasse, whose amiable character and conversational
charm had endeared her at once to the circle of her patroness, arranged to see her personal friends — among whom were
d'Alembert, Turgot, Chastellux, and Marmontel — in her own
apartments for an hour before the marquise appeared. When
this came to the knowledge of the latter, she fell into a violent
rage at what she chose to regard as a treachery to herself,
and dismissed her companion at once. The result was the
opening of a rival salon which carried off many of her favorite
guests, notably d'Alembert, to whom she was much attached.
" If she had died fifteen years earlier, I should not have lost
d'Alembert," was her sympathetic remark when she heard of
the death of Mlle. de Lespinasse.

But the most striking point in the career of this worldly
woman was her friendship for Horace Walpole. When they first
met she was nearly seventy, blind, ill-tempered, bitter, and hopelessly *ennuyée.* He was not yet fifty, a brilliant, versatile man
of the world, and saw her only at long intervals. Their curious

correspondence extends over a period of fifteen years, ending only with her death.

In a letter to Grayson, after meeting her, he writes: "Mme. du Deffand is now very old and stone blind, but retains all her vivacity, wit, memory, judgment, passion, and agreeableness. She goes to operas, plays, suppers, Versailles; gives supper twice a week; has everything new read to her; makes new songs and epigrams — aye, admirably — and remembers every one that has been made these fourscore years. She corresponds with Voltaire, dictates charming letters to him, contradicts him, is no bigot to him or anybody, and laughs both at the clergy and the philosophers. In a dispute, into which she easily falls, she is very warm, and yet scarce ever in the wrong; her judgment on every subject is as just as possible; on every point of conduct as wrong as possible; for she is all love and hatred, passionate for her friends to enthusiasm, still anxious to be loved — I don't mean by lovers — and a vehement enemy openly."

The acquaintance thus begun quickly drifted into an intimacy. Friendship she calls this absorbing sentiment, but it has all the caprices and inconsistencies of love. Fed by the imagination, and prevented by separation from wearing itself out, it became the most permanent interest of her life. There is something curiously pathetic in the submissive attitude of this blind, aged, but spirited woman — who scoffs at sentiment and confesses that she could never love anything — towards the man who criticizes her, scolds her, crushes back her too ardent feeling, yet calls her his dear old friend, writes her a weekly letter, and modestly declares that she "loves him better than all France together."

The spirit of this correspondence greatly modifies the impression which her own words, as well as the facts of her career, would naturally give us. We find in the letters of this period little of the freshness and spontaneity that lent such a charm to the letters of Mme. de Sévigné and her contemporaries. Women still write of the incidents of their lives, the people they meet, their jealousies, their rivalries, their loves, and their follies; but they think, where they formerly mirrored the world about them. They analyze, they compare, they criticize, they formulate their own emotions, they add opinions to facts. The gaiety, the sparkle, the wit, the play of feeling, is not there. Occasionally there is the tone of passion, as in the letters of Mlle. Aïssé and Mlle. de Lespinasse, but this is rare. Even passion has grown sophisticated and deals with phrases. There is more or less artificiality in the exchange of written thoughts. Mme. du Deffand thinks while she writes, and what she sees takes always the color of her own intelligence. She complains of her inability to catch the elusive quality, the clearness, the flexibility of Mme. de Sévigné, whom she longs to rival because Walpole so admires her. But if she lacks the vivacity, the simplicity, the poetic grace of her model, she has qualities not less striking, though less lovable. Her keen insight is unfailing. With masterly penetration she grasps the essence of things. No one has portrayed so concisely and so vividly the men and women of her time. No one has discriminated between the shades of character with such nicety. No one has so clearly fathomed the underlying motives of action. No one has forecast the outcome of theories and events with such prophetic vision. The note of bitterness and cynicism is always there. The nature of the woman reveals itself in every line: keen, dry, critical, with clear ideals which she can never hope to attain. But we feel that she has stripped off the rags of pretension and brought us face to face with realities. "All that I can do is to love you with all my heart, as I have done for about fifty years," wrote Voltaire. "How could I fail to love you? Your soul seeks always the true; it is a quality as rare as truth itself." So far does she carry her hatred of insincerity that one is often tempted to believe she affects a freedom from affectation. "I am so fatigued with the vanity of others that I avoid the occasion of having any myself," she writes. Is there not here a trace of the quality she so despises?

But beneath all this runs the swift undercurrent of an absorbing passion. A passion of friendship it may be, but it forces itself through the arid shells of conventionalism; it is at once the agony and the consolation of a despairing soul. Heartless, Mme. du Deffand is called, and her life seems to

27

prove the truth of the verdict; but these letters throb and palpitate with feeling which she laughs at, but cannot still. It is the cry of the soul for what it has not; what the world cannot give; what it has somehow missed out of a cold, hard, restless, and superficial existence. With a need of loving, she is satisfied with no one. There is something wanting, even in the affection of her friends. "*Ma grand'maman,*" she says to the gentle Duchesse de Choiseul, "you *know* that you love me, but you do not *feel* it."

Devouring herself in solitude, she despises the society she cannot do without. "Men and women appear to me puppets who go, come, talk, laugh, without thinking, without reflecting, without feeling," she writes. She confesses that she has a thousand troubles in assembling a choice company of people who bore her to death. "One sees only masks, one hears only lies," is her constant refrain. She does not want to live, but is afraid to die; she says she is not made for this world, but does not know that there is any other. She tries devotion, but has no taste for it. Of the light that shines from within upon so many darkened and weary souls she has no knowledge. Her vision is bounded by the tangible, which offers only a rigid barrier, against which her life flutters itself away. She dies as she has lived, with a deepened conviction of the nothingness of existence. "Spare me three things," she said to her confessor in her last moments; "let me have no questions, no reasons, and no sermons." Seeing Wiart, her faithful servitor, in tears, she remarks pathetically, as if surprised, "You love me then?" "Divert yourself as much as you can," was her final message to Walpole. "You will regret me, because one is very glad to know that one is loved." She commends to his care and affection Tonton, her little dog.

Strong but not gentle, brilliant but not tender, too penetrating for any illusions, with a nature forever at war with itself, its surroundings, and its limitations, no one better points the moral of an age without faith, without ideals, without the inner light that reveals to hope what is denied to sense.

The influence of such a woman, with her gifts, her energy, her power, and her social prestige, can hardly be estimated.

It was not in the direction of the new drift of thought. " I am not a fanatic as to liberty," she said ; " I believe it is an error to pretend that it exists in a democracy. One has a thousand tyrants in place of one." She had no breadth of sympathy, and her interests were largely personal ; but in matters of style and form her taste was unerring. Pitiless in her criticisms, she held firmly to her ideals of clear, elegant, and concise expression, both in literature and in conversation. She tolerated no platitudes, no pretension, and left behind her the traditions of a society that blended, more perfectly, perhaps, than any other of her time, the best intellectual life with courtly manners and a strict observance of *les convenances.*

*The Women
of the
French Salons*

CHAPTER XV

MADEMOISELLE DE LESPINASSE

*A Romantic Career — Companion of Mme. du Deffand —
Rival Salons — Association with the Encyclopedists —
D'Alembert — A Heart Tragedy — Impassioned Letters
— A Type Unique in her Age.*

INSEPARABLY connected with the name of Mme.
du Deffand is that of her companion and rival,
Mlle. de Lespinasse, the gifted, charming, tender and loving woman who presided over one
of the most noted of the philosophical salons;
who was the chosen friend and *confidante* of
the Encyclopedists; and who died in her prime of a broken
heart, leaving the world a legacy of letters that rival those of
Héloïse or the poems of Sappho, as "immortal pictures of
passion." The memory of her social triumphs, remarkable as
they were, pales before the singular romance of her life. In
the midst of a cold, critical, and heartless society, that adored
talent and ridiculed sentiment, she became the victim of a

passion so profound, so ardent, so hopeless, that her powerful intellect bent before it like a reed before a storm. She died of that unsuspected passion, and years afterwards these letters found the light and told the tale.

The contrast between the two women so closely linked together is complete. Mme. du Deffand belonged to the age of Voltaire by every fiber of her hard and cynical nature. What she called love was a fire of the intellect which consumed without warming. It was a violent and fierce prejudice in favor of those who reflected something of herself. The tenderness of self-sacrifice was not there. Mlle. de Lespinasse was of the later era of Rousseau; the era of exaggerated feeling, of emotional delirium, of romantic dreams; the era whose heroine was the loving and sentimental *Julie*, for whose portrait she might have sat, with a shade or so less of intellect and brilliancy. But it was more than a romantic dream that shadowed and shortened the life of Mlle. de Lespinasse. She had a veritable heart of flame, that consumed not only itself but its frail tenement as well.

Julie-Jeanne-Eléonore de Lespinasse, who was born at Lyons in 1732, had a birthright of sorrow. Her mother, the Comtesse d'Albon, could not acknowledge this fugitive and nameless daughter, but after the death of her husband she received her on an inferior footing, had her carefully educated, and secretly gave her love and care. Left alone and without resources at fifteen, Julie was taken, as governess and companion, into the family of a sister who was the wife of Mme. du Deffand's brother. Here the marquise met her on one of her visits and heard the story of her sorrows. Tearful, sad, and worn out by humiliations, the young girl had decided to enter a convent. "There is no misfortune that I have not experienced," she wrote to Guibert many years afterwards. "Some day, my friend, I will relate to you things not to be found in the romances of Prévost nor of Richardson. . . I ought naturally to devote myself to hating; I have well fulfilled my destiny; I have loved much and hated very little. Mon Dieu, my friend, I am a hundred years old." Mme. du Deffand was struck with her talent and a certain indefinable fascination of manner which afterwards became so potent. "You have gaiety," she wrote to her, "you are capable of sentiment; with these qualities you will be charming so long as you are natural and without pretension." After a negotiation of some months, Mlle. de Lespinasse went to Paris to live with her new friend. The history of this affair has been already related.

Parisian society was divided into two factions on the merits of the quarrel — those who censured the ingratitude of the younger woman, and those who accused the marquise of cruelty and injustice. But many of the oldest friends of the latter aided her rival. The Maréchale de Luxembourg furnished her apartments in the Rue de Belle-Chasse. The Duc de Choiseul procured her a pension, and Mme. Geoffrin gave her an annuity. She carried with her a strong following of eminent men from the salon of Mme. du Deffand, among whom was d'Alembert, who remained faithful and devoted to the end. It is said that President Hénault even offered to marry her, but how, under these circumstances, he managed to continue in the good graces of his lifelong friend, the unforgiving marquise, does not appear. A letter which he wrote to Mlle. de Lespinasse throws a direct light upon her character, after making due allowance for the exaggeration of French gallantry.

You are cosmopolitan; you adapt yourself to all situations. The world pleases you; you love solitude. Society amuses you, but it does not seduce you. Your heart does not give itself easily. Strong passions are necessary to you, and it is better so, for they will not return often. Nature, in placing you in an ordinary position, has given you something to relieve it. Your soul is noble and elevated, and you will never remain in a crowd. It is the same with your person. It is distinguished and attracts attention, without being beautiful. There is something *piquante* about you. . . . You have two things which do not often go together: you are sweet and strong; your gaiety adorns you and relaxes your nerves, which are too tense. . . . You are extremely refined; you have divined the world.

The age of portraits was not quite passed, and the privilege of seeing one's self in the eyes of one's friends was still accorded, a fact to which we owe many striking if sometimes rather highly colored pictures. A few words from d'Alembert are of twofold interest. He writes some years later:

The regard one has for you does not depend alone upon your external charms; it depends, above all, upon your intellect and your character. That which distinguishes you in society is the art of saying to every one the fitting word and that art is very simple with you; it consists in never speaking of yourself to others, and much of themselves. It is an infallible means of pleasing; thus you please every one, though it happens that all the world pleases you; you know even how to avoid repelling those who are least agreeable.

This epitome of the art of pleasing may be commended for its wisdom, aside from the very delightful picture it gives of an amiable and attractive woman. Again he writes:

The excellence of your tone would not be a distinction for one reared in a court, and speaking only the language she has learned. In you it is a merit very real and very rare. You have brought it from the seclusion of a province, where you met no one who could teach you. You were, in this regard, as perfect the day after your arrival at Paris as you are to-day. You found yourself, from the first, as free, as little out of place in the most brilliant and most critical society as if you had passed your life there; you have felt its usages before knowing them, which implies a justness and fineness of tact very unusual, an exquisite knowledge of *les convenances*.

It was her innate tact and social instinct, combined with rare gifts of intellect and great conversational charm, that gave this woman without name, beauty, or fortune so exceptional a position, and her salon so distinguished a place among the brilliant centers of Paris. As she was not rich and could not give costly dinners, she saw her friends daily from five to nine, in the interval between other engagements. This society was her chief interest, and she rarely went out. "If she made an exception to this rule, all Paris was apprised of it in advance," says Grimm. The most illustrious men of the State, the Church, the Court, and the Army, as well as celebrated foreigners and men of letters, were sure to be found there. "Nowhere was conversation more lively, more brilliant, or better regulated," writes Marmontel. . . . "It was not with fashionable nonsense and vanity that every day during four hours, without languor or pause, she knew how to make herself interesting to a circle of sensible people." Caraccioli went from her salon one evening to sup with Mme. du Deffand. "He was intoxicated with all the fine works he had heard read there," writes the latter. "There was a eulogy of one named Fontaine by M. de Condorcet. There were translations of Theocritus; tales, fables by I know not whom. And then some eulogies of Helvétius, an extreme admiration of the *esprit* and the talents of the age ; in fine, enough to make one stop the ears. All these judgments false and in the worst taste." A hint of the rivalry between the former friends is given in a letter from Horace Walpole. "There is at Paris," he writes, "a Mlle. de Lespinasse, a pretended *bel esprit*, who was formerly a humble companion of Mme. du Deffand, and betrayed her and used her very ill. I beg of you not to let any one carry you thither. I dwell upon this because she has some enemies so spiteful as to try to carry off all the English to Mlle. de Lespinasse."

But this "pretended *bel esprit*" had socially the touch of genius. Her ardent, impulsive nature lent to her conversation a rare eloquence that inspired her listeners, though she never drifted into monologue, and understood the value of discreet silence. "She rendered the marble sensible, and made matter talk," said Guibert. Versatile and suggestive herself, she knew how to draw out the best thoughts of others. Her swift insight caught the weak points of her friends, and her gracious adaptation had all the fascination of a subtle flattery. Sad as her experience had been, she had nevertheless been drawn into the world most congenial to her tastes. "Ah, how I dislike not to love that which is excellent," she wrote later. "How difficult I have become ! But is it my fault? Consider the education I have received with Mme. du Deffand. President Hénault, Abbé Bon, the Archbishop of Toulouse, the Archbishop of Aix, Turgot, d'Alembert, Abbé de Boismont—these are the men who have taught me to speak, to think, and who have deigned to count me for something."

It was men like these who thronged her own salon, together with such women as the Duchesse d'Anville, friend of the economists, the Duchesse de Châtillon whom she loved so passionately, and others well-known in the world of fashion and letters. But its tone was more philosophical than that of Mme. du Deffand. Though far from democratic by taste or temperament, she was so from conviction. The griefs and humiliations of her life had left her peculiarly open to the new social and political theories which were agitating France. She liked free discussion, and her own large intelligence, added to her talent for calling out and giving point to the ideas of others, went far towards making the cosmopolitan circle over which she presided one of the most potent forces of the time. Her influence may be traced in the work of the Encyclopedists, in which she

MLLE. DE LESPINASSE.

was associated, and which she did more than any other woman to aid and encourage. As a power in the making of reputations and in the election of members to the Academy she shared with Mme. Geoffrin the honor of being a legitimate successor of Mme. de Lambert. Chastellux owed his admission largely to her, and on her deathbed she secured that of La Harpe.

But the side of her character which strikes us most forcibly at this distance of time is the emotional. The personal charm which is always so large a factor in social success is of too subtle a quality to be caught in words. The most vivid portrait leaves a divine something to be supplied by the imagination, and the fascination of eloquence is gone with the flash of the eye, the modulation of the voice, or some fleeting grace of manner. But passion writes itself out in indelible characters, especially when it is a rare and spontaneous overflow from the heart of a man or woman of genius, whose emotions readily crystallize into form.

Her friendship for d'Alembert, loyal and devoted as it was, seems to have been without illusions. It is true she had cast aside every other consideration to nurse him through a dangerous illness, and as soon as he was able to be removed, he had taken an apartment in the house where she lived, which he retained until her death. But he was not rich, and marriage was not to be thought of. On this point we have his own testimony. "The one to whom they marry me in the gazettes is indeed a person respectable in character, and fitted by the sweetness and charm of her society to render a husband happy," he writes to Voltaire; "but she is worthy of an establishment better than mine, and there is between us neither marriage nor love, but mutual esteem, and all the sweetness of friendship. I live actually in the same house with her, where there are besides ten other tenants; this is what has given rise to the rumor." His devotion through so many years, and his profound grief at her loss, as well as his subsequent words, leave some doubt as to the tranquillity of his heart, but the sentiments of Mlle. de Lespinasse seem never to have passed the calm measure of an exalted and sympathetic friendship. It was remarked that he lost much of his prestige, and that his society, which had been so brilliant, became infinitely more miscellaneous and infinitely less agreeable after the death of the friend whose tact and finesse had so well served his ambition.

Not long after leaving Mme. du Deffand she met the Marquis de Mora, a son of the Spanish ambassador, who became a constant *habitué* of her salon. Of distinguished family and large fortune, brilliant, courtly, popular, and only twenty-four, he captivated at once the fiery heart of this attractive woman of thirty-five. It seems to have been a mutual passion, as during one brief absence of ten days he wrote her twenty-two letters. But his family became alarmed and made his delicate health a pretext for recalling him to Spain. Her grief at the separation enlisted the sympathy of d'Alembert. At her request he procured from his physician a statement that the climate of Madrid would prove fatal to M. de Mora, whose health had steadily failed since his return home, and that if his friends wished to save him they must lose no time in sending him back to Paris. The young man was permitted to leave at once, but he died *en route* at Bordeaux.

In the mean time Mlle. de Lespinasse, sad and inconsolable, had met M. Guibert, a man of great versatility and many accomplishments, whose genius seems to have borne no adequate fruit. We hear of him later through the passing enthusiasm of Mme. de Staël, who in her youth, made a pen-portrait of him, sufficiently flattering to account in some degree for the singular passion of which he became the object. Mlle. de Lespinasse was forty. He was twenty-nine, had competed for the Académie Française, written a work on military science, also a national tragedy which was still unpublished. She was dazzled by his brilliancy, and when she fathomed his shallow nature, as she finally did, it was too late to disentangle her heart. He was a man of gallantry, and was flattered by the preference of a woman much in vogue, who had powerful friends, influence at the Academy, and the ability to advance his interest in many ways. He clearly condescended to be loved, but his own professions have little of the true ring.

Distracted by this new passion on one side, and by remorse for her disloyalty to the old one, on the other, the health of Mlle. de Lespinasse, naturally delicate and already undermined, began to succumb to the hidden struggle. The death of M. de Mora solved one problem; the other remained. M. Guibert wished to advance his fortune by a brilliant marriage without losing the friend who might still be of service to him. She sat in judgment upon her own fate, counseled him, aided him in his choice, even praised the woman who became his wife, hoping still, perhaps, for some repose in that exaltation of friendship which is often the last consolation of passionate souls. But she was on a path that led to no haven of peace. There was only a blank wall before her, and the lightning impulses of her own heart were forced back to shatter her frail life. The world was ignorant of this fresh experience; and, believing her crushed by the death of M. de Mora, sympathized with her sorrow and praised her fidelity. She tried to sustain a double rôle—smiles and gaiety for her friends, tears and agony for the long hours of solitude. The tension was too much for her. She died shortly afterwards at the age of forty-three. "If to think, to love, and to suffer is that which constitutes life, she lived in these few years many ages," said one who knew her well.

It was not until many years later, when those most interested were gone, that the letters to Guibert, which form her chief title to fame, were collected, and, curiously enough, by his widow. Then for the first time the true drama of her life was unveiled. It is impossible in a few extracts to convey an adequate idea of the passion and devotion that runs through these letters. They touch the entire gamut of emotion, from the tender melancholy of a lonely soul, the inexpressible sweetness of self-forgetful love, to the tragic notes of agony and despair. There are many brilliant passages in them, many flashes of profound thought, many vivid traits of the people about her; but they are, before all, the record of a soul that is rapidly burning out its casket.

"I prefer my misery to all that the world calls happiness or pleasure," she writes. "I shall die of it, perhaps, but that is better than never to have lived."

"I have no more the strength to love," she says again: "my soul fatigues me, torments me; I am no more sustained by anything. I have every day a fever; and my physician, who is not the most skilful of men, repeats to me without ceasing that I am consumed by chagrin, that my pulse, my respiration announce an active grief, and he always goes out saying, 'We have no cure for the soul.'"

"Adieu, my friend," were her last words to him. "If I ever return to life I shall still love to employ it in loving you; but there is no more time."

One could almost wish that these letters had never come to light. A single grand passion has always a strong hold upon the imagination and the sympathies, but two passions contending for the mastery verge upon something quite the reverse of heroic. The note of heart-breaking despair is tragic enough, but there is a touch of comedy behind it. Though her words have the fire, the devotion, the *abandon* of Héloïse, they leave a certain sense of disproportion. One is inclined to wonder if they do not overtop the feeling.

D'Alembert was her truest mourner, and fell into a profound melancholy after her death. "Yes," he said to Marmontel, "she was changed, but I was not; she no longer lived for me, but I ever lived for her. Since she is no more, I know not why I exist. Ah! why have I not still to suffer those moments of bitterness that she knew so well how to sweeten and make me forget? Do you remember the happy evenings we passed together? Now what have I left? I return home, and instead of herself I find only her shade. This lodging at the Louvre is itself a tomb, which I never enter but with horror." To this "shade" he wrote two expressive and well-considered eulogies, which paint in pathetic words the perfections of his friend and his own desolation. "Adieu, adieu, my dear Julie," says the heartbroken philosopher; "for these eyes which I should like to close forever fill with tears in tracing these last lines, and I see no more the paper on which I write." His grief called out a sympathetic letter from Frederick the Great, which shows the philosophic warrior and king in a new light. There is a touch of bitter irony in the inflated eulogy of Guibert, who gave the too-loving woman a death-blow in furthering his ambition, then exhausted his vocabulary in laments and praises. Perhaps he hoped to borrow from this friendship a fresh ray of immortality.

Whatever we may think of the strange inconsistencies of Mlle. de Lespinasse, she is doubly interesting to us as a type that contrasts strongly with that of her age. Her exquisite tact, her brilliant intellect, her conversational gifts, her personal charm made her the idol of the world in which she lived. Her influence was courted, her salon was the resort of the most distinguished men of the century, and while she loved to discuss the great social problems which her friends were trying to solve, she forgot none of the graces. With the intellectual strength and grasp of a man, she preserved always the taste, the delicacy, the tenderness of a woman. Her faults were those of a strong nature. Her thoughts were clear and penetrating, her expression was lively and impassioned. But in her emotional power she reached the proportion of genius. With " the most ardent soul, the liveliest fancy, the most inflammable imagination that has existed since Sappho," she represents the embodied spirit of tragedy outlined against the cold, hard background of a skeptical, mocking, realistic age. " I love in order to live," she said, " and I live to love." This is the key-note of her life.

CHAPTER XVI

THE SALON HELVÉTIQUE

The Swiss Pastor's Daughter—Her Social Ambition—Her Friends—Mme. de Marchais—Mme. d'Houdetot—Duchesse de Lauzun—Character of Mme. Necker—Death at Coppet —Close of the most Brilliant Period of the Salons.

THERE was one woman who held a very prominent place in the society of this period, and who has a double interest for us, though she was not French, and never quite caught the spirit of the eighteenth-century life whose attractive forms she loved so well. Mme. Necker, whose history has been made so familiar through the interesting memoirs of the Comte d'Haussonville, owes her fame to her marked qualities of intellect and character rather than to the brilliancy of her social talents. These found an admirable setting in the surroundings which her husband's fortune and political career gave her. The Salon Helvétique had a distinctive color of its own, and was always tinged with the strong convictions and exalted ideals of the Swiss pastor's daughter, who passed through this world of intellectual affluence and moral laxity like a white angel of purity—in it, but not of it. The center of a choice and lettered circle which included the most noted men and women of her time, she brought into it not only rare gifts, a fine taste, and genuine literary enthusiasm, but the fresh charm of a noble character and a beautiful family life, with the instincts of duty and right conduct which she inherited from her simple Protestant ancestry. She lacked a little, however, in the tact, the ease, the grace, the spontaneity, which were the essential charm of the French women. Her social talents were a trifle theoretical. "She studied society," says one of her critics, "as she would a literary question." She had a theory of conducting a salon, as she had of life in general, and believed that study would attain everything. But the ability to do a thing superlatively well is by no means always implied in the knowledge of how it ought to be done. Social genius is as purely a gift of nature as poetry or music ; and, of all others, it is the most subtle and indefinable. It was a long step from the primitive simplicity in which Suzanne Curchod passed her childhood on the borders of Lake Leman to the complex life of a Parisian salon ; and the provincial beauty, whose fair face, soft blue eyes, dignified but slightly coquettish manner, brilliant intellect, and sparkling though sometimes rather learned conversation had made her a local queen, was quick to see her own shortcomings. She confessed that she had a new language to learn, and she never fully mastered it. "Mme. Necker has talent, but it is in a sphere too elevated for one to communicate with her," said Mme. du Deffand, though she was glad to go once a week to her suppers at Saint-Ouen, and admitted that in spite of a certain stiffness and coldness she was better fitted for society than most of the *grandes dames.*

The salon of Mme. Necker marks a transition point between two periods, and had two quite distinct phases. One likes best to recall her in the freshness of her early enthusiasm, when she gave Friday dinners, modeled after those of Mme. Geoffrin, to men of letters, and received a larger world in the evening ; when her guests were enlivened by the satire of Diderot, the anecdotes of Marmontel, the brilliancy or learning of Grimm, d'Alembert, Thomas, Suard, Buffon, the Abbé Raynal, and other wits of the day; when they discussed the affairs of the Academy and decided the fate of candidates; when they listened to the recitations of Mlle. Clairon, and the works of many authors known and unknown. It is interesting to recall that *Paul and Virginia* was first read here. But there was apt to be a shade of stiffness, and the conversation had sometimes too strong a flavor of pedantry. "No one knows better or feels more sensibly than you, my dear and very amiable friend," wrote Mme. Geoffrin, "the charm of friendship and its sweetness; no one makes others experience them more fully. But you will never attain that facility, that ease, and that liberty which give to society its perfect enjoyment." The Abbé Morellet complained of the austerity that always held the conversation within certain limits, and the gay little Abbé Galiani found fault with Mme. Necker's coldness and reserve, though he addresses her as his "Divinity" after his return to Naples, and his racy letters give us vivid and amusing pictures of these Fridays, which in his memory are wholly charming.

In spite of her firm religious convictions, Mme. Necker cordially welcomed the most extreme of the philosophers. "I have atheistic friends," she said. "Why not? They are unfortunate friends." But her admiration for their talents by no means extended to their opinions, and she did not permit the discussion of religious questions. It was at one of her own dinners that she started the subscription for a statue of Voltaire, for whom she entertained the warmest friendship. One may note here, as elsewhere, a fine mental poise, a justness of spirit, and a discrimination that was superior to natural prejudices. Sometimes her frank simplicity was misunderstood. "There is a Mme. Necker here, a pretty woman and a *bel esprit*, who is infatuated with me; she persecutes me to have me at her house," wrote Diderot to Mlle. Volland, with an evident incapacity to comprehend the innocent appreciation of a pure-hearted woman. When he knew her better, he expressed his regret that he had not known her sooner. "You would certainly have inspired me with a taste for purity and for delicacy," he says, "which would have passed from my soul into my works." He refers to her again as "a woman who possesses all that the purity of an angelic soul adds to an exquisite taste."

Among the many distinguished foreigners who found their way into this pleasant circle was her early lover, Gibbon. The old days were far away when she presided over the literary coterie at Lausanne, speculated upon the mystery of love, talked of the possibility of tender and platonic friendships between men and women, after the fashion of the *précieuses*, and wept bitter tears over the faithlessness of the embryo historian. The memory of her grief had long been lost in the fullness of subsequent happiness, and one readily pardons her natural complacency in the brilliancy of a position which took little added luster from the fame of the man who had wooed and so easily forgotten her.

This period of Mme. Necker's career shows her character on a very engaging side. Loving her husband with a devotion that verged upon idolatry, she was rich in the friendship of men like Thomas, Buffon, Grimm, Diderot, and Voltaire, whose respectful tone was the highest tribute to her dignity and her delicacy. But the true nature of a woman is best seen in her relations with her own sex. There are a thousand fine reserves in her relations with men that, in a measure, veil her personality. They doubtless call out the most brilliant qualities of her intellect, and reveal her character, in some points, on its best and most lovable side; but the rarer shades of generous and unselfish feeling are more clearly seen in the intimate friendships, free from petty vanities and jealous rivalries, rich in cordial appreciation and disinterested affection, which we often find among women of the finest type. It is impossible that one so serious and so earnest as Mme. Necker should have cherished such passionate friendships for her own sex, if she had been as cold or as calculating as she has been sometimes represented. Her intimacy with Mme. de Marchais, of which we have so many pleasant details, furnishes a case in point.

This graceful and vivacious woman, who talked so eloquently upon philosophical, political, and economic questions, was the center of a circle noted for its liberal tendencies. A friend of Mme. de Pompadour, at whose suppers she often sang; gifted, witty, and, in spite of a certain seriousness, retaining always

MME. NECKER.

FROM A PRINT.

the taste, the elegance, the charming manners which were her
native heritage, she attracted to her salon not only a distinguished literary company, but many men and women from the
great world of which she only touched the borders. Mme.
Necker had sought the aid and advice of Mme. de Marchais in

the formation of her own salon, and had taken for her one of
those ardent attachments so characteristic of earnest and susceptible natures.   She confided to her all the secrets of her heart;
she felt a double pleasure when her joys and her little troubles
were shared with this sympathetic companion.   " I had for her
a passionate affection," she says.   " When I first saw her
my whole soul was captivated.   I thought her one of those
enchanting fairies who combine all the gifts of nature and
of magic.   I loved her; or, rather, I idolized her."   So pure,
so confiding, so far above reproach herself, she refuses to see
the faults of one she loves so tenderly.   Her letters glow with
exalted sentiment.   " Adieu, my charming, my beautiful, my
sweet friend," she writes.   " I embrace you.   I press you to
my bosom; or, rather, to my soul, for it seems to me that no
interval can separate yours from mine."

But the character of Mme. de Marchais was evidently not
equal to her fascination.   Her vanity was wounded by the
success of her friend.   She took offense at a trifling incident
that touched her self-love.   " The great ladies have disgusted
me with friendship," she wrote, in reply to Mme. Necker's
efforts to repair the breach.   They returned to each other the
letters so full of vows of eternal fidelity, and were friends no
more.   Apparently without any fault of her own, Mme. Necker
was left with an illusion the less, and the world has another
example to cite of the frail texture of feminine friendships.

She was not always, however, so unfortunate in her choice.
She found a more amiable and constant object for her affections
in Mme. d'Houdetot, a charming woman who, in spite of her
errors, held a very warm place in the hearts of her cotemporaries.   We have met her before in the philosophical circles of
La Chevrette, and in the beautiful promenades of the valley
of Montmorency, where Rousseau offered her the incense of a
passionate and poetic love.   She was facile and witty, graceful
and gay, said wise and thoughtful things, wrote pleasant verses
which were the exhalations of her own heart, and was the center
of a limited though distinguished circle; but her chief attraction
was the magic of a sunny temper and a loving spirit.   " He
only is unhappy who can neither love, nor work, nor die," she

writes. Though more or less linked with the literary coteries of her time, Mme. d'Houdetot seems to have been singularly free from the small vanities and vulgar ambitions so often met there. She loved simple pleasures and the peaceful scenes of the country. "What more have we to desire when we can enjoy the pleasures of friendship and of nature?" she writes. "We may then pass lightly over the small troubles of life." She counsels repose to her more restless friend, and her warm expressions of affection have always the ring of sincerity, which contrasts agreeably with the artificial tone of the time. Mme. d'Houdetot lived to a great age, preserving always her youthfulness of spirit and sweet serenity of temper, in spite of sharp domestic sorrows. She took refuge from these in the lifelong friendship of Saint-Lambert, for whom Mme. Necker has usually a gracious message. It is a curious commentary upon the manners of the age that one so rigid and severe should have chosen for her intimate companionship two women whose lives were so far removed from her own ideal of reserved decorum. But she thought it best to ignore errors which her world did not regard as grave, if she was conscious of them at all.

One finds greater pleasure in recalling her ardent and romantic attachment to the granddaughter of the Maréchale de Luxembourg, the lovely Amélie de Boufflers, Duchesse de Lauzun, whose pen-portrait she sketched so gracefully and so tenderly; whose gentle sweetness and shy delicacy, in the rather oppressive glare of her surroundings, suggest a modest wild flower astray among the pretentious beauties of the hothouse, and whose untimely death on the scaffold has left her fragrant memory entwined with a garland of cypress. But we cannot dwell upon the intimate phases of this friendship, whose fine quality is shown in the few scattered leaves of a correspondence overflowing with the wealth of two rare though unequally gifted natures.

At a later period her husband's position in the ministry, and the pronounced opinions of her brilliant daughter, gave to the salon of Mme. Necker a marked political and semi-revolutionary coloring. Her inclinations always led her to literary diversions, rather than to the discussion of economic questions, but as Mme. de Staël gradually took the scepter that was falling from her hand, she found it difficult to guide the conversation into its old channels.   Her pale, thoughtful face, her gentle manner, her soft and penetrating voice, all indicated an exquisitely feminine quality quite in unison with the spirit of urbanity and politeness that was even then going out of fashion.   Her quiet and earnest though interesting conversation was somewhat overshadowed by the impetuous eloquence of Mme. de Staël, who gave the tone to every circle into which she came.   " I am more and more convinced that I am not made for the great world," she said to the Duchesse de Lauzun, with an accent of regret.   " It is Germaine who should shine there and who should love it, for she possesses all the qualities which put her in a position to be at once feared and sought."

If she was allied to the past, however, by her tastes and her sympathies, she belonged to the future by her convictions, and her many-sided intellect touched upon every question of the day. Profoundly religious herself, she was broadly tolerant ; always delicate in health, she found time amid her numerous social duties to aid the poor and suffering, and to establish the hospital that still bears her name.   Her letters and literary records reveal a woman of liberal thought and fine insight, as well as scholarly tastes.   If she lacked a little in the facile graces of the French women, she had to an eminent degree the qualities of character that were far rarer in her age and sphere.   Though she was cold and reserved in manner, beneath the light snow which she brought from her native hills beat a heart of warm and tender, even passionate, impulses.   Devoted wife, loyal friend, careful mother, large-minded and large-souled woman, she stands conspicuous, in a period of lax domestic relations, for the virtues that grace the fireside as well as for the talents that shine in the salon.

But she was not exempt from the sorrows of a nature that exacts from life more than life can give, and finds its illusions vanish before the cold touch of experience.   She had her hours of darkness and of suffering.   Even the love that was the source of her keenest happiness was also the source of her sharpest griefs. In the days of her husband's power she missed the exclusive attention she craved. There were moments when she doubted the depth of his affection, and felt anew that her "eyes were wedded to eternal tears." She could not see without pain his extreme devotion to her daughter, whose rich nature, so spontaneous, so original, so foreign to her own, gave rise to many anxieties and occasional antagonisms. This touches the weak point in her character. She was not wholly free from a certain egotism and intellectual vanity, without the imagination to comprehend fully an individuality quite remote from all her preconceived ideas. She was slow to accept the fact that her system of education was at fault, and her failure to mold her daughter after her own models was long a source of grief and disappointment. She was ambitious too, and had not won her position without many secret wounds. When misfortunes came, the blows that fell upon her husband struck with double force into her own heart. She was destined to share with him the chill of censure and neglect, the bitter sting of ingratitude, the lonely isolation of one fallen from a high place, whose friendship and whose favors count no more.

In the solitude of Coppet, where she died at fifty-seven, during the last and darkest days of the Revolution, perhaps she realized in the tireless devotion of her husband and the loving care of Mme. de Staël the repose of heart which the brilliant world of Paris never gave her.

With all her gifts, which have left many records that may be read, and in spite of a few shadows that fall more or less upon all earthly relations, not the least of her legacies to posterity was the beautiful example, rarer then than now, of that true and sympathetic family life in which lies the complete harmony of existence, a safeguard against the storms of passion, a perennial fount of love that keeps the spirit young, the tranquillity out of which spring the purest flowers of human happiness and human endeavor.

There were many salons of lesser note which have left agreeable memories. It would be pleasant to recall other clever and beautiful women whose names one meets so often in the chronicles of the time, and whose faces, conspicuous for their clear, strong outlines, still look out upon us from the galleries that perpetuate its life; but the list is too long and would lead us too far. From the moving procession of social leaders who made the age preceding the Revolution so brilliant I have chosen only the few who were most widely known, and who best represent its dominant types and its special phases.

The most remarkable period of the literary salons was really closed with the death of Mme. du Deffand, in 1780. Mme. Geoffrin had already been dead three years, and Mlle. de Lespinasse, four. Some of the most noted of the philosophers and men of letters were also gone, others were past the age of forming fresh ties, the young men belonged to another generation, and no new drawing-rooms exactly replaced the old ones. Mme. Necker still received the world that was wont to assemble in the great salons, Mme. de Condorcet presided over a rival coterie, and there were numerous small and intimate circles; but the element of politics was beginning to intrude, and with it a degree of heat which disturbed the usual harmony. The reign of *esprit*, the perpetual play of wit had begun to pall upon the tastes of people who found themselves face to face with problems so grave and issues so vital. There was a slight reaction towards nature and simplicity. "They may be growing wiser," said Walpole, "but the intermediate change is dullness." For nearly half a century learned men and clever women had been amusing themselves with utopian theories, a few through conviction, the majority through fashion, or egotism, or the vanity of saying new things, just as the world is doing to-day. The doctrines put forth by Montesquieu, vivified by Voltaire, and carried to the popular heart by Rousseau had been freely discussed in the salons, not only by philosophers and statesmen, but by men of the world, poets, artists, and pretty women. The sparks of thought with which they played so lightly filtered slowly through the social strata. The talk of the drawing-room at last reached the street. But the torch of truth which, held aloft, serves as a beacon star to guide the world towards some longed-for ideal becomes often a deadly explosive when it falls among the poisonous vapors of inflammable human passions.

Liberty, equality, fraternity assumed a new and fatal significance in the minds of the hungry and restless masses who,
embittered by centuries of wrong, were ready to carry these
phrases to their immediate and living conclusions. They had
found their watchwords and their hour. The train was already
laid beneath this complex social structure, and the tragedy that
followed carried to a common ruin court and salon, philosophers
and *beaux esprits*, innocent women and dreaming men.

That the salons were unconscious instruments in hasten-
ing the catastrophe, which was sooner or later inevitable, is undoubtedly true. Their influence in the dissemination of thought
was immense. The part they played was, to a limited extent,
precisely that of the modern press, with an added personal
element. They moved in the drift of their time, directed its
intelligence, and reflected its average morality. As centers of
serious conversation they were distinctly stimulating. It is
quite possible that they stimulated the intellect to the exclusion
of the more solid qualities of character, and that they were the
source of a vast amount of affectation. It was the fashion to
have *esprit*, and those who were deficient in an article so essential to success were naturally disposed to borrow it, or to put
on the semblance of it. But no phase of life is without its
reverse side, and the present generation cannot claim freedom
from pretension of the same sort. It is not unlikely that in
expanding the intelligence they established new standards of
distinction, which in a measure weakened the old ones. But
if they precipitated the downfall of the court they began by
rivaling, it was in the logical course of events, which few were
wise enough to foresee, much less to determine.

It is worthy of remark that this reign of women, in which
the manners and forms of modern society found their initiative
and their models, was not a reign of youth, or beauty, though
these qualities are never likely to lose their own peculiar
fascination. It was, before all things, a reign of intelligence,
the ascendency of women who had put on the hues of age
without laying aside the permanent charm of a fully developed
personality. It was intelligence blended with practical knowledge of the world and with the graceful amenities that height-

30

ened while half disguising its power. The women of the present have different aims. They are no longer content with the rôle of inspirer. Their methods are more direct. They depend less upon finesse, more upon inherent right and strength. But it is to the women who shone so conspicuously in France for more than two hundred years that we may trace the broadened intellectual life, the unfettered activities, the wide and beneficent influence of the women of to-day.

The Women
of the
French Salons

Chapter XVII

SALONS OF THE REVOLUTION — MADAME ROLAND

Change in the Character of the Salons—Mme. de Condorcet—
Mme. Roland's Story of Her Own Life—A Marriage of
Reason—Enthusiasm for the Revolution—Her Modest Sa-
lon—Her Tragical Fate.

HE salons of the Revolution were no longer simply the fountains of literary and artistic criticism, the centers of wit, intelligence, knowledge, philosophy, and good manners, but the rallying-points of parties. They took the tone of the time and assumed the character of political clubs. The salon of 1790 was not the salon of 1770. A new generation had arisen, with new ideals and a new spirit that made for itself other forms or greatly modified the old ones. It was not led by philosophers and *beaux esprits* who evolved theories and turned them over as an intellectual diversion, but by men of action, ready to test these theories and force them to their logical conclusions. Mirabeau, Vergniaud, and Robespierre had succeeded Voltaire, Diderot, and d'Alembert. Impelled towards one end, by vanity, ambition, love of glory, or genuine conviction, these men and their colleagues turned the salon, which had so long been the school of public opinion, into an engine of revolution. The exquisite flower of the eighteenth century had blossomed, matured, and fallen. Perhaps it was followed by a plant of sturdier growth, but the rare quality of its beauty was not repeated. The time was past when the gentle touch of women could temper the violence of clashing opinions, or subject the discussion of vital questions to the inflexible laws of taste. No tactful hostess could hold in leading-strings these fiery spirits. The voices that had charmed the old generation were silent. Of the women who had made the social life of the century so powerful and so famous, many were quietly asleep before the storm broke ; many were languishing in prison cells, with no outlook but the scaffold ; some were pining in the loneliness of exile ; and a few were buried in a seclusion which was their only safeguard.

But nature has always in reserve fresh types that come to the surface in a great crisis. The women who made themselves felt and heard above the din of revolution, though by no means deficient in the graces, were mainly distinguished for quite other qualities than those which shine in a drawing-room or lead a coterie. They were either women of rare genius and the courage of their convictions, or women trained in the stern school of a bitter experience, who found their true *milieu* in the midst of stirring events. The names of Mme. de Staël, Mme. Roland, and Mme. de Condorcet readily suggest themselves as the most conspicuous representatives of this stormy period. With different gifts and in different measure, each played a prominent rôle in the brief drama to which they lent the inspiration of their genius and their sympathy, until they were forced to turn back with horror from that carnival of savage passions which they had unconsciously helped to let loose upon the world.

The salon of the young, beautiful, and gifted Mme. de Condorcet had its roots in the old order of things. During the ministry of Necker it was in some degree a rival of the Salon Helvétique, and included many of the same guests ; later it became a rendezvous for the revolutionary party. The Marquis de Condorcet was not only philosopher, *savant, littéra-teur*, a member of two academies, and among the profoundest thinkers of his time, but a man of the world, who inherited the tastes and habits of the old *noblesse.* His wife, whom he had married late in life, was Sophie de Grouchy, sister of the Maréchal, and was noted for remarkable talents, as well as for surpassing beauty. Belonging by birth and associations to the aristocracy, and by her pronounced opinions to the radical side of the philosophic party, her salon was a center in which two worlds met. In its palmy days people were only speculating upon the borders of an abyss which had not yet opened visibly before them. The revolutionary spirit ran high, but had not passed the limits of reason and humanity. Mme. de Condorcet, who was deeply tinged with the new doctrines, presided with charming grace, and her youthful beauty lent an added fascination to the brilliancy of her intellect and the rather grave eloquence of her conversation. In her drawing-room were gathered men of letters and women of talent, nobles and scientists, philosophers and *beaux esprits.* Turgot and Malesherbes represented its political side; Marmontel, the Abbé Morellet, and Suard lent it some of the wit and vivacity that shone in the old salons. Literature, science, and the arts were discussed here, and there was more or less reading, music, or recitation. But the tendency was towards serious conversation, and the tone was often controversial.

The character of Condorcet was a sincere and elevated one. "He loved much and he loved many people," said Mlle. de Lespinasse. He aimed at enlightening and regenerating the world, not at overturning it; but, like many others, strong souls and true, he was led from practical truth in the pursuit of an ideal one. His wife, who shared his political opinions, united with them a fiery and independent spirit that was not content with theories. Her philosophic tastes led her to translate Adam Smith, and to write a fine analysis of the *Moral Sentiments.* But the sympathy of which she spoke so beautifully, and which gave so living a force to the philosophy it illuminated, if not directed by broad intelligence and impartial judgment, is often like the *ignis fatuus* that plays over the

poisonous marsh and lures the unwary to destruction. For a
brief day the magical influence of Mme. de Condorcet was felt
more or less by all who came within her circle.   She inspired
the equable temper of her husband with her own enthusiasm,
and urged him on to extreme measures from which his gentler
soul would have recoiled.   When at last he turned from those
scenes of horror, choosing to be victim rather than oppressor,
it was too late.   Perhaps she recalled the days of her power
with a pang of regret when her friends had fallen one by one
at the scaffold, and her husband, hunted and deserted by those
he tried to serve, had died by his own hand, in a lonely cell, to
escape a sadder fate; while she was left, after her timely release from prison, to struggle alone in poverty and obscurity,
for some years painting water-color portraits for bread.   She
was not yet thirty when the Revolution ended, and lived far
into the present century; but though the illusions of her youth
had been rudely shattered, she remained always devoted to her
liberal principles and a broad humanity.

The woman, however, who most fitly represents the spirit of
the Revolution, who was at once its inspiration, its heroine, and
its victim, is Mme. Roland.   It is not as the leader of a salon
that she takes her place in the history of her time, but as one
of the foremost and ablest leaders of a powerful political party.
Born in the ranks of the *bourgeoisie*, she had neither the prestige of a name nor the distinction of an aristocratic lineage.
Reared in seclusion, she was familiar with the great world by
report only.   Though brilliant, even eloquent in conversation
when her interest was roused, her early training had added to
her natural distaste for the spirit, as well as the accessories, of
a social life that was inevitably more or less artificial.   She
would have felt cramped and caged in the conventional atmosphere of a drawing-room in which the gravest problems were
apt to be forgotten in the flash of an epigram or the turn of a
bon mot.   The strong and heroic outlines of her character were
more clearly defined on the theater of the world.   But at a
time when the empire of the salon was waning, when vital interests and burning convictions had for the moment thrown
into the shade all minor questions of form and *convenance*, she

took up the scepter in a simpler fashion, and, disdaining the arts of a society of which she saw only the fatal and hopeless corruption, held her sway over the daring and ardent men who gathered about her by the unassisted force of her clear and vigorous intellect.

It would be interesting to trace the career of the thoughtful and precocious child known as Manon or Marie Phlipon, who sat in her father's studio with the burin of an engraver in one hand and a book in the other, eagerly absorbing the revolutionary theories which were to prove so fatal to her, but it is not the purpose here to dwell upon the details of her life. In the solitude of a prison cell and under the shadow of the scaffold she told her own story. She has introduced us to the simple scenes of her childhood, the modest home on the Quai de l'Horloge, the wise and tender mother, the weak and unstable father. We are made familiar with the tiny recess in which she studies, reads, and makes extracts from the books which are such strange companions for her years. We seem to see the grave little face as it lights with emotion over the inspiring pages of Fénelon or the chivalrous heroes of Tasso, and sympathize with the fascination that leads the child of nine years to carry her Plutarch to mass instead of her prayer-book. She portrays for us her convent life with its dreams, its exaltations, its romantic friendships, and its ardent enthusiasms. We have vivid pictures of the calm and sympathetic Sophie Cannet, to whom she unburdens all her hopes and aspirations and sorrows; of the lively sister Henriette, who years afterward, in the generous hope of saving her early friend, proposed to exchange clothes and take her place in the cells of Sainte-Pélagie. In the long and commonplace procession of suitors that files before us, one only touches her heart. La Blancherie has a literary and philosophic turn, and the young girl's imagination drapes him in its own glowing colors. The opposition of her father separates them, but absence only lends fuel to this virgin flame. One day she learns that his views are mercenary, that he is neither true nor disinterested, and the charm is broken. She met him afterward in the Luxembourg gardens with a feather in his hat, and the last illusion vanished.

There is an idyllic charm in these pictures so simply and gracefully sketched. She sees with the vision of one lying down to sleep after a life of pain, and dreaming of the green fields, the blue skies, the running brooks, the trees, the flowers, that make so beautiful a background for youthful loves and hopes. Perhaps we could wish sometimes that she were a little less frank. We miss a touch of delicacy in this nature that was so strong and self-poised. We are sorry that she dismissed La Blancherie quite so theatrically. There is a trace too much of consciousness in her fine self-analysis, perhaps a little vanity, and we half suspect that her unchildlike penetration and precocity of motive was sometimes the reflection of an after-thought. But it is to be remembered that, even in childhood, she had lived in such close companionship with the heroes and moralists of the past that their sentiments had become her own. She doubtless posed a little to herself, as well as to the world, but her frankness was a part of that uncompromising truth-fulness which scorned disguises of any sort, and led her to paint faults and virtues alike.

Family sorrows—the death of the mother whom she adored, and the unworthiness of her father—combined to change the current of her free and happy life, and to deepen a natural vein of melancholy. In her loneliness of soul the convent seemed to offer itself as the sole haven of peace and rest. The child, who loved Fénelon, and dreamed over the lives of the saints, had in her much of the stuff out of which mystics and fanatics are made. Her ardent soul was raised to ecstasy by the stately ceremonial of the Church; her imagination was captivated by its majestic music, its mystery, its solemnity, and she was wont to spend hours in rapt meditation. But her strong fund of good sense, her firm reason fortified by wide and solid reading, together with her habits of close observation and analysis, saved her from falling a victim to her own emotional needs, or to chimeras of any sort. She had drawn her mental nourish-ment too long from Voltaire, Rousseau, Montesquieu, the Eng-lish philosophers, and classic historians, to become permanently a prey to exaggerated sensibilities, though it was the same temperament, fired by a sense of human inequality and wrong,

MME. ROLAND.

31

that swept her at last along the road that led to the scaffold. At twenty-six the vocation of the *religieuse* had lost its fascination; the pious fervor of her childhood had vanished before the skepticism of her intellect, its ardent friendships had grown dim, its fleeting loves had proved illusive, and her romantic dreams ended in a cold marriage of reason.

It may be noted here that though Mme. Roland had lost her belief in ecclesiastical systems, and, as she said, continued to go to mass only for the "edification of her neighbors and the good order of society," there was always in her nature a strong undercurrent of religious feeling. Her faith had not survived the full illumination of her reason, but her trust in immortality never seriously wavered. The Invocation that was among her last written words is the prayer of a soul that is conscious of its divine origin and destiny. She retained, too, the firm moral basis that was laid in her early teachings, and which saved her from the worst errors of her time. She might be shaken by the storms of passion, but one feels that she could never be swept from her moorings.

Tall and finely developed, with dark brown hair; a large mouth whose beauty lay in a smile of singular sweetness; dark, serious eyes with a changeful expression which no artist could catch; a fresh complexion that responded to every emotion of a passionate soul; a deep, well-modulated voice; manners gentle, modest, reserved, sometimes timid with the consciousness that she was not readily taken at her true value —such was the *personnelle* of the woman who calmly weighed the possibilities of a life which had no longer a pleasant outlook in any direction, and, after much hesitation, became the wife of a grave, studious, austere man of good family and moderate fortune, but many years her senior.

It was this marriage, into which she entered with all seriousness, and a devotion that was none the less sincere because it was of the intellect rather than the heart, that gave the final tinge to a character that was already laid on solid foundations. Strong, clear-sighted, earnest, and gifted, her later experience had accented a slightly ascetic quality which had been deepened also by her study of antique models. Her tastes were grave and severe. But they had a lighter side. As a child she had excelled in music, dancing, drawing, and other feminine accomplishments, though one feels always that her distinctive talent does not lie in these things. She is more at home with her thoughts. There was a touch of poetry, too, in her nature, that under different circumstances might have lent it a softer and more graceful coloring. She had a natural love for the woods and the flowers. The single relief to her somber life at La Plâtière, after her marriage, was in the long and lonely rambles in the country, whose endless variations of hill and vale and sky and color she has so tenderly and so vividly noted. In her last days a piano and a few flowers lighted the darkness of her prison walls, and out of these her imagination reared a world of its own, peopled with dreams and fancies that contrasted strangely with the gloom of her surroundings. This poetic vein was closely allied to the keen sensibility that tempered the seriousness of her character. With the mental equipment of a man, she combined the rich sympathy of a woman. Her devotion to her mother was passionate in its intensity; her letters to Sophie throb with warmth and sentiment. She is tender and loving, as well as philosophic and thoughtful. Her emotional ardor was doubtless partly the glow of youth and not altogether in the texture of a mind so eminently rational; but there were rich possibilities behind it. A shade of difference in the mental and moral atmosphere, a trace more or less of sunshine and happiness are important factors in the peculiar combination of qualities that make up a human being. The marriage of Mme. Roland led her into a world that had little color save what she brought into it. Her husband did not smile upon her friends. Sympathy other than that of the intellect she does not seem to have had. But her story is best told in her own words, written in the last days of her life.

"In considering only the happiness of my partner, I soon perceived that something was wanting to my own. I had never, for a single instant, ceased to see in my husband one of the most estimable of men, to whom I felt it an honor to belong; but I have often realized that there was a lack of equality between us, that the ascendency of an overbearing character, added to that of twenty years more of age, gave him too much superiority. If we lived in solitude, I had many painful hours to pass; if we went into the world, I was loved by men of whom I saw that some might touch me too deeply. I plunged into work with my husband, another excess which had its inconvenience; I gave him the habit of not knowing how to do without me for anything in the world, nor at any moment.

"I honor, I cherish my husband, as a sensible daughter adores a virtuous father to whom she would sacrifice even her lover; but I have found the man who might have been that lover, and remaining faithful to my duties, my frankness has not known how to conceal the feelings which I subjected to them. My husband, excessively sensitive both in his affections and his self-love, could not support the idea of the least change in his influence; his imagination darkened, his jealousy irritated me; happiness fled; he adored me, I sacrificed myself for him, and we were miserable.

"If I were free, I would follow him everywhere to soften his griefs and console his old age; a soul like mine leaves no sacrifices imperfect. But Roland was embittered by the thought of sacrifice, and the knowledge once acquired that I had made one ruined his happiness; he suffered in accepting it, and could not do without it."

The sequel to this tale is told in allusions and half-revelations, in her letters to Buzot, which glow with suppressed feeling; in her touching farewell to one whom she dared not to name, but whom she hoped to meet where it would not be a crime to love; in those final words of her *Last Thoughts*—"Adieu. . . . No, it is from thee alone that I do not separate; to leave the earth is to approach each other."

Beneath this semi-transparent veil the heart-drama of her life is hidden.

For the sake of those who would be pained by this story, as well as for her own, we would rather it had never been told. We should like to believe that the woman who worked so nobly with and for the man who died by his own hand five days after her death, because he could stay no longer in a world where such crimes were possible, had lived in the full perfection of domestic sympathy. But, if she carried with her an incurable wound, one cannot help regretting that her Spartan courage had not led her to wear the mantle of silence to the end. Posterity is curious rather than sympathetic, and the world is neither wiser nor better for these needless soul-revelations. There is always a certain malady of egotism behind them. But it is often easier to scale the heights of human heroism than to still the cry of a bruised spirit. Mme. Roland had moments of falling short of her own ideals, and this was one of them. Pure, loyal, self-sustained as she was, her strong sense of verity did not permit the veil which would have best served the interests of the larger truth. It is fair to say that she thought the malicious gossip of her enemies rendered this statement necessary to the protection of her fame. Perhaps, after all, she shows here her most human and lovable if not her strongest side. We should like Minerva better if she were not so faultlessly wise.

The outbreak of the Revolution found Mme. Roland at La Plâtière, where she shared her husband's philosophic and economic studies, brought peace into a discordant family, attended to her household duties and the training of her child, devoted many hours to generous care for the sick and poor, and reserved a little leisure for poetry and the solitary rambles she loved so well. The first martial note struck a responsive chord in her heart. Her opportunity had come. Embittered by class distinctions over which she had long brooded, saturated with the sentiments of Rousseau, and full of untried theories constructed in the closet, with small knowledge of the wide and complex interests with which it was necessary to deal, she centered all the hitherto latent energies of her forceful nature upon the quixotic effort to redress human wrongs. Her birth, her intellect, her character, her temperament, her education, her associations—all led her towards the rôle she played so heroically. She had a keen appreciation for genuine values, but none whatever for factitious ones. Her inborn hatred of artificial distinctions had grown with her years and colored all her estimates of men and things. When she came to Paris she noted with a sort of indignation the superior poise and courtesy of the men in the Assembly who had been reared in the habit of power. It added fuel to her enmity towards institutions in which reason, knowledge, and integrity paid homage to fine language and distinguished manners. She found even Vergniaud too refined and fastidious in his dress for a successful republican leader. Her old contempt for a "philosopher with a feather" had in no wise abated. With such principles ingrained and fostered, it is not difficult to forecast the part Mme. Roland was destined to play in the coming conflict of classes. Whatever we may think of the wisdom of her attitude towards the Revolution, she represented at least its most sincere side. As she stood white-robed and courageous at the foot of the scaffold, facing the savage populace she had laid down her life to befriend, perhaps her perspectives were truer. Experience had given her an insight into the characters of men which is not to be gained in the library, nor in the worship of dead heroes. If it had not shaken her faith in human perfectibility, it had taught her at least the value of tradition in chaining brutal human passions.

The tragical fate of Mme. Roland has thrown a strong light upon the modest little salon in which the unfortunate Girondists met four times a week to discuss the grave problems that confronted them. A salon in the old sense it certainly was not. It had little in common with the famous centers of conversation and *esprit*. It was simply the rallying-point of a party. The only woman present was Mme. Roland herself, but at first she assumed no active leadership. She sat at a little table outside of the circle, working with her needle, or writing letters, alive to everything that was said, venturing sometimes a word of counsel or a thoughtful suggestion, and often biting her lips to repress some criticism that she feared might not be within her province. She had left her quiet home in the country fired with a single thought — the regeneration of France. The men who gathered about her were in full accord with her generous aims. It was not to such enthusiasms that the old salons lent themselves. They had been often the centers of political intrigues, as in the days of the Fronde; or of religious partizanship, as during the troubles of Port Royal; they had ranged themselves for and against rival candidates for literary or artistic honors; but they had preserved, on the whole, a certain cosmopolitan character. All shades of opinion were represented, and social brilliancy was the end sought, not the triumph of special ideas. It is indeed true that earnest convictions were, to some extent, stifled in the salons, where charm and intelligence counted for so much, and the sterling qualities of character for so little. But the etiquette, the urbanity, the measure, which assured the outward harmony of a society that courted distinction of every kind, were quite foreign to the iconoclasts who were bent upon leveling all distinctions. The Revolution, which attacked the whole superstructure of society, was antagonistic to its minor forms as well, and it was the revolutionary party alone which was represented in the salon of Mme. Roland. Brissot, Vergniaud, Pétion, Guadet, and Buzot were leaders there—men sincere and ardent, though misguided, and unable to cope with the storm they had raised, to be themselves swept away by its pitiless rage. Robespierre, scheming and ambitious, came there, listened, said little, appropriated for his own ends, and bided his time. Mme. Roland had small taste for the light play of intellect and wit that has no outcome beyond the meteoric display of the moment, and she was impatient with the talk in which an evening was often passed among these men without any definite results. As she measured their strength, she became more outspoken. She communicated to them a spark of her own energy. The most daring moves were made at her bidding. She urged on her timid and conservative husband, she drew up his memorials, she wrote his letters, she was at once his stimulus and his helper. Weak and vacillating men yielded to her rapid insight, her vigor, her earnestness, and her persuasive eloquence. This was probably the period of her greatest influence. Many of the swift changes of those first months may be traced to her salon. The moves which were made in the Assembly were concocted there, the orators who triumphed found their inspiration there. Still, in spite of her energy, her strength, and her courage, she prides herself upon maintaining always the reserve and decorum of her sex.

If she assumed the favorite rôle of the French woman for a short time while her husband was in the ministry, it was in a sternly republican fashion. She gave dinners twice a week to her husband's political friends. The fifteen or twenty men who met around her table at five o'clock were linked by political interests only. The service was simple, with no other luxury than a few flowers. There were no women to temper the discussions or to lighten their seriousness. After dinner the guests lingered for an hour or so in the drawing-room, but by nine o'clock it was deserted. She received on Friday, but what a contrast to the Fridays of Mme. Necker in those same apartments! It was no longer a brilliant company of wits, *savants*, and men of letters, enlivened by women of beauty, *esprit*, rank, and fashion. There was none of the diversity of taste and thought which lends such a charm to social life. Mme. Roland tells us that she never had an extended circle at any time, and that, while her husband was in power, she made and received no visits, and invited no women to her house. She saw only her husband's colleagues, or those who were interested in his tastes and pursuits, which were also her own. The world of society wearied her. She was absorbed in a single purpose. If she needed recreation, she sought it in serious studies.

It is always difficult to judge what a man or a woman might have been under slightly altered conditions. But for some single circumstance that converged and focused their talents, many a hero would have died unknown and unsuspected. The key that unlocks the treasure-house of the soul is not always found, and its wealth is often scattered on unseen shores. But it is clear that the part of Mme. Roland could never have been a distinctively social one. She lived at a time when great events brought out great qualities. Her clear intellect, her positive convictions, her boundless energy, and her ardent enthusiasm, gave her a powerful influence in those early days of the Revolution, that looked towards a world reconstructed but not plunged into the dark depths of chaos, and it is through this that she has left a name among the noted women of France. In more peaceful times her peculiar talent would doubtless have led her towards literature. In her best style she has rare vigor and simplicity. She has moments of eloquent thought. There are flashes of it in her early letters to Sophie, which she begs her friend not to burn, though she does not hope to rival Mme. de Sévigné, whom she takes for her model. She lacked the grace, the lightness, the wit, the humor of this model, but she had an earnestness, a serious depth of thought, that one does not find in Mme. de Sévigné. She had also a vein of sentiment that was an underlying force in her character, though it was always subject to her masculine intellect. She confesses that she should like to be the annalist of her country, and longs for the pen of Tacitus, for whom she has a veritable passion. When one reads her sharp, incisive pen-portraits, drawn with such profound insight and masterly skill, one feels that her true vocation was in the world of letters. At the close she verges a little upon the theatrical, as sometimes in her young days. But when she wrote her final records she felt her last hours slipping away. Life, with its large possibilities undeveloped and its promises unfulfilled, was behind her. Darkness was all around her, eternal silence before her. And she had lived but thirty-nine years.

Mme. Roland does not really belong to the world of the salons, though she has been included among them by some of her own cotemporaries. She was of quite another *genre*. She represents a social reaction in which old forms are adapted to new ideas and lose their essential quality by the change. But she foreshadows a type of woman that has had great influence since the salons have lost their prestige. She relied neither upon the reflected light of a coterie, the arts of the courtier, nor the subtle power of personal attraction ; but, firm in her convictions, clear in her purposes, and unselfish in her aims, she laid down her interests, and, in the end, her life, upon the altar of liberty and humanity. She could hardly be regarded, however, as herself a type. She was cast in a rare mold and lived under rare conditions. She was individual, as were Hypatia, Joan of Arc, and Charlotte Corday — a woman fitted for a special mission which brought her little but a martyr's crown and a permanent fame.

32

The Women of the French Salons

CHAPTER XVIII

MADAME DE STAËL

Supremacy of Her Genius — Her Early Training — Her Sensibility — A Mariage de Convenance — Her Salon — Anecdote of Benjamin Constant — Her Exile — Life at Coppet — Secret Marriage — Close of a Stormy Life.

HE fame of all other French women is more or less overshadowed by that of one who was not only supreme in her own world, but who stands on a pinnacle so high that time and distance only serve to throw into stronger relief the grand outlines of her many-sided genius. Without the simplicity and naturalness of Mme. de Sévigné, the poise and judgment of Mme. de Lafayette, or the calm foresight and diplomacy of Mme. de Maintenon, Mme. de Staël had a brilliancy of imagination, a force of passion, a grasp of intellect, and a diversity of gifts that belonged to none of these women. It is not possible within the limits of a brief chapter to touch even lightly upon the various phases of a character so complex and talents so versatile. One can only gather a few scattered traits and indicate a few salient points in a life of which the details are already familiar.   As woman, novelist, philosopher, *littérateur*, and conversationist, she has marked, if not equal, claims upon our attention.   To speak of her as simply the leader of a salon is to merge the greater talent into the less, but her brilliant social qualities in a measure brought out and illuminated all the others.   It was not the gift of reconciling diverse elements, and of calling out the best thoughts of those who came within her radius, that distinguished her.   Her personality was too dominant not to disturb sometimes the measure and harmony which fashion had established.   She did not listen well, but her gift was that of the orator, and, taking whatever subject was uppermost into her own hands, she talked with an irresistible eloquence that held her auditors silent and enchained.   Living as she did in the world of wit and talent which had so fascinated her mother, she ruled it as an autocrat.

The mental coloring of Mme. de Staël was not taken in the shade, as that of Mme. Roland had been.   She was reared in the atmosphere of the great world.   That which her eager mind gathered in solitude was subject always to the modification which contact with vigorous living minds is sure to give.   The little Germaine Necker who sat on a low stool at her mother's side, charming the cleverest men of her time by her precocious wit; who wrote extracts from the dramas she heard, and opinions upon the authors she read; who made pen-portraits of her friends, and cut out paper kings and queens to play in the tragedies she composed; whose heart was always overflowing with love for those around her, and who had supreme need for an outlet to her sensibilities, was a fresh type in that age of keen analysis, cold skepticism, and rigid forms.   The serious utterances of her childhood were always suffused with feeling. She loved that which made her weep.   Her sympathies were full and overflowing, and when her vigorous and masculine intellect took the ascendency it directed them, but only partly held them in check.   It never dulled nor subdued them.   The source of her power, as also of her weakness, lay perhaps in her vast capacity for love.   It gave color and force to her rich and versatile character.   It animated all she did and gave point to all she wrote. It found expression in the eloquence of her conversation, in the exaltation and passionate intensity of her affections, in the fervor of her patriotism, in the self-forgetful generosity that brought her very near the verge of the scaffold. Here was the source of that indefinable quality we call genius — not genius of the sort which Buffon has defined as patience, but the divine flame that crowns with life the dead materials which patience has gathered.

It was impossible that a child so eager, so sympathetic, so full of intellect and *esprit*, should not have developed rapidly in the atmosphere of her mother's salon. Whether it was the best school for a young girl may be a question, but a character like that of Mme. de Staël is apt to go its own way in whatever circumstances it finds itself. She was the despair of Mme. Necker, whose educational theories were altogether upset by this precocious daughter who refused to be cast in a mold. But she was habituated to a high altitude of thought. Men like Marmontel, La Harpe, Grimm, Thomas, and the Abbé Raynal delighted in calling out her ready wit, her brilliant repartee, and her precocious ideas. Surrounded thus from childhood with all the appointments as well as the talent and *esprit* that made the life of the salons so fascinating; inheriting the philosophic insight of her father, the literary gifts of her mother, to which she added a genius all her own; heir also to the spirit of conversation, the facility, the enthusiasm, the love of pleasing which are the Gallic birthright, she took her place in the social world as a queen by virtue of her position, her gifts, and her heritage. Already, before her marriage, she had changed the tone of her mother's salon. She brought into it an element of freshness and originality which the dignified and rather precise character of Mme. Necker had failed to impart. She gave it also a strong political coloring. This influence was more marked after she became the wife of the Swedish ambassador, as she continued for some time to pass her evenings in her mother's drawing-room, where she became more and more a central figure. Her temperament and her tastes were of the world in which she lived, but her reason and her expansive sympathies led her to ally herself with the popular cause;

hence she was, to some extent, a link between two conflicting interests.

It was in 1786 that Mme. de Staël entered the world as a married woman. This marriage was arranged for her after the fashion of the time, and she accepted it as she would have accepted anything tolerable that pleased her idolized father and revered mother. When only ten years of age, she observed that they took great pleasure in the society of Gibbon, and she gravely proposed to marry him, that they might always have this happiness. The full significance of this singular proposition is not apparent until one remembers that the learned historian was not only rather old, but so short and fat as to call out from one of his friends the remark that when he needed a little exercise he had only to take a turn of three times around M. Gibbon. The Baron de Staël had an exalted position, fine manners, a good figure, and a handsome face, but he lacked the one thing that Mme. de Staël most considered, a commanding talent. She did not see him through the prism of a strong affection which transfigures all things, even the most commonplace. What this must have meant to a woman of her genius and temperament, whose ideal of happiness was a sympathetic marriage, it is not difficult to divine. It may account, in some degree, for her restlessness, her perpetual need of movement, of excitement, of society. But, whatever her domestic troubles may have been, they were of limited duration. She was quietly separated from her husband in 1798. Four years later she decided to return to Coppet with him, as he was unhappy and longed to see his children. He died *en route.*

The period of this marriage was one of the most memorable of France, the period when noble and generous spirits rallied in a spontaneous movement for national regeneration. Mme. de Staël was in the flush of hope and enthusiasm, fresh from the study of Rousseau and her own dreams of human perfectibility; radiant, too, with the reflection of her youthful fame. Among those who surrounded her were the Montmorencys, Lafayette, and Count Louis de Narbonne, whose brilliant intellect and charming manners touched her perhaps too deeply for her peace of mind. There were also Barnave, Chénier, Talleyrand, Mirabeau, Vergniaud, and many others of the active leaders of the Revolution. A few women mingled in her more intimate circle, which was still of the old society. Of these were the ill-fated Duchesse de Gramont, Mme. de Lauzun, the Princesse de Poix, and the witty, lovable Maréchale de Beauvau. As a rule, though devoted to her friends and kind to those who sought her aid, Mme. de Staël did not like the society of women. Perhaps they did not always respond to her elevated and swiftly flowing thoughts; or it may be that she wounded the vanity of those who were cast into the shade by talents so conspicuous and conversation so eloquent, and who felt the lack of sympathetic *rapport*. Society is *au fond* republican, and is apt to resent autocracy, even the autocracy of genius, when it takes the form of monologue. It is contrary to the social spirit. The salon of Mme. de Staël not only took its tone from herself, but it was a reflection of herself. She was not beautiful, and she dressed badly; indeed, she seems to have been singularly free from that personal consciousness which leads people to give themselves the advantages of an artistic setting, even if the taste is not inborn. She was too intent upon what she thought and felt, to give heed to minor details. But in her conversation, which was a sort of improvisation, her eloquent face was aglow, her dark eyes flashed with inspiration, her superb form and finely poised head seemed to respond to the rhythmic flow of thoughts that were emphasized by the graceful gestures of an exquisitely molded hand, in which she usually held a sprig of laurel. "If I were queen," said Mme. de Tessé, "I would order Mme. de Staël to talk to me always."

But this center in which the more thoughtful spirits of the old régime met the brilliant and active leaders of the new was broken up by the storm which swept away so many of its leaders, and Mme. de Staël, after lingering in the face of dangers to save her friends, barely escaped with her life on the eve of the September massacres of 1792. "She is an excellent woman," said one of her contemporaries, "who drowns all her friends in order to have the pleasure of angling for them."

Mme. de Staël resumed her place and organized her salon anew in 1795. But it was her fate to live always in an atmo-

MADAME DE STAËL.

FROM THE PAINTING BY GÉRARD.

sphere surcharged with storms. She was too republican for the
aristocrats, and too aristocratic for the republicans. Distrusted
by both parties and feared by the Directoire, she found it ad-
visable after a few months to retire to Coppet. Less than two
years later she was again in Paris. Her friends were then in
power, notably Talleyrand. "If I remain here another year
I shall die," he had written her from America, and she had
generously secured the repeal of the decree that exiled him, a
kindness which he promptly forgot. Though her enthusiasm
for the republic was much moderated, and though she had been
so far dazzled by the genius of Napoleon as to hail him as a
restorer of order, her illusions regarding him were very short-
lived. She had no sympathy with his aims at personal power.
Her drawing-room soon became the rallying-point for his
enemies and the center of a powerful opposition. But she had
a natural love for all forms of intellectual distinction, and her
genius and fame still attracted a circle more or less cosmopolitan.
Ministers of state and editors of leading journals were among
her guests. Joseph and Lucien Bonaparte were her devoted
friends. The small remnant of the *noblesse* that had any inclination to return to a world which had lost its charm for them
found there a trace of the old politeness. Mathieu de Montmorency, devout and charitable; his brother Adrien, delicate in
spirit and gentle in manners; Narbonne, still devoted and
diplomatic, and the Chevalier de Boufflers, gay, witty, and
brilliant, were of those who brought into it something of the
tone of the past régime. There were also the men of the new
generation, men who were saturated with the principles of the
Revolution though regretting its methods. Among these were
Chénier, Regnault, and Benjamin Constant.

The influence of Mme. de Staël was at its height during this
period. Her talent, her liberal opinions, and her persuasive
eloquence gave her great power over the constitutional leaders.
The measures of the Government were freely discussed and
criticized in her salon, and men went out with positions well
defined and speeches well considered. The Duchesse d'Abrantes
relates an incident which aptly illustrates this power and its
reaction upon herself. Benjamin Constant had prepared a

brilliant address. The evening before it was to be delivered, Mme. de Staël was surrounded by a large and distinguished company. After tea was served he said to her:

"Your salon is filled with people who please you; if I speak to-morrow, it will be deserted. Think of it."

"One must follow one's convictions," she replied, after a moment's hesitation.

She admitted afterward that she would never have refused his offer not to compromise her, if she could have foreseen all that would follow.

The next day she invited her friends to celebrate his triumph. At four o'clock a note of excuse; in an hour, ten. From this time her fortunes waned. Many ceased to visit her salon. Even Talleyrand, who owed her so much, came there no more.

In later years she confessed that the three men she had most loved were Narbonne, Talleyrand, and Mathieu de Montmorency. Her friendship for the first of these reached a passionate exaltation which had a profound and not altogether wholesome influence upon her life. How completely she was disenchanted is shown in a remark she made long afterward of a loyal and distinguished man : " He has the manners of Narbonne and a heart." It is a character in a sentence. Mathieu de Montmorency was a man of pure motives, who proved a refuge of consolation in many storms, but her regard for him was evidently a gentler flame that never burned to extinction. Whatever illusions she may have had as to Talleyrand — and they seem to have been little more than an enthusiastic appreciation of his talent — were certainly broken by his treacherous desertion in her hour of need. Not the least among her many sorrows was the bitter taste of ingratitude.

But Napoleon, who, like Louis XIV., sought to draw all influences and merge all power in himself, could not tolerate a woman whom he felt to be in some sense a rival. He thought he detected her hand in the address of Benjamin Constant which lost her so many friends. He feared the wit that flashed in her salon, the satire that wounded, the criticism that measured his motives and his actions. He recognized the power of a coterie of brilliant intellects led by a genius so inspiring.

His brothers, knowing her vulnerable point and the will with which she had to deal, gave her a word of caution.   But the advice and intercession of her friends were alike without avail. The blow which she so much feared fell at last, and she found herself an exile and a wanderer from the scenes she most loved.

We have many pleasant glimpses of her life at Coppet, but a shadow always rests upon it.   A few friends still clung to her through the bitter and relentless persecutions that form one of the most singular chapters in history, and offer the most remarkable tribute to her genius and her power.   We find here Schlegel, Sismondi, Mathieu de Montmorency, Prince Augustus, Monti, Mme. Récamier, and many other distinguished visitors of various nationalities.   The most prominent figure perhaps was Benjamin Constant, brilliant, gifted, eloquent, passionate, vain, and capricious, the torturing consolation and the stormy problem of her saddest years.   She revived the old literary diversions.   At eleven o'clock, we are told, the guests assembled at breakfast, and the conversations took a high literary tone. They were resumed at dinner, and continued often until midnight.   Here, as elsewhere, Mme. de Staël was queen, holding her guests entranced by the magic of her words.   " Life is for me like a ball after the music has ceased," said Sismondi when her voice was silent.   She was a veritable *Corinne* in her *esprit*, her sentiment, her gift of improvisation, and her underlying melancholy.   But in this choice company hers was not the only voice, though it was heard above all the others.   Thought and wit flashed and sparkled.   Dramas were played—the *Zaïre* and *Tancred* of Voltaire, and tragedies written by herself.   Mme. Récamier acted the *Aricie* to Mme. de Staël's *Phédre.*   This life, that seems to us so fascinating, has been described too often to need repetition.   It had its tumultuous elements, its passionate undercurrents, its romantic episodes.   But in spite of its attractions Mme. de Staël fretted under the peaceful shades of Coppet. Its limited horizon pressed upon her.   The silence of the snow-capped mountains chilled her.   She looked upon their solitary grandeur with "magnificent horror."   The repose of nature was an "infernal peace" which plunged her into gloomier depths of *ennui* and despair.   To some one who was admiring the beauties of Lake Leman she replied: "I should like better the gutters of the Rue du Bac." It was people, always people, who interested her. "French conversation exists only in Paris," she said, "and conversation has been from infancy my greatest pleasure." Restlessly she sought distraction in travel, but wherever she went the iron hand pressed upon her still. Italy fostered her melancholy. She loved its ruins, which her imagination draped with the fading colors of the past and associated with the desolation of a living soul. But its exquisite variety of landscape and color does not seem to have touched her. "If it were not for the world's opinion," she said, "I would not open my window to see the Bay of Naples for the first time, but I would travel five hundred leagues to talk with a clever man whom I have not met." Germany gave her infinite food for thought, but her "astonishing volubility," her "incessant movement," her constant desire to know, to discuss, to penetrate all things wearied the moderate Germans, as it had already wearied the serious English. "Tell me, Monsieur Fichte," she said one day, "could you in a short time, a quarter of an hour for example, give me a glimpse of your system and explain what you understand by your *me ;* I find it very obscure." The philosopher was amazed at what he thought her impertinence, but made the attempt through an interpreter. At the end of ten minutes she exclaimed, "That is sufficient, Monsieur Fichte. That is quite sufficient. I comprehend you perfectly. I have seen your system in illustration. It is one of the adventures of Baron Münchhausen." "We are in perpetual mental tension," said the wife of Schiller. Even Schiller himself grew tired. "It seems as if I were relieved of a malady," he said, when she left.

It was this excess of vivacity and her abounding sensibility that constituted at once her fascination and her misfortune. Her beliefs were enthusiasms. Her friendships were passions. "No one has carried the religion of friendship so far as myself," she said. To love, to be loved was the supreme need of her soul; but her love was a flame that irradiated her intellect and added brilliancy to the life it consumed. She paints in *Corinne* the passions, the struggles, the penalties, and the sorrows of a woman of genius. It is a life she had known, a life of which she had tasted the sweetest delights and experienced the most cruel disenchantments. *Corinne* at the Capitol, *Corinne* thinking, analyzing, loving, suffering, triumphing, wearing a crown of laurel upon her head and an invisible crown of thorns upon her heart — it is Mme. de Staël self-revealed by the light of her own imagination.

It was in a moment of weakness and weariness, when her idols had one after another been shattered, and all the pleasant vistas of her youth seemed shut out forever, that she met M. de Rocca, a wounded officer of good family, but of little more than half her years, whose gentle chivalric character commanded her admiration, whose suffering touched her pity, and whose devotion won her affection. " I will love her so much that she will end by marrying me," he said, and the result proved his penetration. This marriage, which was a secret one, has shadowed a little the brilliancy of her fame, but if it was a weakness to bend from her high altitude, it was not a sin, though more creditable to her heart than to her worldly wisdom. At all events it brought into her life a new element of repose, and gave her a tender consolation in her closing years.

When at last the relentless autocrat of France found his rock-bound limits, and she was free to return to the spot which had been the goal of all her dreams, it was too late. Her health was broken. It is true her friends rallied around her, and her salon, opened once more, retook a little of its ancient glory. Few celebrities who came to Paris failed to seek the drawing-room of Mme. de Staël, which was still illuminated with the brilliancy of her genius and the splendor of her fame. But her triumphs were past, and life was receding. Her few remaining days of weakness and suffering, darkened by vain regrets, were passed more and more in the warmth and tenderness of her devoted family, in the noble and elevated thought that rose above the strife of politics into the serene atmosphere of a Christian faith. At her death-bed Chateaubriand did her tardy justice. "*Bon jour*, my dear Francis; I suffer, but that does not prevent me from loving you," she said to one who had been her critic, but never her friend. Her magnanimity was as unfailing as her generosity, and it may be truly said that she never cherished a hatred.

The life of Mme. de Staël was in the world. She embodied the French spirit; she could not conceive of happiness in a secluded existence; a theater and an audience were needed to call out her best talents. She could not even bear her griefs alone. The world was taken into her confidence. She demanded its sympathy. She chanted exquisite requiems over her dead hopes and her lost illusions, but she chanted them in costume, never quite forgetting that her rôle was a heroic one. She added, however, to the gifts of an improvisatrice something infinitely higher and deeper. There was no problem with which she was not ready to deal. She felt the pulse-beats in the great heart of humanity, and her tongue, her pen, her purse, and her influence were ever at the bidding of the unfortunate. She traversed all fields of thought, from the pleasant regions of poetry and romance to the highest altitudes of philosophy. We may note the drift of her ardent and imaginative nature in the youthful tales into which she wove her romantic dreams, her fancied griefs, her inward struggles, and her tears. In the pages of *Corinne* we read the poetry, the sensibility, the passion, the melancholy, the thought of a matured woman whose youth of the soul neither sorrow nor experience could destroy. We may divine the direction of her sympathies, and the fountain of her inspiration, in her letters on Rousseau, written at twenty, and foreshadowing her own attitude towards the theories which appealed so powerfully to the generous spirits of the century. We may follow the active and scholarly workings of her versatile intellect in her pregnant thoughts on literature, on the passions, on the Revolution; or measure the clearness of her insight, the depth of her penetration, the catholicity of her sympathies, and the breadth of her intelligence in her profound and masterly, if not always accurate, studies of Germany. The consideration of all this pertains to a critical estimate of her character and genius which cannot be attempted here.

It has grown to be somewhat the fashion to depreciate the literary work of Mme. de Staël. Measured by present standards she leaves something to be desired in logical precision;

she had not the exactness of the critical scholar, nor the simplicity of the careful artist; the luxuriance of her language often
obscures her thought. She is talking still, and her written
words have the rapid, tumultuous flow of conversation, together
with its occasional negligences, its careless periods, its sudden
turns, its encumbered phrases. Misguided she sometimes was,
and carried away by the resistless rush of ideas that, like the
mountain torrent, gathered much debris along their course. But
her rapid judgments, which have the force of inspiration, are in
advance of her time, though in the main correct from her own
point of view, while her flaws in workmanship are more than
counterbalanced by that inward illumination which is Heaven's
richest and rarest gift. But who cares to dwell upon the
shadows that scarcely dim the brilliancy of a genius so rare and
so commanding? They are but spots on the sun that are only
discovered by looking through a glass that veils its radiance.
It is just to weigh her by the standards of her own age. Born
at its highest level, she soared far above her generation. She
carried within herself the vision of a statesman, the penetration
of a critic, the insight of a philosopher, the soul of a poet, and
the heart of a woman. If she was not without faults she had
rare virtues. No woman has ever exercised a wider or more
varied influence. With one or two exceptions, none stands on
so high a pinnacle. George Sand was a more finished artist;
George Eliot was a greater novelist, a more accurate scholar,
and a more logical thinker; but in versatility, in intellectual
spontaneity, in brilliancy of conversation and natural eloquence
of thought she is without a rival. Her moral standards, too,
were above the average of her time. Her ideals were high
and pure. The wealth of her emotions and the rich coloring
of sentiment in which her thoughts and feelings were often
clothed left her open to possible misconceptions. It was her
fate to be grossly misunderstood, to miss the domestic happiness she craved, to be the victim of a sleepless persecution, to
pass her best years in a dreary exile from the life she most
loved, to be maligned by her enemies and betrayed by her
friends. Her very virtues were construed into faults and turned
against her. Though we may not lift the veil from her intimate

life, we may fairly judge her by her own ideals and her dominant traits. The world, which is rarely indulgent, has been in the main just to her motives and her character. "I have been ever the same, intense and sad," were among her last words. "I have loved God, my father, and liberty." But she was a victim to the contradictory elements in her own nature, and walked always among storms. This nature, so complex, so rich, so ardent, so passionate, could it ever have found permanent repose?

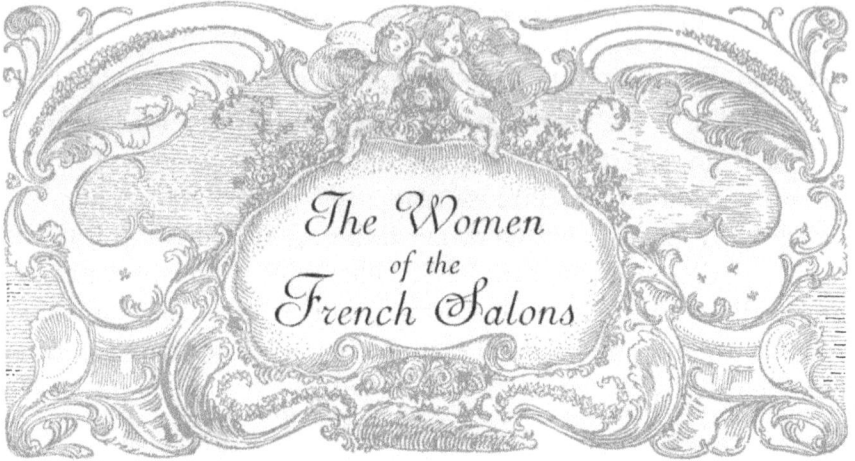

Chapter XIX

THE SALONS OF THE EMPIRE AND RESTORATION—
MADAME RÉCAMIER

*A Transition Period—Mme. de Montesson—Mme. de Genlis—
Revival of the Literary Spirit—Mme. de Beaumont—Mme.
de Remusat—Mme. de Souza—Mme. de Duras—Mme. de
Krüdener—Fascination of Mme. Récamier—Her Friends—
Her Convent Salon—Chateaubriand—Decline of the Salon.*

IN its best sense, society is born, not made. A
crowd of well-dressed people is not necessarily
a society. They may meet and disperse with
no other bond of union than a fine house and
lavish hospitality can give. It may be an assembly without unity, flavor, or influence. In
the social chaos that followed the Revolution, this truth found
a practical illustration. The old circles were scattered. The
old distinctions were virtually destroyed, so far as edicts can
destroy that which lies in the essence of things. A few who
held honored names were left, or had returned from a long
exile, to find themselves bereft of rank, fortune, and friends;

264

but these had small disposition to form new associations, and few points of contact with the *parvenus* who had mounted upon the ruins of their order. The new society was composed largely of these *parvenus*, who were ambitious for a position and a life of which they had neither the spirit, the taste, the habits, nor the mellowing traditions. Naturally they mistook the gilded frame for the picture. Unfamiliar with the gentle manners, the delicate sense of honor, and the chivalrous instincts which underlie the best social life, though not always illustrated by its individual members, they were absorbed in matters of etiquette of which they were uncertain, and exacting of non-essentials. They regarded society upon its commercial side, contended over questions of precedence, and, as one of the most observing of their contemporaries has expressed it, "bargained for a courtesy and counted visits." "I have seen quarrels in the imperial court," she adds, "over a visit more or less long, more or less deferred." Perhaps it is to be considered that in a new order which has many aggressive elements, this balancing of courtesies is not without a certain *raison d'être* as a protection against serious inroads upon time and hospitality; but the fault lies behind all this, in the lack of that subtle social sense which makes the discussion of these things superfluous, not to say impossible.

It was the wish of Napoleon to reconstruct a society that should rival in brilliancy the old courts. With this view he called to his aid a few women whose name, position, education, and reputation for *esprit* and fine manners he thought a sufficient guarantee of success. But he soon learned that it could not be commanded at will. The reply of the Duchesse d'Abrantes, who has left us so many pleasant reminiscences of this period, in which she was an actor as well as an observer, was very apt.

"You can do all that I wish," he said to her; "you are all young, and almost all pretty; ah, well! a young and pretty woman can do anything she likes."

"Sire, what your Majesty says may be true," she replied, "but only to a certain point. . . . If the Emperor, instead of his guard and his good soldiers, had only conscripts who would

34

recoil under fire, he could not win great battles like that of
Austerlitz.   Nevertheless, he is the first general in the world."
    But this social life was to serve a personal end.   It was to
furnish an added instrument of power to the autocrat who ruled,
to reflect always and everywhere the glory of Napoleon.   The
period which saw its cleverest woman in hopeless exile, and its
most beautiful one under a similar ban for the crime of being
her friend, was not one which favored intellectual supremacy.
The empire did not encourage literature, it silenced philosophy,
and oppressed the talent that did not glorify itself.   Its blighting
touch rested upon the whole social fabric.   The finer elements
which, to some extent, entered into it were lost in the glitter
of display and pretension.   The true spirit of conversation was
limited to private coteries that kept themselves in the shade,
and were too small to be noted.
    The salon which represented the best side of the new
régime was that of Mme. de Montesson, wife of the Duc
d'Orléans, a woman of brilliant talents, finished manners, great
knowledge of the world, fine gifts of conversation, and, what
was equally essential, great discrimination and perfect tact.
If her niece, Mme de. Genlis, is to be trusted, she had more
ambition than originality, her reputation was superior to her
abilities, and her beauty covered many imperfections.   But she
had experience, *finesse*, and prestige.   Napoleon was quick to
see the value of such a woman in reorganizing a court, and
treated her with the greatest consideration, even asking her
to instruct Josephine in the old customs and usages.   Her salon,
however, united many elements which it was impossible to
fuse.   There were people of all parties and all conditions, a
few of the nobles and returned *émigrés*, the numerous members
of the Bonaparte family, the new military circle, together with
many people of influence "not to the manner born."   Mme.
de Montesson revived the old amusements, wrote plays for
the entertainment of her guests, gave grand dinners and brilliant fêtes.   But the accustomed links were wanting.   Her
salon simply illustrates a social life in a state of transition.
    Mme. de Genlis had lived much in the world before the
Revolution, and her position in the family of the Duc d'Orléans,

MARQUISE DE MONTESSON.

FROM A LITHOGRAPH BY BELLIARD.

together with her great versatility of talent, had given her a certain vogue. Author, musician, teacher, moralist, critic, poser, egotist, *femme d'esprit*, and friend of princes, her romantic life would fill a volume and cannot be even touched upon in a few lines. After ten years of exile she returned to Paris, and her salon at the Arsenal was a center for a few celebrities.

Many of these names have small significance to-day. A few men like Talleyrand, La Harpe, Fontanes, and Cardinal Maury were among her friends, and she was neutral enough, or diplomatic enough, not to give offense to the new govern-

MME. DE GENLIS.

FROM A PRINT AFTER A DRAWING BY DEVERIA.

ment. But she was a woman of many affectations, and in spite of her numerous accomplishments, her cleverness, and her literary fame, the circle she gathered about her was never noted for its brilliancy or its influence. As a historic figure, she is more remarkable for the variety of her voluminous work, her educational theories, and her observations upon the world in which she lived, than for talents of a purely social order.

One is little inclined to dwell upon the ruling society of this period. It had neither the dignity of past traditions nor freedom of intellectual expression. Its finer shades were drowned in loud and glaring colors. The luxury that could be commanded counted for more than the wit and intelligence that could not.

As the social elements readjusted themselves on a more natural basis, there were a few salons out of the main drift of the time in which the literary spirit flourished once more, blended with the refined tastes, the elegant manners, and the amiable courtesy that had distinguished the old régime. But the interval in which history was made so rapidly, and the startling events of a century were condensed into a decade, had wrought many vital changes. It was no longer the spirit of the eighteenth century that reappeared under its revived and attractive forms. We note a tone of seriousness that had no permanent place in that world of *esprit* and skepticism, of fine manners and lax morals, which divided its allegiance between fashion and philosophy. The survivors of so many heart-breaking tragedies, with their weary weight of dead hopes and sad memories, found no healing balm in the cold speculation and scathing wit of Diderot or Voltaire. Even the devotees of philosophy gave it but a half-hearted reverence. It was at this moment that Chateaubriand, saturated with the sorrows of his age, and penetrated with the hopelessness of its philosophy, offered anew the truths that had sustained the suffering and broken-hearted for eighteen centuries, in a form so sympathetic, so fascinating, that it thrilled the sensitive spirits of his time, and passed like an inspiration into the literature of the next fifty years. The melancholy of *René* found its divine consolation in the *Genius of Christianity*. It was this spirit that lent a new and softer coloring to the intimate social life that blended in some degree the tastes and manners of the old *noblesse* with a refined and tempered form of modern thought. It recalls, in many points, the best spirit of the seventeenth

century. There is a flavor of the same seriousness, the same
sentiment. It is the sentiment that sent so many beautiful
women to the solitude of the cloister, when youth had faded
and the air of approaching age began to grow chilly. But it
is not to the cloister that these women turn. They weave romantic tales out of the texture of their own lives, they repeat
their experiences, their illusions, their triumphs, and their disenchantments. As the day grows more somber and the evening shadows begin to fall, they meditate, they moralize, they
substitute prayers for dreams. But they think also. The
drama of the late years had left no thoughtful soul without
earnest convictions. There were numerous shades of opinion,
many finely drawn issues. In a few salons these elements were
delicately blended, and if they did not repeat the brilliant
triumphs of the past, if they focused with less power the intellectual light which was dispersed in many new channels,
they have left behind them many fragrant memories. One is
tempted to linger in these temples of a goddess half-dethroned.
One would like to study these women who added to the social
gifts of their race a character that had risen superior to many
storms, hearts that were mellowed and purified by premature
sorrow, and intellects that had taken a deeper and more serious
tone from long brooding over the great problems of their time.
But only a glance is permitted us here. Most of them have
been drawn in living colors by Sainte-Beuve, from whom I
gather here and there a salient trait.

Who that is familiar with the fine and exquisite thought of
Joubert can fail to be interested in the delicate and fragile
woman whom he met in her supreme hour of suffering, to find
in her a rare and permanent friend, a literary *confidante*, and an
inspiration? Mme. de Beaumont — the daughter of Mont-
morin, who had been a colleague of Necker in the Ministry —
had been forsaken by a worthless husband, had seen father,
mother, brother, perish by the guillotine, and her sister escape
it only by losing her reason, and then her life, before the fatal
day. She, too, had been arrested with the others, but was so
ill and weak that she was left to die by the roadside *en route* to
Paris — a fate from which she was saved by the kindness of a

peasant. It was at this moment that Joubert befriended her. These numerous and crushing sorrows had shattered her health, which was never strong, but during the few brief years that remained to her she was the center of a coterie more distinguished for quality than numbers. Joubert and Chateaubriand were its leading spirits, but it included also Fontanes, Pasquier,

MME. DE BEAUMONT.

FROM A PRINT AFTER THE PAINTING BY DE LA TOUR.

Mme. de Vintimille, Mme. de Pastoret, and other friends who had survived the days in which she presided with such youthful dignity over her father's salon. The fascination of her fine and elevated intellect, her gentle sympathy, her keen appreciation of talent, and her graces of manner lent a singular charm to her presence. Her character was aptly expressed by this device which Rulhière had suggested for her seal: " *Un souffle m'agite et rien ne m'ébranle.*" Chateaubriand was enchanted with a nature so pure, so poetic, and so ardent. He visited her daily, read to her *Atala* and *René*, and finished the *Genius of Christianity* under her influence. He was young then, and that she loved him is hardly doubtful, though the

friendship of Joubert was far truer and more loyal than the
passing devotion of this capricious man of genius, who seems
to have cared only for his own reflection in another soul.   But
this sheltered nook of thoughtful repose, this conversational
oasis in a chaotic period had a short duration.   Mme. de Beau-

MME. DE RÉMUSAT.

FROM A PRINT.

mont died at Rome, where she had gone in the faint hope of
reviving her drooping health, in 1803.   Chateaubriand was
there, watched over her last hours with Bertin, and wrote eloquently of her death.   Joubert mourned deeply and silently
over the light that had gone out of his life.

   We have pleasant reminiscences of the amiable, thoughtful,
and *spirituelle* Mme. de Rémusat, who has left us such vivid
records of the social and intimate life of the imperial court.   A
studious and secluded childhood, prematurely saddened by the
untimely fate of her father in the terrible days of 1794, an early

and congenial marriage, together with her own wise penetration and clear intellect, enabled her to traverse this period without losing her delicate tone or serious tastes. She had her quiet retreat into which the noise and glare did not intrude, where a few men of letters and thoughtful men of the world

MME. DE SOUZA.

FROM A PRINT DRAWN BY CHRÉTIEN.

revived the old conversational spirit. She amused her idle hours by writing graceful tales, and, after the close of her court life and the weakening of her health, she turned her thoughts towards the education and improvement of her sex. Blended with her wide knowledge of the world, there is always a note of earnestness, a tender coloring of sentiment, which culminates towards the end in a lofty Christian resignation.

We meet again, at this time, a woman known to an earlier generation as Mme. de Flahaut, and made familiar to us through the pens of Talleyrand and Gouverneur Morris. She saw her

35

husband fall by the guillotine, and, after wandering over Europe for years as an exile, became the wife of M. de Souza, and, returning to Paris, took her place in a quiet corner of the un-accustomed world, writing softly colored romances after the

MME. DE DURAS.

FROM A PRINT AFTER THE PAINTING BY MME. ROUCHIER.

manner of Mme. de La Fayette, wearing with grace the honors her literary fame brought her, and preserving the tastes, the fine courtesies, the gentle manners, the social charms, and the delicate vivacity of the old régime.

One recalls, too, Mme. de Duras, whose father, the noble and fearless Kersaint, was the companion of Mme. Roland at the scaffold; who drifted to our own shores until the storms had passed, and, after saving her large fortune in Martinique, returned matured and saddened to France. As the wife of the Duc de Duras, she gathered around her a circle of rank, talent, and distinction. Chateaubriand, Humboldt, Cuvier, de Mont-morency were among her friends. What treasures of thought and conversation do these names suggest! What memories

MME. DE KRÜDENER.

FROM THE PORTRAIT IN THE LOUVRE.

of the past, what prophecies for the future! Mme. de Duras, too, wore gracefully the mantle of authorship with which she united pleasant household cares. She, too, put something of the sad experiences of her own life into romances which reflect the melancholy of this age of restlessness and lost illusions. She, too, like many of the women of her time whose youth had been blighted by suffering, passed into an exalted Christian strain. The friend of Mme. de Staël, the literary *confidante* of Chateaubriand, the woman of many talents, many virtues, and many sorrows, died with words of faith and hope and divine consolation on her lips.

The devotion of Mme. de Chantal, the mysticism of Mme. Guyon, find a nineteenth-century counterpart in the spiritual illumination of Mme. de Krüdener. Passing from a life of luxury and pleasure to a life of penitence and asceticism, singularly blending worldliness and piety, opening her salon with prayer, and adding a new sensation to the gay life of Paris, this adviser of Alexander I. and friend of Benjamin Constant, who put her best life into the charming romances which ranked next to *Corinne* and *Delphine* in their time; this beautiful woman, novelist, prophetess, mystic, *illuminée*, fanatic, with the passion of the South and the superstitious vein of the far North, disappeared from the world she had graced, and gave up her life in an ecstasy of sacrifice in the wilderness of the Crimea.

It is only to indicate the altered drift of the social life that flowed in quiet undercurrents during the Empire and came to the surface again after the Restoration; to trace lightly the slow reaction towards the finer shades of modern thought and modern morality, that I touch—so briefly and so inadequately— upon these women who represent the best side of their age, leaving altogether untouched many of equal gifts and equal note.

There is one, however, whose salon gathered into itself the last rays of the old glory, and whose fame as a social leader has eclipsed that of all her contemporaries. Mme. Récamier, "the last flower of the salons," is the woman of the century who has been, perhaps, most admired, most loved, and most written about. It has been so much the fashion to dwell upon her marvelous beauty, her kindness, and her irresistible fascination, that she has become, to some extent, an ideal figure invested with a subtle and poetic grace that folds itself about her like the invisible mantle of an enchantress. Her actual relations to the world in which she lived extended over a long period, terminating only on the threshold of our own generation. Without strong opinions or pronounced color, loyal to her friends rather than to her convictions, of a calm and happy temperament, gentle in character, keenly appreciative of all that was intellectually fine and rare, but without exceptional gifts herself, fascinating in manner, perfect in tact, with the beauty of an angel and the heart of a woman—she presents a fitting close to the long reign of the salons.

We hear of her first in the bizarre circles of the Consulate, as the wife of a man who was rather father than husband, young, fresh, lovely, accomplished, surrounded by the luxuries of wealth, and captivating all hearts by that indefinable charm of manner which she carried with her to the end of her life. Both at Paris and at her country house at Clichy she was the center of a company in which the old was discreetly mingled with the new, in which enmities were tempered, antagonisms softened, and the most discordant elements brought into harmonious *rapport*, for the moment, at least, by her gracious word or her winning smile. Here we find Adrien and Mathieu de Montmorency, who already testified the rare friendship that was to outlive years and misfortunes; Mme. de Staël before her exile; Narbonne, Barrère, Bernadotte, Moreau, and many distinguished foreigners. Lucien Bonaparte was at her feet; La Harpe was devoted to her interests; Napoleon was trying in vain to draw her into his court, and treasuring up his failure for another day. The salon of Mme. Récamier was not in any sense philosophical or political, but after the cruel persecution of La Harpe, the banishment of Mme. de Staël, and the similar misfortunes of other friends, her sympathies were too strong for her diplomacy, and it gradually fell into the ranks of the opposition. It was well known that the emperor regarded all who went there as his enemies, and this young and innocent woman was destined to feel the full bitterness of his petty displeasure.   We cannot trace here the incidents of her varied career, the misfortunes of the father to whom she was a ministering angel, the loss of her husband's fortune and her own, the years of wandering and exile, the second period of brief and illusive prosperity, and the swift reverses which led to her final retreat.   She was at the height of her beauty and her fame in the early days of the Restoration, when her salon revived its old brilliancy, and was a center in which all parties met on neutral ground.   Her intimate relations with those in power gave it a strong political influence, but this was never a marked feature, as it was mainly personal.

But the position in which one is most inclined to recall Mme. Récamier is in the convent of Abbaye-aux-Bois, where, divested of fortune and living in the simplest manner, she preserved for nearly thirty years the fading traditions of the old salons.   Through all the changes which tried her fortitude and revealed the latent heroism of her character, she seems to have kept her sweet serenity unbroken, bending to the passing storms with the grace of a facile nature, but never murmuring at the inevitable.   One may find in this inflexible strength and gentleness of temper a clue to the subtle fascination which held the devoted friendship of so many gifted men and women, long after the fresh charm of youth was gone.

The intellectual gifts of Mme. Récamier, as has been said before, were not of a high or brilliant order.   She was neither profound nor original, nor given to definite thought.   Her letters were few, and she has left no written records by which she can be measured.   She read much, was familiar with current literature, also with religious works.   But the world is slow to accord a twofold superiority, and it is quite possible that the fame of her beauty has prevented full justice to her mental abilities.   Mme. de Genlis tells us that she had a great deal of *esprit*.   It is certain that no woman could have held her place as the center of a distinguished literary circle and the *confidante* and adviser of the first literary men of her time, without a fine intellectual appreciation.   "To love what is great," said Mme. Necker, "is almost to be great one's self."   Ballanche advised her to translate Petrarch, and she even began the work, but it was never finished. "Believe me," he writes, "you have at your command the genius of music, flowers, imagination, and elegance. . . . Do not fear to try your hand on the golden lyre of the poets." He may have been too much blinded by a friendship that verged closely upon a more passionate sentiment to be an altogether impar-

MME. RECAMIER.

FROM THE PAINTING BY DAVID.

tial critic, but it was a high tribute to her gifts that a man of such conspicuous talents thought her capable of work so exacting. Her qualities were those of taste and a delicate imagination rather than of reason. Her musical accomplishments were always a resource. She sang, played the harp and piano, and we hear of her during a summer at Albano playing the organ at vespers and high mass. She danced exquisitely, and it was her ravishing grace that suggested the shawl dance of *Corinne* to Mme. de Staël and of *Valérie* to Mme. de Krüdener. One can fancy her, too, at Coppet, playing the rôle of the angel to

Mme. de Staël's Hagar—a spirit of love and consolation to the stormy and despairing soul of her friend.

But her real power lay in the wonderful harmony of her nature, in the subtle penetration that divined the chagrins and weaknesses of others, only to administer a healing balm; in the delicate tact that put people always on the best terms with themselves, and gave the finest play to whatever talents they possessed. Add to this a quality of beauty which cannot be caught by pen or pencil, and one can understand the singular sway she held over men and women alike. Mme. de Krüdener, whose salon so curiously united fashion and piety, worldliness and mysticism, was troubled by the distraction which the entrance of Mme. Récamier was sure to cause, and begged Benjamin Constant to write and entreat her to make herself as little charming as possible. His note is certainly unique, though it loses much of its piquancy in translation:

I acquit myself with a little embarrassment of a commission which Mme. de Krüdener has just given me. She begs you to come as little beautiful as you can. She says that you dazzle all the world, and that consequently every soul is troubled and attention is impossible. You cannot lay aside your charms, but do not add to them.

In her youth she dressed with great simplicity and was fond of wearing white with pearls, which accorded well with the dazzling purity of her complexion.

Mme. Récamier was not without vanity, and this is the reverse side of her peculiar gifts. She would have been more than mortal if she had been quite unconscious of attractions so rare that even the children in the street paid tribute to them. But one finds small trace of the petty jealousies and exactions that are so apt to accompany them. She liked to please, she wished to be loved, and this inevitably implies a shade of coquetry in a young and beautiful woman. There is an element of fascination in this very coquetry, with its delicate subtleties and its shifting tints of sentiment. That she carried it too far is no doubt true; that she did so wittingly is not so certain. Her victims were many, and if they quietly subsided into friends, as they usually did, it was after many struggles and heartburnings. But if she did not exercise her power with invariable discretion, it seems to have been less the result of vanity than a lack of decision and an amiable unwillingness to give immediate pain, or to lose the friend with the lover. With all her fine qualities of heart and soul, she had a temperament that saved her from much of the suffering she thoughtlessly inflicted upon others. The many violent passions she roused do not seem to have disturbed at all her own serenity. The delicate and chivalrous nature of Mathieu de Montmorency, added to his years, gave his relations to her a half-paternal character, but that he loved her always with the profound tenderness of a loyal and steadfast soul is apparent through all the singularly disinterested phases of a friendship that ended only with his life.

Prince Augustus, whom she met at Coppet, called up a passing ripple on the surface of her heart, sufficiently strong to lead her to suggest a divorce to her husband, whose relations to her, though always friendly, were only nominal. But he appealed to her generosity, and she thought of it no more. Why she permitted her princely suitor to cherish so long the illusions that time and distance do not readily destroy is one of the mysteries that are not easy to solve. Perhaps she thought it more kind to let absence wear out a passion than to break it too rudely. At all events, he cherished no permanent bitterness, and never forgot her. At his death, nearly forty years later he ordered her portrait by Gérard to be returned, but her ring was buried with him.

The various phases of the well-known infatuation of Benjamin Constant, which led him to violate his political principles and belie his own words rather than take a course that must result in separation from her, suggest a page of highly colored romance. The letters of Mlle. de Lespinasse scarcely furnish us with a more ardent episode in the literature of hopeless passion. The worshipful devotion of Ampère and Ballanche would form a chapter no less interesting, though less intense and stormy.

But the name most inseparably connected with Mme. Récamier is that of Chateaubriand. This friendship, of an unquestioned sort that seems to have gone quite out of the world, had all the phases of a more tender sentiment, and goes far towards disproving the charge of coldness that has often been brought against her. It was begun after she had reached the dreaded forties, by the death-bed of Mme. de Staël, and

MME. SWETCHINE.
FROM A PRINT.

lasted more than thirty years. It seems to have been the single sentiment that mastered her. One may trace in the letters of Chateaubriand the restless undercurrents of this life that was outwardly so serene. He writes to her from Berlin, from England, from Rome. He confides to her his ambitions, tells her his anxieties, asks her counsel as to his plans, chides her little jealousies, and commends his wife to her care and attention. This recalls a remarkable side of her relations with the world. Women are not apt to love formidable rivals, but the wives of her friends apparently shared the admiration with which their husbands regarded her. If they did not love her, they exchanged friendly notes, and courtesies that were often more than cordial. She consoles Mme. de Montmorency in her sorrow, and Mme. de Chateaubriand asks her to cheer her husband's gloomy moods. Indeed, she roused little of that bit-. ter jealousy which is usually the penalty of exceptional beauty or exceptional gifts of any sort. The sharp tongue of Mme. de Genlis lost its sting in writing of her. She idealized her as *Athénaïs*, in the novel of that name, which has for its background the beauties of Coppet, and vaguely reproduces much of its life. The pious and austere Mme. Swetchine, whose prejudices against her were so strong that for a long time she did not wish to meet her, confessed herself at once a captive to her "penetrating and indefinable charm." Though she did not always escape the shafts of malice, no better tribute could be offered to the graces of her character than the indulgence with which she was regarded by the most severely judging of her own sex.

But she has her days of depression. Chateaubriand is absorbed in his ambitions and sometimes indifferent; his antagonistic attitude towards Montmorency, who is far the nobler character of the two, is a source of grief to her. She tries in vain to reconcile her rival friends. Once she feels compelled to tear herself from an influence which is destroying her happiness, and goes to Italy. But she carries within her own heart the seeds of unrest. She still follows the movements of the man who occupies so large a space in her horizon, sympathizes from afar with his disappointments, and cares for his literary interest, ordering from Tenerani a bas-relief of a scene from *The Martyrs*.

After her return her life settles into more quiet channels. Chateaubriand, embittered by the chagrins of political life, welcomed her with the old enthusiasm. From this time he devoted himself exclusively to letters, and sought his diversion in the convent-salon which has left so wide a fame, and of which he was always the central figure. The petted man of genius was moody and capricious. His colossal egotism found its best solace in the gentle presence of the woman who flattered his restless vanity, anticipated his wishes, studied his tastes, and watched every shadow that flitted across his face. He was in the habit of writing her a few lines in the morning; at three o'clock he visited her, and they chatted over their tea until four, when favored visitors began to arrive. In the evening it was a little world that met there. The names of Ampère, Tocqueville, Montalembert, Merimée, Thierry, and Sainte-Beuve suggest the literary quality of this circle, in which were seen from time to time such foreign celebrities as Sir Humphry and Lady Davy, Maria Edgeworth, Humboldt, the Duke of Hamilton, the gifted Duchess of Devonshire, and Miss Berry. Lamartine read his *Méditations* and Delphine Gay her first poems. Rachel recited, and Pauline Viardot, Garcia, Rubini, and Lablache sang. Delacroix, David, and Gérard represented the world of art, and the visitors from the *grand monde* were too numerous to mention. In this brilliant and cosmopolitan company, what resources of wit and knowledge, what charms of beauty and elegance, what splendors of rank and distinction were laid upon the altar of the lovely and adored woman, who recognized all values, and never forgot the kindly word or the delicate courtesy that put the most modest guests at ease and brought out the best there was in them!

One day in 1847 there was a vacant place, and the faithful Ballanche came no more from his rooms across the street. A year later Chateaubriand died. After the death of his wife he had wished to marry Mme. Récamier, but she thought it best to change nothing, believing that age and blindness had given her the right to devote herself to his last days. To her friends she said that if she married him, he would miss the pleasure and variety of his daily visits.

Old, blind, broken in health and spirit, but retaining always the charm which had given her the empire over so many hearts, she followed him in a few months.

Mme. Récamier represents better than any woman of her time the peculiar talents that distinguished the leaders of some of the most famous salons. She had tact, grace, intelligence, appreciation, and the gift of inspiring others. The cleverest men and women of the age were to be met in her drawing-room. One found there genius, beauty, *esprit*, elegance, courtesy, and the brilliant conversation which is the Gallic heritage. But not even her surpassing fascination added to all these attractions could revive the old power of the salon. Her coterie was charming, as a choice circle gathered about a beautiful, refined, accomplished woman, and illuminated by the wit and intelligence of thoughtful men, will always be; but its influence was limited and largely personal, and it has left no perceptible traces. Nor has it had any noted successor. It is no longer coteries presided over by clever women that guide the age and mold its tastes or its political destinies. The old conditions have ceased to exist, and the prestige of the salon is gone.

The causes that led to its decline have been already more or less indicated. Among them, the decay of aristocratic institutions played only a small part. The salons were *au fond* democratic in the sense that all forms of distinction were recognized so far as they were amenable to the laws of taste, which form the ultimate tribunal of social fitness in France. But it cannot be denied that the code of etiquette which ruled them had its foundation in the traditions of the *noblesse*. The genteel manners, the absence of egotism and self-assertion, as of disturbing passions, the fine and uniform courtesy which is the poetry of life, are the product of ease and assured conditions. It is struggle that destroys harmony and repose, whatever stronger qualities it may develop, and the greater mingling of classes which inevitably resulted in this took something from the exquisite flavor of the old society. The increase of wealth, too, created new standards that were fatal to a life in which the resources of wit, learning, and education in its highest sense were the chief attractions. The greater perfection of all forms of public amusement was not without its influence. Men drifted, also, more and more into the one-sided life of the club. Considered as a social phase, no single thing has been more disastrous to the unity of modern society than this.   But the most formidable enemy of the salon has been the press.   Intelligence has become too universal to be focused in a few drawing-rooms.   Genius and ambition have found a broader arena.   When interest no longer led men to seek the stimulus and approval of a powerful coterie, it ceased to be more than an elegant form of recreation, a theater of small talents, the diversion of an idle hour.   When the press assumed the sovereignty, the salon was dethroned.

www.ingramcontent.com/pod-product-compliance
Lightning Source LLC
LaVergne TN
LVHW061258060426
835509LV00013B/1482